DATE DUE

NOV 1 0 2004			
NOV 2 4 2004			
JAN 1 1 2005			
FEB 8 2005			
FEB 2 6 2005			
DE 2 2 '05			
MR 0 6 '09			

Demco, Inc. 38-293

ALSO BY PETER G. PETERSON

Gray Dawn

Will America Grow Up Before It Grows Old?

Facing Up

On Borrowed Time

RUNNING ON EMPTY

RUNNING ON EMPTY

•

How the Democratic and Republican Parties Are Bankrupting Our Future and What Americans Can Do About It

•

PETER G. PETERSON

FARRAR, STRAUS AND GIROUX

New York

Farrar, Straus and Giroux
19 Union Square West, New York 10003

Distributed in Canada by Douglas & McIntyre Ltd.
Printed in the United States of America
First edition, 2004

Library of Congress Control Number: 2004104298
ISBN-13: 978-0-374-25287-8
ISBN-10: 0-374-25287-4

Designed by Abby Kagan

www.fsgbooks.com

5 7 9 10 8 6

To my wife, Joan Ganz Cooney,

who is always there with

brilliant insight and wise judgment

about the right thing to say or do

CONTENTS

PREFACE: WHY THIS BOOK NOW?

Less than three short years after America absorbed the double blows of 9/11 and the collapse of the bubble economy, a new mood of triumphalism reemerged in many quarters. Saddam Hussein was dragged from his spider hole and humiliated before the world. Inflation and interest rates remained low while productivity and profits soared. The stock market roared back and investors began reading their statements again. So quick was the rise in manufacturing and consumption that freight backed up on the nation's railroads and waterways.

Yet if it seemed the dawn of another "Morning in America," many Americans still felt a chill in the air: at what price did America purchase its recovery? Yes, nearly everyone agreed that tax cuts and a big run in federal spending had helped to stimulate the economy. Everyone agreed the Fed had been right to cut interest rates. But even after three big tax cuts in a row, a boom in home refinancing, and zero percent auto loans, the economy was slow to produce jobs, personal savings rates skidded to historic lows, and the nation faced ballooning budget and trade deficits stretching as far as the eye can see.

Meanwhile, the oldest baby boomers are just a few years away from retirement. Today, Social Security still runs a sizable cash-flow surplus, which covers the roughly equal cash-flow deficit in Medicare. But official projections show that within fifteen years both programs will be paying out far more in benefits than they collect in taxes, with Medicare's red ink far surpassing that of Social Security. Indeed, if one looks at Social Security and Medicare together, including both Medicare's hospital and physician programs, they go from a modest combined cash-flow deficit of about $25 billion in 2003 to an unthinkable annual cash-flow deficit of $783 billion in 2020 (or $519 billion in today's dollars). And that annual deficit is projected to reach $4.3 *trillion* (that's $4,300 billion) by 2040 (or $1.6 trillion in today's dollars). No longer will Congress be able to use Social Security tax dollars to pay for Medicare's deficits or for other government operations. Unless Social Security and, in particular, Medicare benefits are brought under control, the government will face stark options: either draconian cuts in defense, education, transportation, the criminal justice and other programs, or huge tax hikes—or, of course, both.

What were the politicians preparing to do about all this? The Republicans wanted to make all of their recent tax cuts permanent, while also pushing for big increases in spending on defense, homeland security, energy subsidies, and miscellaneous pork. Meanwhile, the Democrats vowed to do away with the tax cuts for the rich, preserve tax cuts for the middle class, put new money into education, health care, highway construction, and miscellaneous pork while promising to do nothing about the big deficits in Social Security and Medicare—except perhaps to make them *bigger*. After a costly new expansion of Medicare to pay for prescription drugs, the Democrats complained it "didn't go far enough," thereby suggesting we make an already unsustainable program even more unsustainable.

America was back, but for how long? Were we celebrating an economic Pyrrhic victory?

Buried deep in the financial pages, telltale signs are appearing that suggest America may well be headed for a financial meltdown. In January 2004 the staff of the International Monetary Fund, who normally worry about profligate nations like Argentina, took direct aim at the United States, warning the world that we are careening toward insolvency. They point to a huge and growing imbalance between what the federal government has promised to pay in future benefits and what it can reasonably expect to collect in future taxes. Its long-term structural deficit now exceeds 500 percent of gross domestic product. Closing that gap, the IMF calculated, "would require an immediate and permanent 60 percent hike in the federal income tax, or a 50 percent cut in Social Security and Medicare benefits."

Adding to the gathering fiscal storm is America's growing dependence on foreign capital. Because Americans import far more goods and services than they export, and because the federal government borrows so much and Americans save so little, the American economy is increasingly owned by, or indebted to, foreigners. This is America's *other* deficit, the so-called current-account deficit, which indicates how much of our birthright we are selling off to foreigners, or promising to pay them in future interest payments. Last year the United States imported capital from foreigners at an unprecedented rate—four billion dollars every working day.

These "twin deficits"—the U.S. budget deficit and America's current-account deficit—pose a dual challenge. Today's budget deficits consume so much of the nation's meager savings that we must turn to other countries to finance our home mortgages, credit card balances, and the business investments that fuel our growth. Thus, if foreigners stopped providing us with so much easy money, interest rates would likely shoot up, the dollar would likely sink, and the economy would likely stall. This flow of easy money also reduces pressure on our government to cut its own reckless borrowing, and on ordinary Americans to reduce their consumption and increase their savings.

For a long time this arrangement has been a boon for American consumers. This borrowing from abroad allowed us to buy lots of cheap imports, even if it caused many Americans to get hooked on credit and others to lose their jobs to foreign competition. Fred Bergsten, director of the Institute for International Economics, observes, "We finally understand the true meaning of supply-side economics. Foreigners supply most of the goods and all of the money."

But the arrangement cannot last indefinitely: we have for too long consumed far more than we have produced as a nation. International economists agree that the odds of severe adjustment problems mount rapidly once an economy exceeds a current account deficit of 5 percent of GDP. In 2003 our current-account deficit just reached that mark. It is now half again as large, as a percentage of GDP, as our previous record set in 1987, a year that saw a one-third drop in the dollar and a still legendary stock market crash. And New York Fed economists expect the current-account deficit to climb still higher.

Taking the longer view, we must also remember our creditors, notably western Europe and Japan, are aging even more rapidly than the United States. They will eventually need their savings at home to pay for their own retirement systems, which are even more costly than our own. China, another major U.S. creditor, is also aging rapidly, while also needing huge amounts of capital to finance its own industrial expansion.

America's twin deficits are causing some of the world's shrewdest financial minds to raise alarms. When two such experienced and understated executives as Bob Rubin, former secretary of Treasury, and Paul Volcker, former chairman of the Federal Reserve Board, join the many others who fear these twin deficits, I listen. Bob Rubin says we are confronting "a day of serious reckoning." In referring to our "fecklessness," Rubin warns that "the traditional immunity of advanced countries like America to the third-world-style crisis isn't a birthright." Volcker predicts we face a 75 percent chance of a crisis within five years.

America's twin deficits are now so large, and our savings rate so low, that there is a real danger that investors around the world will simply lose faith in the dollar. According to Steve Roach, chief economist of Morgan Stanley, "it's hard to conceive of a more unstable disequilibrium." For the first time in his seventy-two years, Warren Buffett, the Nebraska sage, is purchasing foreign currencies. Britain's prominent fund manager and financial commentator Marshall Auerback says America has entered into a banana-republic-style "debt trap." Many experts use the metaphor of a "hard landing"—a moment that will bring a further sharp drop in the dollar, a big spike in interest rates, a stock market plunge, and a paralyzed U.S. economy, with devastating aftershocks to the global economy.

In truth, no one can be sure what kind of landing is coming—soft, hard, or even crash. But a landing it will be, not a takeoff. We won't take off because right now we are not saving nearly enough in our households and businesses. In fact, Americans have the lowest personal savings rate in the developed world. What's worse, a growing share of what little we do save—right now that share is three-quarters—is devoured by our federal budget deficits. Our twin deficits pose huge risks to our economy that we should not, and need not, be taking. We are not paying our own way. As a nation, we are running on empty.

The world is increasingly alarmed by America's profligacy. It's not just the staff of the International Monetary Fund who lecture us as if we were a banana republic. Global leaders at the

Davos World Economic Forum and other venues speculate openly about how long the dollar will remain the world's reserve currency, and about whether the U.S. financial system will take down the global economy when it implodes. And it's not just our problem. It's the world's problem. America must learn to redirect its entire economy away from imports and toward exports—which is to say, toward higher rates of savings. Yet at the same time, the rest of the developed nations must redirect their economies away from exports and toward imports—which is to say, toward higher rates of consumption. Everyone must break out of old habits. Like two runners joined in a three-legged race, they must move at the same time if they want to prevent both from tumbling to the ground.*

Why this book now? Because the hour is getting late. Because, while our problems are not yet intractable, both political parties are increasingly incorrigible. They are not facing our problems, they are running from them. They are locked into a politics of denial, distraction, and self-indulgence that can only be overcome if readers like you take back this country from the ideologues and spin doctors of both the left and the right. I believe a critical mass of ordinary Americans now sense that the country is on the wrong economic course and are willing to do something about it. I fervently hope so. We can't expect politicians to do it for us. We the people must make it possible for politicians to do the right thing.

Over the last quarter century I have published four books and many articles warning about how the combination of mount-

*Rebalancing the world economy requires global coordination, that is, a major effort to make sure that the developed countries restructure their economies in these fundamentally different directions. See chapter seven of my 2000 book *Gray Dawn*, "Toward Global Solutions to a Global Problem: An Open Letter."

ing debt, pay-as-you-go retirement programs, and population aging would, if left unattended, one day undermine America's economic foundations. I noted that developed countries around the world had experienced a sharp and unexpected decline in birth rates that would result in ever fewer workers being available to support ever more retirees. I noted that as countries like Japan came to have more elders than children, their spending on health care and pensions would make it far more difficult for them to continue underwriting America's trade and budget deficits. I noted that the tax cuts pushed by both Ronald Reagan and George W. Bush did not, as promised, pay for themselves, but led to an explosion of government debt. I raised the question—still unanswered—that was the title of one of the books: *Will America Grow Up Before It Grows Old?*

I'd like to think this work has made a difference, but have to admit that for most of that time the public's enthusiasm was (shall I say) restrained. The subject was dreary, and the predicted disaster far off in the future. But time passes. In June of 2003 I wrote a piece for *The New York Times Magazine* titled "Deficits and Dysfunction: How the Republican and Democratic Parties Are Robbing Our Future." I was astonished by what happened next. I was flooded with letters and calls from Republicans, Independents, and Democrats who shared my anxieties not simply about our country's finances but about how their own political parties were conspiring to turn a difficult, long-term challenge into a looming crisis.

It's not hard to see why so many Americans are now reexamining their assumptions about the future, and about the two major political parties that would each presume to take them there. To begin with, America's old-age crisis looms ever larger, ever closer, and is ever harder to ignore. Once, when experts warned about the long-term deficits projected for Social Security and Medicare, they spoke about the implications for young adults and future generations. I myself used to invoke the names of my nine grandchildren, Alexandra, Peter Cary,

Steven, Chloe, Jack, Alexander, Beau, Eliza, and Drew. But by now reform has been so long deferred that it's not only young folks but fifty- and sixty-year-olds who have to worry.

The oldest baby boomers, born in 1946, are just five years away from the median age of retirement on Social Security (sixty-three). Roughly one-third of all boomers have virtually no retirement savings, and another third have saved far too little to meet their retirement needs. Roughly 20 percent never had children. Due to rising rates of disability in midlife, which health experts suspect are triggered by rising rates of obesity, many boomers are already beset by costly and chronic health conditions. At the same time, improved life expectancy means that many will be collecting Social Security and Medicare for 20 or 30 percent of their lifetimes.

In late February 2004 Fed chairman Alan Greenspan reminded Congress yet again about the fiscal elephant in the room: the cost of the baby boom generation's retirement. He even suggested that some benefits would have to be cut. Predictably, and in unison, the Democratic presidential candidates shouted: "No, no, a thousand times no! Just repeal Bush's tax cuts for the rich." Meanwhile, Republicans edged away from Greenspan, as if pointing to the elephant was a very rude thing to do. After all, at a time when the federal government should be building up big surpluses to prepare for the aging of the boomers, the Republicans are presiding over huge deficits, and engaging in still another reckless experiment with "grow your way out" supply-side economics. It's hard to say which party is being more irresponsible.

Americans cannot tax their way out of these deficits. Just financing the projected increases in Social Security and Medicare through higher contributions would require payroll taxes to rise by 50 percent by 2020, and by 200 to 350 percent by 2040, according to the Social Security Administration. And need I remind you that these payroll taxes would fall heavily on the middle class and low-income workers?

If Democrats believe entitlement reform is an avoidable issue, they should consult the ten Democratic members of President Clinton's Commission on Entitlement Reform, who found unanimously that the cost of entitlement programs like Social Security and Medicare, plus interest on the national debt, will consume all federal spending by 2030 and deemed these programs "unsustainable." That finding, made in 1994, came *before* the three recent tax cuts and the big recent Medicare expansion.

Nor can America use tax cuts to "grow our way out" of the kinds of deficits we now face. Even if the supply-side prescription somehow brought America sustained economic growth, a robust economy would by itself cause Social Security benefits, which are tied to wages, to become more generous, while also further inflating health care costs.

Nor can we balance the budget without taking on major entitlement programs like Social Security and Medicare. In 2003 entitlements and interest on the national debt accounted for nearly two-thirds of federal spending, and on our current course, as I pointed out earlier, will account for much more in the future. During the 1990s we were able to absorb the growth of entitlement spending through large post-Cold War cuts in defense spending, which fell from over 5 to 3 percent of GDP. We also took advantage of favorable demographics. It was a decade in which a relatively small generation (born in the 1930s) was retiring and a relatively large generation (born in the 1950s) was hitting its peak income-earning and tax-paying years. Over the coming decade all of these trends will be reversing themselves—with a vengeance.

To the crisis of the twin deficits add the crisis of the twin towers. However one feels about President Bush's handling of the war on terror or the invasion of Iraq, there is no denying that since 9/11 America faces new and costly burdens for peacekeeping abroad and for defense of the homeland. With the number of U.S. military troops down from 2 million in

1990 to just 1.4 million today, and with military commitments continuing to expand, individual soldiers and sailors draw more frequent, prolonged, and dangerous assignments. National Guard units across the country are already failing to meet their recruiting targets. The Army Reserves reports a shortfall in reenlistments.

Four divisions, representing nearly half the army's active-duty strength, are now officially in the two lowest categories of readiness. The tempo of operations in Iraq, warns a recent War College study, has "stressed the U.S. Army to the breaking point." A common criticism of our defense structure is that "we have a ten-division army with a twelve-division list of priorities." Yet even if we could attract the personnel needed to fill such a gap, the Defense Department estimates that it would cost nearly $40 billion annually just for personnel-related expenses. The Business Executives for National Security is an organization not known for its friendliness to the military-industrial complex. Nonetheless, its executive director, General Charles Boyd, writes me that a range of budget experts in this field believe that implementing a "transformation strategy" while maintaining current defense capabilities will be "hugely costly."

The new requirements for homeland defense are putting other new pressures on the budget. A Council on Foreign Relations task force finds that emergency responders are "dangerously under-funded, dangerously unprepared." Stephen Flynn, a leading expert on homeland security for the council, estimates that the cost of preparing for just three obvious vulnerabilities to terrorism—equipping our emergency responders, expanding our medical facilities, and protecting our ports—comes to about $120 billion over five years.

Meanwhile, even if our traditional allies like France and Germany had proved eager to help out with international security and nation-building, their capacity to contribute will decline over time because of the severe aging of *their* populations.

Already the cost of old-age benefits in Europe has crowded out spending on the military, to the point that European powers could play only a limited military role in Kosovo. In Germany and France, as well as in countries such as Japan, Italy, and Spain, the cost of old-age benefits is projected to consume between a quarter and a third of their GDP by 2040. In other words, the ability of America's traditional allies to project power overseas, or even to commit serious resources to foreign aid, is fast fading. And indeed, we too will face the wrenching issue of funding guns or canes, weapons or walkers.

No longer does anyone talk glibly about an imminent "end of history," in which the rest of the world will soon become peaceable, orderly, and democratic. Instead, we worry about violent conspiracies and rogue nations, loose nukes and portable biolabs, code reds and mass evacuations.

The seeping in of such realities awakens a new mood in our country. Americans know their nation is still strong. They know that American productivity and military strength are unrivaled. They know we have made great progress in making America a fair and tolerant society. But when they look to their political leaders, they see them overlooking or denying obvious challenges that can no longer be deferred. As during the era leading up to the Civil War, the American people don't see statesmen working together and don't hear voices of moderation or common sense. Instead, they are accosted by ideologues and operators who play on fears and resentments, making big problems out of small ones and small problems out of big ones.

Like millions of other Americans, I didn't always feel this way. As it happened, I was born a Republican, and for most of my life it felt easy and right to be one. My father was a Greek immigrant and small businessman who taught me to value thrift, stewardship, individual responsibility, and compassion for the poor. He started out as a railroad dishwasher who slept in a caboose to save on rent. He settled in Kearney, Nebraska, and used his savings to start the inevitable Greek restaurant. With the help of my mother, he ran it 24/7 for twenty-five years so that my brother and I could "get the best education money can buy." Meanwhile, if an unemployed person came to the back door of the Central Café asking to be fed—and during the Great Depression there were countless numbers—none went hungry as long as they were willing to do some honest labor.

These values were reinforced when I arrived at the University of Chicago and learned from its famed economists about the virtues of open markets, the hazards of too much government, and of course the importance of fiscal responsibility. From Milton Friedman I learned that in public finance, as in life, there is no such thing as a free lunch. You borrow today, you pay tomorrow. As for permanent tax cuts, Friedman taught us they were a fine idea as long as we remembered that they were not tax cuts at all unless accompanied by permanent spending cuts. Otherwise, they were simply a shift in taxes to future taxpayers—which is to say a tax cut for us, but a tax increase on our children.

Later in my career, as a CEO, I often observed firsthand how much economic damage could be wrought by excessive regulation, but also how much a well run government could benefit the needy. I've been appalled by the costly damage done by a favorite special interest group of the Democrats, the trial lawyers, but I remind myself they also stood by the struggle of minorities to regain and protect civil rights. While later serving in government as a Republican, there were low moments. Watergate, for instance—especially since at the time I was serving as President Nixon's secretary of commerce. It was also difficult to watch Nixon preside over another big increase in entitlement spending, or to hear him proclaim, "We're all Keynesians now." But my experience in the Nixon White House still did not shake my faith in the party of Lincoln—the party that freed the slaves, brought the vote to women, and stood, I thought, for government that paid its own way.

But what did at last begin to shake my faith in the GOP was Ronald Reagan's supply-side gospel.

I voted for Reagan with high expectations in 1980. But when I had a chance to study his first budget, I was incredulous. This supply-side Reagan budget was indeed, as his own vice president had once said, based on "voodoo economics." It was an amalgam of psychology, expectations, and theological certitudes. In one giant leap of faith, we were to have the biggest tax cut in history, the biggest defense increases in history, and an unprecedented Republican affirmation of Ponzi-scheme financing for vital programs like Social Security and Medicare. And yes, all this and budget and trade surpluses, too—just in time for the next election.

This is not the time to revisit the big budget battles of the 1980s. Suffice it to say the supply-side revolution did not work as advertised. The Reagan tax cuts and defense buildup did provide some badly needed stimulus coming out of a tough recession. I have no quarrel with using short-term deficits to give a kick start to a stalled economy. And I do not doubt that punitive marginal income tax rates (at 70 percent when Reagan was elected) were a genuine source of economic drag. But because the supply-siders insisted on broad and large tax cuts through good times and bad, and because neither party had the guts to take on the rapid increase in spending, what grew most during Reagan's term was federal debt, which rose from 26 to 43 percent of GDP.

Those numbers would look even worse if they included all the additional borrowing that went on "off the books" and that is only now coming due. In 1983 Congress enacted and Reagan signed a giant payroll tax hike. The plan, championed by Alan Greenspan, was to "prefund" the baby boom generation's Social Security benefits. Instead, under Reagan and every president since, the money has been used to pay for growth in

Medicare and the rest of the budget, so that when baby boomers finally do go to collect their benefits, they'll find their Social Security trust funds stuffed only with IOUs.

Although President Ronald Reagan made many positive, even historic contributions to American history, the tripling of the national debt that occurred during his White House tenure is certainly not among them. Remarkably, President George W. Bush and those around him today seem unaware of this. At a 2002 policy strategy meeting, Vice President Dick Cheney reportedly announced that "Reagan proved deficits don't matter."

I certainly hoped a new George W. Bush administration would do better. By the time of his inauguration in 2001, virtually every policy wonk of every political affiliation recognized that unsustainable cost growth in old-age entitlements was a serious problem—now that the huge baby boom generation, 77 million strong, was about to become the senior boom. When a senior Bush administration official asked me in early 2001 for my thoughts on entitlement reform, I immediately spoke my mind. "You people have a God-sent opportunity," I told him. I reminded him that the Treasury had recently affirmed the size of Social Security's and Medicare's staggering, multitrillion-dollar, long-term unfunded liabilities, and that meanwhile we had big cash-flow budget surpluses building up. "Why not take the trillions of dollars of surpluses out of the hands of the government?" I asked. "You know that if you don't sequester them, Congress will spend them. By starting to fund some sort of personal retirement accounts to supplement Social Security, you would, in effect, return those surpluses to the people. That way, you could also fulfill your campaign promise—and do it in a way that would help solve one of the largest fiscal challenges in our history."

"Great idea," he said. "Let me try it on at the senior White House level." The answer came later back: "Sorry, Pete. Tax cuts come first."

Somehow they always do in this administration. Supply-side theory has mutated into a kind of "any cut, anytime" attitude. No matter which taxes are reduced, and no matter how far, Bush's economic team is inclined to believe—and of course his political team agrees—that reducing them still further will ultimately raise more revenue. By that ephemeral logic, why not go for massive surpluses by eliminating taxes altogether?

This tax cut ideology is not fact-driven. It is faith-driven. The elect simply "know" they are right, untroubled by their changing, competing, and even contradictory rationales. One day, it's short-term stimulus. The next, trickle-down economics. The day after, investment economics. Some Republicans say their tax cuts are a way to close the deficit. Others say the reverse—that larger deficits are necessary to "starve the beast" of government, as if future Congresses will only spend what we can afford. Grover Norquist, the Republican tax radical, says, "I don't want to abolish government. I simply want to reduce it to the size where I can drag it into the bathroom and drown it in the bathtub." Norquist and other extremists should be careful what they wish for. A small government run by libertarians is not the likely outcome if a shredded social safety net leaves millions of elders in poverty, or if mounting debts cause the economy to crash. Remember whence the New Deal came.

I've only met George W. Bush twice, before he was President, and found him charming, friendly, and straightforward. He seemed to know I was concerned about the viability of our entitlement programs and asked what I thought about the issue. I told him entitlement reform was both a philosophical and moral issue. "What do you mean by that?" he asked. I told him that I thought the philosophical issue was whether a modern, media-driven democracy that only focuses on immediate crises could respond effectively to a very different kind of threat—a silent, slow-motion, long-term crisis like entitlements. He enthusiastically agreed that America could, and that reforming

Social Security would be one of his highest priorities. I believed him at the time. He himself probably believed it.

He then asked what I meant about Social Security and other entitlements being a moral issue. I took him through the official numbers on the huge payroll taxes and the huge debt that we would be passing on to our children. I told him if looking out for our children's future was a definitive test of our morality, then long-term tax cuts, particularly for us fat cats in the room, should wait until entitlement reforms had been completed. He visibly stiffened, as though hit in the gut. "I don't think tax cuts are immoral." "Governor," I said, "I didn't say long-term tax cuts were immoral. I said they were immoral until we have taken care of our long-term obligations to our children."

That ended the conversation. It was there and then that I sensed that to George W. Bush, tax cuts were an obligation driven by faith, not a policy guided by evidence.

Once Bush took office, he set up a Social Security Commission. Again, I believe that at the time he was very sincere about wanting to tackle this major national challenge. This commission, with his own appointees, came up with three options for reform—at least one of which was very plausible. But George W's commitment to "Social Security reform" has resembled Bill Clinton's to "entitlement reform"—sincere, but not really a priority. Bush and Clinton both chose to ignore the findings of their own commissions.

Former chairman of the Council of Economic Advisors Charles Shultze once characterized America's slow-growing fiscal crisis by saying, "The problem is not that the wolf is at the door. It's more like termites in the woodwork." By now the termites have done more damage to the house than a wolf ever could. Politicians may try to distract us from the crunching noises we now hear in the beams. They may chant high-minded phrases like "We shall not pass on our problems to future generations," or "No child left behind." They may demagogically declare that a deficit-financed tax cut is just a return of "your money," while the resulting debt somehow belongs to the ages. They may tell you that the first priority for dealing with runaway health care costs is to add new benefits. These are all pleasing thoughts, but who can really believe them anymore?

Echoing the libertarian Cato Institute, which refers to the "Republican Spending Explosion," *The Economist* magazine calls Bush "the most profligate president since Vietnam. George W. Bush's self-proclaimed party of small government has turned itself into the party of unlimited spending." Former House Republican leader Richard Armey recently declared, "I am upset about spending. There is no way I can pin that on the Democrats. Republicans own the town now." According to my fellow Nebraskan, conservative Republican senator Chuck Hagel, "We have become loose from our moorings." Stephen Moore, a leading Republican supply-side advocate, said this about the president: "He likes bigger government."

In sum, this administration and the Republican Congress have presided over the biggest, most reckless deterioration of America's finances in history. It includes a feast of pork, inequitable and profligate tax cuts, and a major new expansion of Medicare that is unaccompanied by any serious measures to control its exploding cost. Even before the new prescription drug benefit, Medicare accounted for three-fourths of America's stunning multi-trillion-dollar unfunded liabilities. It's almost as if today's Republicans have decided that a legitimate goal of supply-side economics is to increase the supply of government.

During the Vietnam War, conservatives relentlessly pilloried Lyndon Johnson for his fiscal irresponsibility. He only wanted guns and butter. Today, so-called conservatives are outpandering LBJ. They must have it all: guns, butter, *and* tax cuts. The result has been euphemistically dubbed "big-government conservatism." Bush signed off on the so-called energy bill and such vital expenditures as $200 million for an indoor "tropical rain forest" in Iowa. Senator John McCain observed, "The name of this bill should be the 'Leave No Lobbyist Behind Act of 2003.' Given the magnitude of the largesse offered in this bill, I feel somewhat like a mosquito in a nudist colony. I hardly know where to begin." Lewis L. Gould, author of the book *Grand Old Party*, sums it up eloquently: "A conservatism that makes no demands and enforces no responsibilities is largely a rhetorical posture."

But let me be clear: the same can be said of a liberal theology that simply brokers benefits among contending pressure groups, conferring entitlements but not responsibilities, unable to put just claims before merely noisy ones. Drew Johnson of the National Taxpayers Union Foundation has reviewed the budget proposals of each of the 2004 Democratic presidential contenders. Every candidate disparaged the "Bush" budget deficits. Yet every one of them—all eight—proposed substantial spending increases, averaging a stunning 21.5 percent rise in annual federal outlays.

In other words, though I often complain about my Republican brethren, I understand full well that the Democratic Party has also strayed far from its traditional principles. Democratic leaders once stood up to the "haves" on behalf of the "have-nots." But by the 1980s party ideologues were defending windfall benefits for affluent retirees while telling downwardly mobile younger workers they had no right to oppose hikes in regressive payroll taxes to pay for the largesse the ideologues so merrily bestowed.

Michael Kinsley, then editor of *The New Republic*, wrote that the Democratic vision of a Great Society had yielded to a "Grandfather Clause Society" in which leaders doted on those who were already well protected while leaving the young to fend for themselves. Then and now, leading Democrats regularly reaffirm their commitment to a "social insurance" scheme under which government puts the cost of supporting affluent retirees disproportionately on the backs of low-income workers while telling those low-income workers that if they expect to collect in their turn, their own children in turn will have to pay even higher taxes.

With faith-driven catechisms that are largely impervious to analysis or evidence, and that seem removed from any kind of serious political morality, both political parties have formed an unholy alliance—an undeclared war on the future. An undeclared war, that is, on our children. From neither party do we hear anything about sacrificing today for a better tomorrow. In some ways, our most formidable challenge may be our leaders' baffling indifference to our fiscal metastasis. As former Treasury Secretary Larry Summers puts it, "the only thing we have to fear is the lack of fear itself."

This book spells out the dimensions and causes of the coming fiscal meltdown, the unthinkable payroll taxes, and the unprecedented debts, as well as some proposed reforms. We have squandered many of the easy solutions that would have been available had we acted in the 1970s and 1980s to meet the predictable needs of an aging society. There is no longer time, for example, to allow the miracle of compound interest to defray much of the cost of the boomers' retirement. The trillions our government has already borrowed from outside our country makes interest payments a leading export, even as foreigners buy up more and more of our leading companies. The question to ask is not whether this will end. As my Nixon administration colleague Herbert Stein used to say, "If something is unsustainable, it tends to stop." Rather, the question is whether it will stop sooner, and on terms we set, or later, and on terms driven by events that are beyond our control.

The American Dream has been very good to me—as it has for many of us. But as do you, I want that American Dream to be there for my children and grandchildren. In that spirit, I remind you of the 1980 presidential campaign, when Ronald Reagan galvanized the American electorate with these famous words: "I want to ask every American: Are you better off now than you were four years ago?" Perhaps we are ready for a candidate who rephrases that line: "I want to ask every American, young people especially: Is *your future* better off now than it was four years ago—now that you and your generation are saddled with these large new unfunded liabilities and the higher taxes that must eventually accompany them?"

Recent history suggests it will take a rare combination of bold presidential leadership and enlightened bipartisanship to forge a reform program equal to the challenge. It may also require (I hope I am wrong!) a fiscal or economic emergency that wakes us up and shakes us from our complacency. Still, as grim as all this may sound at times, it is not too late. Nor are the sacrifices unthinkable. To save Social Security, it is sufficient to stop offering bigger and bigger benefits to each new generation of retirees. Medicare and Medicaid pose far more daunting fiscal challenges, as well as chilling life-and-death choices and moral dilemmas. But there are ways not only to make health care more affordable but to improve the quality of the health care as well.

Yes, we'll also have to conquer our addiction to foreign capital and force ourselves to save more, but learning to live within our means and to invest in our children will bring not only material but spiritual and psychic rewards. My striving immigrant father and mother and millions like them knew the happiness and self-respect that only comes when you know you are building a better world for yourself and the next generation. This is the American Dream, and it can be restored.

RUNNING ON EMPTY

Chapter 1

BANKRUPT PARTIES, BANKRUPT NATION

When the towers fell, I was out of town attending a corporate board meeting (which promptly adjourned) and spent the rest of the day watching cable news and trying to call my wife and family in Manhattan. Four days later, when I finally managed to get a plane home, I saw a New York—and an America—transformed. I saw parents doting on their kids and neighbors helping neighbors and college students lining up to donate blood and cars and streets in a sea of flags. Out of tears and tragedy there came a new sense of community purpose and determination. Like many Americans, I asked myself, Why can't citizenship in a great nation always be like this?

But within a few months our leaders had reverted to their old habits. The nastiness returned. It was business as usual—the same politicians leaping at each other's throats while saying nothing sensible about what America can do or be.

This brought home for me why a growing number of Americans are so disaffected with politics and parties. There seems such a vast gap between what our democracy ought to be and what it is, between the decency of ordinary citizens and the horrible warping of their votes and desires once they get translated into partisan politics. It's gotten so bad that millions of Americans who once worked, led, and campaigned for our major political parties have severed—or are at least rethinking—their attachment to them. These Americans once served as full-fledged "Republicans" and "Democrats." But a growing number now doubt their affiliation. They no longer want to belong to either camp—or at least want to remove the insignia from their old uniforms.

My own example is instructive. As a Republican, I have served as a cabinet member (once), as a presidential commission member (three times), as an all-purpose political ombudsman (many times), and as a relentless crusader for fiscal responsibility whom some would call a crank (throughout). During most of my service, I have been careful not to subscribe to party dogma that violated my common sense, nor assume that a constituency is sacrosanct just because the party says so, nor believe that the other party is automatically the enemy. Yet that's just the problem. Increasingly, those who serve my party are subject to all of these pressures. And I know many Democrats who feel just as I do about their own party.

I believe this political dysfunction poses a clear danger to our nation. It does so by paralyzing our capacity to make elementary fiscal choices—the kind of choices, which, if left unmade by a person or family, would quickly lead to ruining their career or their life. First we had the ideologues of tax and spend. Then we had the ideologues of don't-tax and spend. Today, both have triumphed, with the result that the United States is committed to spending literally trillions of dollars more in personal benefits and collective security over the coming decades than citizens either expect or can afford to pay. The Democrats and the Republicans, with their lopsided and mutually irreconcilable worldviews, have found only one important way to compromise, and this is for both sides to take what they want (low taxing and high spending) and send the bill to our kids. These two parties have launched America into the new century on a course of vast and mounting budget deficits which, if left unaltered, can only end in an economy-shattering crisis or crushing burdens on America's younger generations—or both.

Steered by bankrupt parties, in short, we will soon become a bankrupt nation. That is what this book is about.

What Went Wrong with the Party of Abraham Lincoln

I have been proud to be a Republican. For me, the Republican Party has always embodied the unique American dream of self-direction and unlimited individual achievement—even for those of very modest means (as was my own parents' family). Republicans believe that being a citizen of a "republic" entails duties as well as rights.

Fiscal stewardship has likewise been a bedrock principle of the Grand Old Party since its origins in the 1850s. Republicans have traditionally believed that America should invest in the next generation and that good citizens should never allow government to undermine such efforts by burdening posterity with unsustainable liabilities. When debts are incurred, they are to be paid back as soon as possible. At various times in our history (especially after wars), Republican leaders have honored this principle by advocating and legislating painful budgetary retrenchment, including spending cuts and tax hikes.

At times they overdid a good thing. Herbert Hoover (the only former secretary of commerce to win the presidency, I note without comment) has rightly been condemned for pushing fiscal restraint when he should have been pushing fiscal stimulus. Blame him, if you will, for the severity of the Great Depression or for worshipping at "the temple of the balanced budget." But don't blame him for his intentions—and don't blame the Republican Party for principles of fiscal responsibility that have helped make America the most envied and future-oriented nation on earth. Principles are important only to the extent that they restrain us from what we might otherwise find tempting. Over much of its history a younger, less educated, poorer, and sometimes desperate America was no doubt tempted to borrow from the affluence they (rightly) expected their offspring would someday enjoy. But the people and their leaders chose not to. And today we thank them for it.

Over the last quarter century, unfortuantely, the Grand Old Party has abandoned these original convictions. Without ever renouncing stewardship itself—indeed, while talking incessantly about legacies, endowments, family values, and leaving "no child behind"—the GOP leadership has gradually embraced a more indulgent fiscal philosophy. It now seems to believe that deficit spending energizes America by liberating taxpayers from the need to pay their own way. Deficits have become like aspirin, a sort of fiscal wonder drug. We should take them regularly just to stay healthy and take lots of them whenever we're feeling out of sorts.

With the arrival of Ronald Reagan in the White House, this idea was first introduced as part of an extraordinary "supply-side revolution" in fiscal policy, needed (so the thinking ran) as a onetime fix for an economy gripped by stagflation. To those who worried about large and chronic deficits, they said, Relax, it won't happen—we'll "grow out of them." But we didn't. During Reagan's administration the federal government borrowed more from the public (in inflation-adjusted dollars) than it did during all of World War II. For the first time in U.S. history, people began to explain large swings in interest rates, the stock market, and the exchange-rate value of the dollar by pointing to large, erratic jumps in federal indebtedness.

After George Bush, Sr., famously broke his promise of "no new taxes" in 1990, he lost his party's right wing immediately—and his presidency two years later. Tax cutting thereafter became the GOP's core platform. By 1996 even Bob Dole, who had been a leading deficit hawk during the 1980s, ran for president as a supply-side evangelist. A growing number of Republican leaders argued that deficit finance was nearly always a permissible strategy, though much of this bold talk could be excused as the bluster of a party that didn't have to lead the country. Then, with the Republican takeover of the White House in 2001, the party's tax cut agenda ascended to a new level of irresponsibility. For the first time ever, a Republican leadership in complete control of our national government would embark on a policy of massive and endless debt creation.

The numbers are simply breathtaking. When President George W. Bush entered office, the ten-year budget balance was officially projected to be a surplus of $5.6 trillion—an unexpected blessing, which the new team firmly promised would be used "as a means for shoring up the economic and fiscal environment that our children and grandchildren would inherit." In February of 2001 the new administration's first budget outlined a plan to use at least $2.0 trillion of this surplus to pay down the federal debt. Much of the rest would go for other future-oriented purposes, such as a "contingency reserve," reform of Medicare, and (possibly) a pre-funding of the future cost of Social Security. Amid heady talk about "the largest debt reduction ever achieved by any nation at any time," White House officials publicly worried about how the Federal Reserve would function once the public no longer owned Treasury notes or bonds.

They didn't need to worry long. Soon hit by recession together with the bursting of the stock market bubble, and then by 9/11, the surplus projections fell. When Bush went ahead with two large and heavily back-ended tax cuts in 2001 and 2002, they fell much further. By the end of 2002 all but $1.0 trillion of the ten-year surplus had vanished—with no contingency reserve and nothing done about Medicare or Social Security. Unfazed by this turnaround, the Bush administration pushed a third tax cut package through Congress in the spring of 2003 in the face of huge new fiscal demands, including a war in Iraq and an urgent "homeland security" agenda. By August the Congressional Budget Office (CBO) officially projected the ten-year fiscal balance at a *deficit* of $1.4 trillion.

Along the way, The Concord Coalition (on which I serve as a cofounder) tried to warn policymakers about the perils of this fiscal deterioration. In the spring of 2001 five board members of The Concord Coalition, former senators Sam Nunn and Warren Rudman, former Fed chairman Paul Volcker, former Treasury secretary Bob Rubin, and myself, held a press conference. We argued that fiscal stimulus made plenty of sense so long as it was (first) temporary, (second) targeted at individuals or businesses that would spend it, and (third) not going to worsen our longer-term fiscal outlook. The Bush administration went in the opposite direction on all three counts.

Two years later The Concord Coalition, together with the Committee for Economic Development and the Center on Budget and Policy Priorities, released a statement in which we explained why the growth of the deficit was so dangerous. We explained that the tax cuts would do little to benefit an economy that was already recovering, but would add to long-term deficits that were already unsustainable. Again the administration did not respond with any change in its fiscal policy.

Indeed, there was more red ink yet to come before 2003 was over—this time on the spending side. In November Congress passed and President Bush signed the Medicare Prescription Drug, Improvement, and Modernization Act, the largest legislated entitlement expansion since the heyday of the Great Society. The stated intent was to address the legitimate needs of the small share of poor seniors who have trouble affording prescription drugs. The result, an unfunded universal benefit to all 40 million Medicare beneficiaries, is so expensive that budget experts still have trouble putting any upper limits on its eventual growth. The political goal was clear: to preempt the number one issue on the Democratic agenda.

When the bill came up for its final votes, the CBO declared it would cost $400 billion over the next ten years. Just two months after the bill had passed, the President's Office of Management and Budget (OMB) confessed that under its own assumptions, which were conveniently not released until after the bill was enacted, the cost would be more like $535 billion. Because the program is phased in, moreover, the estimates for the initial decade are deceptively small. In its *second* ten years, this new "Medicare Part D" benefit is expected to cost well over $2 trillion. And even that number is low, since the White House and Congress designed absurd coverage gaps or "doughnut holes" into the benefit formula in the full expectation that seniors would later insist that these holes be filled with more coverage. It's the old sales tactic: hook the customer on the basic home first, then sell the floors and the plumbing.

By January of 2004 the CBO's ten-year fiscal projection had worsened to a deficit of $1.9 trillion. But if you assume, as many prudent forecasters do, that all the recent tax cuts will become permanent (which is what the President wants) and that total "discretionary" or appropriated spending grows as fast as the economy (we have, after all, a very expensive foreign policy agenda), the number is much larger. According to the CBO, it comes to a deficit of $6.0 trillion. That means deficits *averaging* $600 billion per year over the next decade.

Gazing over the Fiscal Brink

So there you have it: in just three years U.S. voters witnessed a negative swing of over $10 trillion in the ten-year federal deficit outlook. By the year 2014, that will amount to $90,000 in additional federal debt for every household. Much of this swing was driven by forces at least partly beyond this administration's control—including the recession, the war on terror, and even the Medicare expansion (since many Republicans feared the other party would kill them politically if they did *not* pass it). Still, at least one-third of the entire ten-year deficit swing can be accounted for by tax cuts imposed solely under the White House's unflagging leadership. And these are large, back-ended tax cuts—with nearly all of the costs arriving after the presumed need for fiscal stimulus has passed. Whatever the president's rationale back in 2001, his team's endless quest for more such reductions even while fiscal projections were plunging suggests that common sense had been blinded by ideological partisanship.

Apparently it is always the right time for a tax cut. Coming into power, the Republican leaders faced a choice between tax cuts and providing genuine funding for the future of Social Security (what a landmark reform this would have been!). They chose tax cuts. After 9/11, they faced a choice between tax cuts and paying for extensive measures needed to protect this nation against further terrorist attacks. They chose tax cuts. After war broke out in the Mideast even while senior lobbies were clamoring for a drug benefit, they faced a choice between tax cuts and galvanizing the nation behind a policy of future-oriented burden-sharing. Again and again, they chose tax cuts.

By February of 2004, with the economy reviving, many Washington hands doubted the White House would persevere in its tax cut plans. Personal income tax revenue, which had hit $1 trillion in 2000, had fallen so far that the CBO projected that it would not reach that dollar mark again until 2007. Why keep cutting and going deeper in debt when the economy no longer needs the boost? The president's FY 2005 budget proved the doubters wrong. It was déjà vu all over again.

In order to justify further tax cuts—while still loudly promising "to cut the federal deficit in half" by 2009—the administration engaged in a disingenuous rhetorical ploy. When arguing for the original tax cuts, the Bush team okayed a congressional gimmick to "sunset" all of the cuts (wink, wink) by the end of the decade, supposedly to prevent any long-term harmful effects on the budget. Now, in its FY 2005 budget, the team argued that making the tax cuts permanent is affordable because only the next five years should matter—failing to mention in this sleight of hand that more than 80 percent of the ten-year revenue loss will occur after the year 2009. Neat, isn't it? The team also proposed new tax-free personal saving and retirement accounts. How to afford them? Make the *payouts* from these accounts tax-exempt (rather than the contributions), so that most of the revenue losses won't occur for decades.

Other budget hurdles were cleared less artfully. Every tax expert knows that Congress must fix the alternative minimum tax or "AMT" before it unfairly hits more and more middle-class taxpayers. The Bush budgeteers agree, but since the fix is costly they decided to patch it one year at a time. Do we still need to do something about Social Security or health insurance? Sure, they said, so long as they don't cost anything. Another war in the Mideast? We'll do an end-run around the budget and fund those through "emergency" appropriations.

Despite the subterfuges, the Bush team could not make its deficit target without yet another stunt, and this one isn't pretty: a one-half percent annual growth cap on all domestic discretionary spending unrelated to homeland security. This amounts to a 10 percent cut over the next five years, in real dollars per capita, in federal spending on everything from justice and education to clean water and immigration. Almost no one in Washington believes that Congress will pay any attention to this "one-half percent" cap. Proposed in a number-fudging budget during an election year—and following several years of rapid spending growth—not even fiscal conservatives take it seriously. Most budget experts believe that deficit spending will increase rapidly with no end in sight. They also understand that, thanks to an impending retirement boom, all of the fiscal projections will get much worse during the next decade.

Loss of fiscal credibility leads to loss of overall credibility—even for a leader with the able command skills of this president. "This will take time and sacrifice," announced President Bush upon declaring war on Iraq. "Yet we will do what is necessary, we will spend what is necessary." What he deftly left unmentioned is *who* will do the sacrificing and *who* will pay for the spending. While America's young men and women were being asked to risk their lives, the president boldly asked the rest of us to "sacrifice" by agreeing to permanent reductions in our own taxes. Such tax cuts, unmatched by spending cuts, are precisely equivalent to shifting even more of our future federal spending burden onto these young soldiers' future income. Keep in mind that these young people, according to official Social Security trustees' numbers, are *already* expected to pay the equivalent of 25 to 40 percent of their payroll into Social Security and Medicare before they retire just to keep these programs solvent.

Relative to the size of our economy, the recent $10 trillion deficit swing is the largest in U.S. history other than during years of total war. With total war, of course, you have the excuse that you expect the emergency to be over soon and thus to be able to pay back the new debt during subsequent years of peace and prosperity. Yet few believe that the major causes of today's deficit projections, most certainly not the war on terror, are similarly short-term. Indeed, the biggest single factor in the projections—the growing cost of senior entitlements—is certain to become much worse just beyond the ten-year horizon when the huge baby boom generation starts retiring in earnest.

Two facts unmentioned in the deficit numbers cited above

will help put the cost of the boomer retirement into focus. First, the deficit projections would be much larger if we took away the "trust-fund surpluses" we are supposed to be dedicating to the future of Social Security and Medicare. And second, the assets in these trust funds, even if we were really accumulating the surpluses—which we were not—are dwarfed by the $27 trillion in total unfinanced liabilities still hanging over both programs. (This is the official number cited in the 2004 federal budget; as we shall see, other estimates of our future fiscal imbalance range much higher, as much as $74 trillion.) A longer time horizon does not justify deficits over the next decade. If anything, the longer-term aging of America is an argument for sizable surpluses over the next decade to prepare for the tide of red ink we know is coming.

How big is the problem, practically speaking? Look at it this way. If we wanted to balance the budget by 2014, on our current track we would either have to raise both individual and corporate income taxes by 38 percent or cut both Social Security and Medicare by 55 percent. Further on, with the Woodstock generation retiring en masse, the trends begin to worsen very quickly. To balance the budget by 2030 (assuming we do nothing until then), we would have to raise all payroll taxes by 100 percent *and* individual income taxes by 50 percent or we would have to cut Social Security and Medicare benefits in half *and* cut all nondefense discretionary spending by half.

"If all these numbers are making your head spin, don't worry; just remember that they are all big, and they are all bad," explains David Walker, comptroller general of the nonpartisan General Accounting Office, which generated the 2030 numbers I have just cited. Walker has a fifteen-year statutory appointment, so he is beholden to no one. He goes on: "Deficits do matter, especially if they are large, structural, and recurring in nature. In addition, our projected budget deficits are not 'manageable' without significant changes in 'status quo' programs. We cannot simply grow our way out of this problem."

RINOs, Starve-the-Beasters, and Big-Government Conservatives

One might suppose that a reasoned debate over this deficit-happy policy would at least be admissible within the discussion tent of the GOP. But party discipline is absolute in the Bush administration. I've seen Republicans get blackballed for merely observing, in point of fact, that national investment is limited by national savings; that large deficits typically reduce national savings; or that higher deficits eventually trigger higher interest rates. (The latter proposition was denied by the former chairman of the Council of Economic Advisers, Glenn Hubbard, until someone inconveniently pointed out that he affirmed it himself in a textbook he wrote before joining the administration.)

I've seen other Republicans get pilloried for picking on the wrong constituency—for suggesting, perhaps, that a tax loophole for a corporation or wealthy retiree is no different, ethically or economically, than a dubious welfare program. Let me mention a fascinating example of this ideological bias. From 1990 to 2002 the Budget Enforcement Act required Congress to follow a "pay-go" rule that made it difficult to enact a permanent new spending hike or tax cut without also enacting an offsetting spending cut or tax hike. The Bush team let the BEA expire at the end of fiscal year 2002. In 2004 they want to reenact the pay-go rule—*but only for spending hikes.* Tax cuts will henceforth always be favored in the budget process. A new tax loophole for (say) offshore banks or vacation homeowners will automatically receive a green light in Congress ahead of a new benefit provision for disabled widows.

Leaders of GOP antitax activists take pride in how effectively their groups can target, and thus intimidate and defeat, any Republican legislator who votes in favor of any tax increase for any reason. "We want to be seen as the tax cut enforcer in the party," says Club for Growth president Stephen Moore, noting that 85 percent of his party's senators and 95 percent of its congressmen have signed antitax "pledges." Even war is no excuse. "Nothing is more important in the face of war than cutting taxes," said House majority leader Tom DeLay while missiles were flying over Iraq, in a dictum that surely would have arched the eyebrow of Abraham Lincoln or Franklin Roosevelt. To be concerned about deficits is to be—that reviled word—a "moderate." "I happen to think moderate Republicanism represents traditional Republicanism," observes Maine senator Olympia Snowe, whose vocal complaints about deficits made her a target of vicious attack ads by the Club for Growth. They have also earned her, along with a shrinking minority of other GOP legislators, the "RINO" label among activists ("Republican in Name Only").

For "supply-side" Republicans, the pursuit of lower taxes has evolved into a religion, indeed a theology that discards any objective evidence that violates the faith. Even after the explosion of federal debt in the eighties, an explosion supply-siders had predicted would never happen, leading prophets like the late Bob Bartley, editorial editor of *The Wall Street Journal*, called for more tax cuts to kick off another "seven fat years." Any tax cut, anytime, always generates prosperity. It may sound illogical, but as Jude Wanniski once put it in his seminal 1978 book, that's just *The Way the World Works*.

For other Republicans, the fat-years language is merely tactical. Many partisan Republicans will admit, in private at least, that the supply-side argument is a charade. But they support tax cuts anyway because they believe that America suffers from too much government and that this is the only strategy that will reduce its size. Shut off government's source of revenue, say these "starve-the-beast" strategists, and the Democrats will have no choice but to shut off spending or risk economic disaster. For too long the politics of pleasure have only helped big-spending Democrats; now, say these partisans, it's time for small-spending Republicans to do some payback.

It's akin to the parent who holds a gun to his child's head in order to get the other parent to agree with him—in an argument over the child's future welfare, no less. But the strategy is not only perverse, it's clearly ineffective. Over the last three years it hasn't persuaded Democrats to become more cooperative or to reduce their spending agenda. If anything, using the deficit threat as a bargaining chip has encouraged many Democrats to grow more cavalier themselves: if you can borrow for your big tax cut, well, we can borrow for our big health insurance plan.

Or why just talk about Democrats? Casual deficits have encouraged *Republicans* to become reckless with outlays—"to spend like drunken sailors," to borrow a phrase from one of several conservative groups expressing growing discomfort with the president's fiscal policy. Excluding homeland security, domestic discretionary outlays have soared 7 percent annually over his first three years, in part due to pork-laden appropriations bills. One bill that (barely) did not pass, a bloated "energy" proposal, was so full of special interest "earmarks"—often a euphemism for pork—to Rust Belt companies and shopping malls that Senator John McCain memorably blasted it as "spending for Hooters and polluters." Another bill that did pass, the 2004 omnibus appropriations package, contained some 7,900 spending items specially "earmarked" for lawmakers' home districts, everything from art exhibits in Iowa to a new senior center in Valdez, Alaska. By all accounts, there is vastly more earmarking today—perhaps five or ten times as much—than there was a decade ago.

It is not clear why President Bush doesn't veto this pork. Maybe he's a "cafeteria Catholic" who likes to pick and choose where to be virtuous. Maybe executive approval on spending is the price he pays for lawmaker approval on taxes. All we know is that he is currently on track to become the first president since James A. Garfield never to veto a bill—and Garfield died after only six months in office. To find a nonvetoing president who served more than a year, you'd have to go all the way back to Millard Fillmore, America's last "Whig" president who later on (by the way) became leader of the Know-Nothing Party. To find one who served a full term, you'd have to go back to John Quincy Adams, and there you're within hailing distance of the founders.

President Bush now promises that he will put domestic appropriations on a very tight leash. But even if we believed him, the fact remains that this leaves out most of the federal budget. In other words, it's hard to be impressed by the starve-the-beast argument when GOP leaders do nothing to reform entitlements, urge greater spending on defense, and allow debt-service costs to rise along with the debt—and when these three functions (benefits, defense, and interest) constitute over four-fifths of all federal outlays. "I don't think you'll find anybody in any party who takes seriously the administration's promise to hold down spending," says well-known conservative Bruce Bartlett. "The president has never made small government a major element of his philosophy."

There's yet another view of Republican intentions, but it's hardly more flattering. According to some observers, the policies of George W. Bush and his congressional allies represent the ascendancy within the GOP of "big-government" conservatism (or, as George Will puts it, "strong-government" conservatism).

Big-government conservatives don't bother much about balanced budgets or the size of government. Abroad, they care about "national greatness" and national security. At home, they care about a powerful and popular government that can put together winning political coalitions. They will embrace big spending to outflank the Democrats and cement the loyalty of Americans whom they regard as their natural constituency—the employed, the affluent, the invested, and the retired. Meanwhile, neoconservatives (who coined the term) want "big government" to help them restore what they allege to be the lost moral fiber of the American people. Few care which political or economic principles are discarded along the way—prompting not only fiscally responsible GOP "moderates" but plenty of GOP libertarians to wonder if the party of the rustic log cabin is turning into the party of imperial bread and circuses.

Is President Bush a big-government conservative? Surely much of the description fits. Surely, too, big government will quickly find favor with any leader, liberal or conservative, at a time when the public is fearful of war and attack. But to explain Bush's embrace of big-government conservatism—if that's what it is—is not to excuse the manner of his embrace. A nation cannot mortgage its long-term future to purchase any "greatness" worthy of the name.

What Went Wrong with the Party of Thomas Jefferson

Not surprisingly, many Democrats have thrown a spotlight on the GOP's internecine quarrel over taxes and spending in order to improve their own party's image with voters, even to the point of claiming to be born-again champions of fiscal responsibility. "Squandering our future" and "disinheriting the next generation" have recently become crowd-pleasing attack lines among Democratic contenders for the White House and Congress.

All this comes from the party that has, over the course of several decades, turned the federal government into a massive entitlements vending machine which operates by dispensing new benefits in return for organized political support and by deferring costs as far as possible into the future. These federal benefits, in real (inflation-adjusted) dollars per capita, have expanded *sixfold* since 1965. This fact undermines Democratic charges that the Republicans have "slashed" our safety net in the "mean" age of Reagan or the Bushes. It also makes many Americans wonder if we've seen anything close to a sixfold improvement in the nation's biggest domestic challenges, from poverty to education.

But some say, Oh no, those old paleoliberals are no longer around. A fresh generation of neoliberal Democrats believes government can be mean and lean, efficient and market-oriented, "steer" the economy without "pulling" the oars, and so on.

Really? Take another look at the six major contenders for the Democratic presidential nomination at the beginning of 2004. Though all of them excoriated Bush for his tax cuts, the four leading "centrists" (John Kerry, Wesley Clark, John Edwards, and Joe Lieberman) refused to roll most of them back except for "the rich" or the "wealthiest" Americans. This means most of the revenue loss would remain. Meanwhile, their web sites brim with "bold" and "generous" and *expensive* new spending programs—for seniors and youth, for energy and the environment, for education and vets, for the disabled and the uninsured. According to one estimate, their proposed new spending agenda ranged from $170 billion per year (for Lieberman) to $369 billion per year (for Dick Gephardt). In all of their two-hundred-odd budget proposals announced by their campaigns or drafted in bills they've submitted to Congress, only two would reduce spending.

Though I welcome any newcomers to the cause of genuine fiscal stewardship, I sincerely doubt that the Democratic Party as a whole is any less dysfunctional than the Republican. It's just dysfunctional in a different way. Like two partners in a troubled marriage, these two parties mirror, react to, and ultimately thrive off the other's pathology. It is said that two type A personalities can sometimes become a successful couple because, in a kind of interlocking neurosis, the rocks in one head fill the holes in the other's. Unfortunately, that never seems to happen in politics.

Yes, today's Republican leaders demonstrate a reckless disregard for widening long-term deficits. But it was the Democrats who, long before Ronald Reagan, labored patiently to purge America of its traditional aversion to deficits. They did so first as Keynesian academics in the 1940s and 1950s. They did so later as the best-and-brightest advisers who successfully urged President Kennedy to abandon the Republicans' "fiscal puritan ethic" in 1962 (explaining why JFK would later become a hero to many GOP supply-siders). They did so still later as the pump-priming allies of Lyndon Johnson. As recently as 1997 thirty-five Democratic senators killed the efforts of a bipartisan Senate majority to pass a balanced budget amendment—and defied the 80 percent of Americans who said they favored the amendment. During the Clinton years, the government's official deficits did go down. But the government's accounting (or "accrual") deficits, which include charges for unfunded liabilities in Social Security and Medicare, continued to climb, and President Clinton did nothing to stop them. If Democrats want to be the antideficit party, they have a lot of history to account for.

Yes, the Republican Party line often boils down to cutting taxes and damning the torpedoes. And yes, by whipping up one-sided popular support for less taxes, the GOP preempts responsible discussion of tax fairness and forces many Democrats to echo weakly, "me too." But it's also true that the Democratic Party line often boils down to boosting outlays and damning the torpedoes. Likewise, Democrats regularly short-circuit any prudent examination of the single biggest spending issue, the future of senior entitlements, by castigating all reformers as heartless Scrooges. No national candidate who says the affordability of these entitlements is a problem or challenge has a prayer of winning a primary. Nothing better reveals the heart of "the Democratic wing of the Democratic Party," as Governor Howard Dean liked to put it, than the furor over Dean's discussions with GOP leaders in the mid-1990s about a plan to reduce the annual growth rate of Medicare from 10 percent to 7 percent. For this apparent outrage, Dean was attacked for weeks. You might have thought he was accused of child abuse or cross burning.

Republicans don't like to gaze at the future of their deficits. But do Democrats enjoy gazing at the future of their favorite programs? Social Security, as officially projected, will be able to pay only 74 percent of its now scheduled benefits by the year 2045. Will Democrats face that fact or bury their heads in the sand? I have often and at great length criticized the free-lunch games of many GOP reform plans for Social Security—such as personal accounts that will be "funded" by deficit-financed contributions. But at least they pretend to have reform plans. *Democrats have nothing.* Or, as Bob Kerrey puts it quite nicely, most of his fellow Democrats propose the "do-nothing plan," a blank sheet of paper that essentially says it is OK to cut benefits by 26 percent across the board whenever the money runs out.

Assuming that Democrats really care about the lower-income widows and orphans who would be most affected by such a cut, I have suggested to them that maybe we ought to introduce an "affluence test" that reduces Social Security for fat cats like me. My reasoning was that, to preserve our safety net for the truly needy, maybe we need to economize on our hammock for the well-off. Put differently, if everyone is on the wagon, who is going to pull it? To my amazement, Democrats angrily respond with slogans like "programs for the poor are poor programs" or "Social Security is a social contract that cannot be broken." (I keep telling them, I don't need these benefits, but they tell me I must get them anyway—for the benefit of others. In other words, we must bribe the rich so they will help the poor.) In 2003 most Democrats, along with the AARP, had trouble swallowing a provision to require the wealthy to pay higher premiums to participate in Medicare. Apparently it doesn't matter that Medicare is already unsustainable, and that the new drug benefit will increase the cost of the program by another 30 percent in 2030. They cling to the mast and are ready to go down with the ship. To most Democratic leaders, federal entitlements are their theology.

To be sure, Republicans can be shameless when they dress up tax cuts in patriotic colors—as though accepting a tax *cut* were somehow equivalent to wartime sacrifice. Yet Democrats do the same with entitlement expansions. When they talk fulsomely about their more expensive benefit proposal, such as a Medicare drug benefit that outspends the GOP plan, they like to say it reflects their stronger commitment to the greatness and generosity of America.

Either way, Republican or Democratic, it's astonishing how we can congratulate ourselves on our own civic virtue when we give ourselves bigger presents and send bigger bills to our kids. In today's Washington, a "courageous" politician is one who takes money from the next generation and passes it out to friends; a "selfish" politician is one who does the reverse.

The same holds for national security and sacred-cow interests. Yes, the GOP has its ties to Main Street and Wall Street. But Democrats cling to their own graven images. In the wake of 9/11, for instance, the Republicans cleverly mousetrapped the bill on terrorism insurance by tying it to litigation reform, and the bill on airport security by tying it to civil service reform. Democrats saw it coming but still couldn't help themselves. They noisily delayed the bills until they passed muster with the trial lawyers' lobby and the government employees' union—a crass favoritism that hurt them in the subsequent 2002 elections. The Republicans, framing the issue as a choice between national security and special interests, were delighted to put them in that box. They knew the Democrats' hands were tied. Loyal supporters must be serviced.

So let's be honest: both parties are the problem. If the Republicans have been culpable for most of the recent follies, it's only because they have recently been pulling the leadership levers. Before them, the Democrats have plenty to answer for. The high priests and assorted ayatollahs of the Republican

Party have never met a tax they didn't want to cut. The revered theologians and ragtag mullahs of the Democratic Party have never met an entitlement program they didn't want to expand.

When in power, the two parties often end up doing injury to the very constituencies they pledge to help. The Republicans champion a family-oriented opportunity society, yet busily rig the economy with debt explosives that sabotage every parent's hopes to raise capital for a new business or pass on assets to their children. The Democrats champion the working classes, yet happily steer their New Deal entitlement ship of state, with all of its top-heavy new rigging, toward an unyielding demographic iceberg that threatens to leave these hard-working Americans adrift without a lifeboat.

When out of power, the two parties have forgotten what it means to constitute an honorable opposition—forgotten, that is, how even the minority party, by force of good example, can serve the country and encourage the majority party to do the right thing. Clever partisans who advise political campaigns like to laugh with delight whenever the opposition candidate takes a dogmatic or demagogic or plain idiotic stand in public. "More leverage and running room for our guy!" they cheer. In truth, even as they cruise to victory, they should be mourning. They will have to live with what happens to their country long after they (and everyone else) will have forgotten about their campaign and even their candidate.

How to Build a Better Future

We all recall the old philosophy riddle: What happens when an irresistible force meets an immovable object? At least one answer to that conundrum lurks somewhere in America's not-so-distant future. The irresistible force is benefit growth in entitlement programs. This growth is automatic. It is linked to the upward march of wages and medical prices, and to the aging of the population. It is scheduled to happen even if Congress never passes another law—and relatively few legislators wish to terminate their careers early by being the first to try to stop it. The immovable object is taxes. Tax bills must start in the House, the GOP majority in the House seems (at this point) very durable, and nearly all of these Republicans have sworn to an oath never to hike a tax. And in any case many Democrats would stand by them.

It's useless to speculate which party has the better excuse for inaction. Yes, benefit spending is the fiscal category that has changed and will change the most over the long haul—in an upward direction—which suggests that it's the Democrats who should yield first on entitlements. On the other hand, all spending promises should in principle be funded until the promises are changed, which suggests it's the Republicans who should yield first on taxes. Behind these arguments lie fundamental differences in each party's vision for America. In one party's "virtuous" America, government is smaller and favors liberty a bit more. In the other party's "decent" America, government is larger and favors equality a bit more. I certainly don't mean to minimize these differences. They are important.

But there are degrees of importance, and only blind ideologues cannot recognize this. Let me explain. Americans may have very different views about whether they would prefer, come the year 2030, to see the federal government both taxing and spending at 18 percent of GDP or to see it both taxing and spending at 32 percent of GDP. Yet very few budget experts, even the most partisan ones, believe that either outcome is likely to wreck our economy and ruin our nation. Now consider a scenario in which by 2030 we are taxing at 18 percent of GDP and spending at 32 percent. This certainly would wreck and ruin us. It would do so long before we even reached 2030. And this is the future, according to the General Accounting Office (GAO), we are now embarked upon if current tax policy and current spending policy get locked in stone. Should this future ever materialize, no one will ever care which party, circa A.D. 2004, was pursuing which vision.

This book is my effort to explain the critical fiscal choices we face as a nation.

Chapters 2, 3, and 4 lay out the overall dimensions of this challenge. In Chapter 2 I examine the budget projections themselves. How do we account for government liabilities? What do the deficit forecasts say? Why are structural deficits so bad, anyway? And how do today's budget plans determine the trade-offs boomers will have to make in their retirement—between their own living standards and those of their children? In Chapters 3 and 4 I cover the two great drivers of future fiscal pressure, the aging of America and the emergence of new dangers abroad. The first driver is part of a historic demographic transformation sweeping over most of the world, excepting only the poorest of countries. It has profound implications for our society, our culture, our family life—and of course our federal budget. This domestic driver alone is enough to break the bank. The second driver encompasses not just the spending needs of America's new war on terror but also the many perils of America's "twin deficit" dependence on foreign borrowing. This global driver accelerates the timetable for necessary action.

Chapters 5, 6, and 7 cover the origins and history of today's partisan gridlock. How did all this get started? Which party did what, and when? Are there lessons to be learned? Many Democrats may not want to hear, in Chapter 5, about their party's central role in setting this whole train of unsustainable promises in motion back in the 1960s and 1970s. Many Republicans may not want to hear, in Chapter 6, about how their party dug America into a deeper hole by trading away fiscal candor for electoral advantage during the 1980s and 1990s. Chapter 7 is all about the myths that each party has invented over the years to justify its lopsided perspective on the budget. To Democrats, endless spending growth is somehow never a problem. To Republicans, endless deficit growth is somehow never a problem. To paraphrase Josh Billings, it's not what our party leaders don't know that gets us in trouble. It's what they know that just ain't so.

In Chapter 8 I try to assess a few of the deeper reasons why our country seems to have difficulty focusing on its long-term fiscal future. Many say that it's the American people who have basically changed in their attitudes and habits. They say that rising individualism, more mobility, weaker family ties, and new forms of fast-paced media (like TV and the Internet) are undermining our sense of community and by extension our connection to the future. It's not hard to find evidence of "short-termitis" or a grab-it-now, live-for-today outlook on life. Yet while some of these trends are real, I believe that most of the responsibility lies with our elected representatives and the dysfunction of their political parties. Most of our bad choices have not been "forced" on Washington by voters. Washington made them on their own—and the fact that most voters do not trust their government is good evidence that they do not feel well represented. Even today's young adults, those who show the most disengagement from political life, can be re-engaged if leaders made a real effort. Sadly, few leaders feel it's worth the trouble.

So what can Americans do about it? In Chapter 9 I outline a few large steps we could take—starting with reforms of Social Security and our major health care programs that would bring long-term spending back in line with long-term revenues and enhance our rate of household savings. I advocate a stronger budget process in Congress to help ensure that America never again wanders near the fiscal precipice. I admit that all these reforms are powerful medicine—but then again so is the challenge we face. Since fiscal policy is designed by politicians, I also outline an agenda that I think would bring new health back to our system of political parties. It consists of a few simple reforms in redistricting, fund-raising, and public education that would help reverse the trend toward partisan gridlock and give the moderate mainstream more reason to get involved. With our party system on the mend, perhaps we can face both the challenge and the medicine.

The last chapter is a letter to the rising generation. Americans these days love to talk about their children—and about the importance of doing all the right things for them. In their families, Americans really are raising a confident, high-achieving, team-playing crop of new kids. Yet the greatest failing in our political system is our inability to translate what we do in our family lives over to what we do in our national life. If we fail our kids collectively as a nation, if we saddle them with unaffordable liabilities and do not leave them the fiscal and economic resources they need to meet their own new challenges, it won't be enough that we "meant" well. Posterity may never entirely forgive us for squandering the national opportunities that our own ancestors safeguarded for us.

When President Bush repeatedly announces to great applause that "I did not take this office to pass on problems to future generations," I believe he is sincere. I believe the enthusiasm of the crowd is genuine. What's missing is any attempt by either his party or the opposition party to educate voters about the very large problems we are indeed passing on to them. And even when voters find out, our parties and leaders offer no real remedies.

Dietrich Bonhoeffer was a German theologian who witnessed firsthand the rise of fascism in Germany. Though he could have fled to America, he stayed in his homeland to help Jews and other persecuted people to safety until he was arrested. Among the many penetrating thoughts he penned while awaiting execution, one has always caught my attention. "The ultimate test of a moral society," Bonhoeffer wrote, "is the kind of world it leaves to its children." Few of us will ever be called on to pay the price he paid. But most of us understand that one essential duty of any citizen is speaking up and taking action when we see a great wrong threatening our republic's future. What is now happening fiscally is a great wrong. And all of us can say or do something to help avert it.

Chapter 2

WHY DEFICITS MATTER TO YOU AND YOUR FUTURE

As red leaves fell in the autumn of 2001, Americans were mesmerized by news of the inglorious collapse of Enron. Through fraudulent accounting artifices, Enron's management had concocted an outrageously misleading portrait of the company's financial health. The annual report for 2000 showed a net income of plus $1 billion. By the time Enron filed for bankruptcy in December of 2001, the public learned that its towering debts amounted to $35 billion—and that its real bottom line for 2000 was probably (no one will ever know for sure) close to minus $5 billion. In the wake of this scandal, which has thus far led to felony indictments for top Enron managers and ruin for Enron's prestigious accounting firm, the U.S. Congress went to work and enacted a sweeping set of corporate regulations called Sarbanes-Oxley to prevent such malfeasance in the future.

That same year, Congress publicly reported that the federal government in FY 2000 ran a record budget surplus of $236 billion. Yet here's the interesting part: if Congress had required itself to follow the same accounting rules it requires of a private-sector corporation (as spelled out in the Employment Retirement Income Securities Act or "ERISA"), it would have shown a jaw-dropping annual deficit of well over $1 *trillion*—that is, $1,000 billion. Keeping crooked books, under Sarbanes-Oxley, is a felony offense. Thus, if Congress had to abide by its own rules, it would have to throw itself in jail for fraudulent accounting.

What is this large annual charge (at least $1.5 trillion) that Congress currently chooses to ignore? It is the cost of amortizing the federal government's unfunded liability for future promised retirement outlays, Social Security and Medicare benefits in particular. That unfunded liability, calculated each year by the Treasury Department, amounted to $27 trillion as of January 1, 2003. It is the total value of benefits that are payable to—minus all the payroll taxes and premiums that are receivable from—every American today aged fifteen and over who is or could be a participant in these programs. Congress doesn't actually have a penny of this money in the bank. That's why the liability is called "unfunded." And that's why ERISA would insist that it be amortized.

Unlike corporate pension plans, government plans can lean on younger and unborn Americans for revenue (we don't call them "pay as you go" for no reason). This is in violation of yet another accounting rule that would apply to a corporate financial officer—but never mind. Let's allow it. Over the next seventy-five years the future contributions of these younger Americans (in excess of *their* benefits) amount to $6 trillion. What's left, the remaining $21 trillion, is the net cash drain on our budget due to all Americans, born and unborn, over the next seventy-five years. It is our nation's fiscal bottom line, expressed in what economists call "present value" terms. It is the amount we would need in hand, beginning today and earning interest, to offset the growing future cash deficits caused by these two programs from now until the year 2078.

Twenty-one trillion dollars is a lot of money. As the federal budget for FY 2004 helpfully reminds us, it "was nearly five times as large as today's publicly held national debt." "Expressed yet another way," explains the U.S. Treasury's Financial Report of the U.S. Government, "the combined shortfall in Social Security and Medicare was eight times the amount of total Government spending in fiscal 2002." Alternatively, it is roughly $200,000 per U.S. household—or double the value of all stocks, bonds, and mutual funds that Americans own.

Maybe you think the estimate appearing in the 2004 federal budget just reflects a bad year and that next year the number will improve. Think again. The trend over time is for the estimates to get worse. In 2000, the unfunded benefit liabilities were pegged at "only" $13 trillion. This year, they're $21 trillion. And by 2005, newly released figures by the Social Security and Medicare trustees, which reflect an acceleration in health-care benefit spending along with the new prescription drug expansion, show that the estimate will likely be much higher than it was in 2004—a huge jump all the way to $33 trillion.

Out-of-Kilter Balance Sheets and Runaway Deficits

Few Americans have heard of this genuine and officially acknowledged $21 trillion liability. What many more have heard about, instead, is something illusory—the $3 trillion in supposed "assets" saved in the Social Security and Medicare trust funds, accumulated surpluses that are supposed to help pay for the boomers' retirement. The bad news is that 3 is a much smaller number than 21. The worse news is that even this $3 trillion has not been saved in any real sense of the word. Any time a federal program like Social Security runs a surplus for the year, the U.S. Treasury spends the surplus immediately on other items. All the program gets back are IOUs from the Treasury for the money taken. The program then puts these IOUs into its trust fund. Nothing has really been saved since, if the program wants to redeem its IOUs, the Treasury will then have to cut spending, hike taxes, or borrow from the public (that is, run a bigger deficit) to raise the cash. These policy choices are identical to the choices the Treasury would face if there were no trust funds at all.

So are these trust funds meaningless? Not entirely. They do represent a blank check that Social Security or Part A of Medicare (Hospital Insurance) may draw on to pay benefits without using any of its own earmarked revenue. That's how these programs are projected to keep operating for many years after they first start to run annual cash deficits. Yet clearly, from the taxpayer's perspective, the trust funds accomplish nothing. Think of it this way. For Christmas, you tell your child you'll cover up to $100 in toy purchases at any time during the coming year. Though your child feels richer, your whole family's balance sheet is unchanged.

You can also see why rising cash deficits in these programs will soon put great pressure on the federal budget—decades before these programs technically "go bankrupt." Imagine giving your child permission to buy toys up to $10,000. You'll start feeling the pain long before your little angel finally maxes out. We too will soon start feeling the pain. Ignored in the recent media scare about how the bankruptcy date for Medicare's Hospital Insurance trust fund has been moved up from 2026 to 2019 is the fact that the HI trust fund is *already* running a cash deficit and that it will run cumulative cash deficits of $467 billion by the time it hits the bottom of its kitty in 2019. Similarly, the Social Security trust funds are projected to run an annual cash deficit of more than $100 billion as early as 2021—twenty years before that program's "bankruptcy" date.

The term Social Security "trust fund" is therefore a fiscal oxymoron since it isn't funded and it can't be trusted. Chalk up this double counting, instead, as yet one more fiscal exercise that would be illegal if anyone but Congress practiced it. As the Congressional Budget Office drily notes: "The assets of the Social Security trust funds do not represent any real stock of resources set aside to pay for benefits in the future."

Unfortunately, not only is our $21 trillion benefit liability undiminished by the trust funds, even this number underestimates the magnitude of our fiscal challenge. The calculation only includes benefit liabilities over the next seventy-five years. If we choose an infinite time horizon (which I will argue in Chapter 7 is more appropriate), the total grows still larger. Estimates vary a bit depending on methodology, but the numbers are all vast: $45 trillion according to a study published by the American Enterprise Institute (2003); $47 trillion in a study from the International Monetary Fund (2004); $50 trillion in a study from the National Center for Policy Analysis (2003); and $60 trillion in a study from the Brookings Institution (2003). In March of 2004 the Social Security and Medicare trustees estimated their unfunded benefit liabilities, using an infinite time horizon, at $74 trillion.

Since the reputations of these institutions run from conservative to liberal to bureaucratic, there can be nothing partisan about the basic message—which is that unless and until we overhaul these benefit programs, we will never catch up to their eventual cost. America can't possibly eliminate such a large liability all at once, yet every year we wait to reduce it, the figure will grow at a compound interest rate as massive future deficits come nearer. Look at it another way. All five numbers exceed the total net worth of the U.S. economy in 2003 ($42 trillion, as calculated by the Fed). Technically, in other words, we really are bankrupt.

Some people find it easier to focus on annual deficits. So consider this. In 2000, Social Security and both parts of Medicare (Hospital Insurance plus Supplementary Medical Insurance) had total outlays of $637 billion. These outlays exceeded the total earmarked revenues of these programs (mostly, payroll taxes and Medicare premiums), generating a modest surplus of $43 billion. That surplus has already disappeared. By the year 2040 these two programs are officially projected to have *annual* outlays of $8.6 trillion and an *annual* cash deficit of $4.3 trillion. By then the combined deficit for just these two programs will be equivalent to 7.4 percent of GDP. Add this to the annual shortfall already built into the unified federal budget from 2005 on (at least 3 percent of GDP) and projected growth in other demographically sensitive programs like Medicaid (say, 2 percent of GDP), and you've easily reached a total program-driven deficit for the entire federal budget of well over 10 percent of GDP. Further, on top of this, add the extra interest costs due to the accelerating accumulation of public debt—and then the interest on the interest costs, and so on.

Well before you even reach 2040, you will find that the whole dynamic spins out of control. With no policy changes, federal spending and federal deficits explode to impossible shares of GDP. In a word, the budget—or the economy—shatters.

This isn't something I'm dreaming up. (Or is the right word "nightmaring up"?) It's something that any reputable budget model will project on a computer—for example, the model used by the U.S. General Accounting Office. The GAO's most recent "do-nothing" projection shows clearly that a federal deficit of 4 percent of GDP in 2013 (a starting point that doesn't seem too scary) will totally metastasize by the 2020s. And by the mid-2030s federal interest costs will start consuming more than half of all federal revenue—a moment we could fairly characterize as the "shattering point." Economists at the IMF reached nearly identical conclusions in 2004 with their own fiscal model.

Remarkably, no matter how large the deficits grow, neither the GAO nor the IMF models assume any upward pressure on interest rates. Consequently, they assume no rise in interest costs in the federal budget nor any slowdown in the future growth rate of the economy or of federal revenue. Plug in these two (more realistic) assumptions, and the shattering point would arrive much sooner. In the year 2023, for example, the publicly held debt under the GAO projection passes 100 percent of GDP. At that point, every 1 percent rise in the interest rate adds 1 percent of GDP to federal outlays. Using the Social Security trustees' projection of GDP in the year 2023, we can project that a 3 percent jump in the interest rate that year would add a catastrophic $800 billion to the annual deficit.

In its report, the IMF took a good look at the growing deficit and concluded, "Closing this gap would require massive adjustments in either tax or spending programs. The longer-term fiscal deficit is also associated with a severe intergenerational imbalance." In plainer words, this approaching train wreck is a clear and present danger to our kids.

No, These Are Not Official Secrets

People sometimes ask me why these dangers are not better known. Is there some conspiracy of silence?

Well, sometimes there are "miniconspiracies." For many years now both the White House and Congress—Democrats, especially—have been reluctant to include much discussion of long-term deficit projections and unfunded liabilities in their official budget documents. Last year the Treasury Department touched off a small scandal by suppressing a report on "generational accounting" that it had commissioned for publication. Clearly, the Bush administration was not eager to throw a spotlight on a daunting problem it had no plan to solve. Yet all in all I would have to say that such hush jobs are not the main cause of our predicament.

No, the truth is even sadder. Every official agency in charge of the budget is issuing plenty of loud warnings: our current fiscal course is catastrophically unsustainable unless we take decisive action soon. It's just our elected political leaders and their parties who see no advantage in listening or responding.

I once had the opportunity to pose this political question to Margaret Thatcher—who as British prime minister was one of the few national leaders ever to succeed in controlling long-term pension costs. "Lady Thatcher," I asked her, "just what do your G-7 leader friends say at their annual meetings about the growing costs of senior benefits? Are they aware of the problem? If so, why don't they agree to do something about it?" She replied, "Oh yes, Mr. Peterson, they are very aware of the impending crisis, but their attitude is this: It's not going to hit on my watch. So why should I take the pain for someone else's gain?" I was reminded of the riff delivered by David Stockman back in the early 1980s when he tried to impersonate a typical member of Congress on the issue of Social Security reform: "I'm just not going to spend a lot of political capital solving some other guy's problem in 2010." Well, guess what? The year 2010 is almost here.

Let me recite the most recent statements from all the relevant official sources. They make for a dirgelike drumbeat:

> "The Social Security and Medicare shortfalls compel change. They must not be left hanging over the heads of our children and grandchildren. The longer the delay in enacting reforms, the greater the danger, and the more drastic the remedies will have to be."
>
> —U.S. Office of Management and Budget, *President's Budget for Fiscal Year 2004* (2003)

> "Without changes to federal programs for the elderly, the aging of the baby-boom generation will cause a historic shift in the U.S. fiscal position in coming decades . . . Federal spending on the major health and retirement programs—Social Security, Medicare, and Medicaid—is projected to grow by

more than two-thirds as a share of the economy by 2030 . . . Consequently, either taxes will need to rise dramatically, spending on other federal programs will have to be cut severely, or federal borrowing will soar."

—Congressional Budget Office,
The Budget and Economic Outlook: An Update (2003)

"The fundamentals of the financial status of Social Security and Medicare remain highly problematic. Although both programs are currently running annual surpluses, these will give way to rapidly rising annual deficits soon after the baby boom generation begins to retire in about 2010. The growing deficits will lead to rapidly mounting pressures on the federal budget in a decade and exhaustion of trust funds in little more than two decades that will not permit payment of currently scheduled benefits. In the long run, these deficits are projected to grow at unsustainable rates."

—Social Security and Medicare Boards of Trustees,
Status of the Social Security and Medicare Programs: Summary of the 2003 Annual Reports (2003)

"The current system is financially unsustainable. Without reform, the promise of Social Security to future retirees cannot be met without eventual resort to benefit cuts, tax increases, or massive borrowing. The time to act is now."

—President's Commission to Strengthen Social Security,
Interim Report (2001)

"In 2008—just four years from now—the first cohort of the baby-boom generation will reach 62, the earliest age at which Social Security retirement benefits may be claimed and the age at which about half of prospective beneficiaries choose to retire; in 2011, these individuals will reach 65 and will thus be eligible for Medicare. At that time, under the intermediate assumptions of the OASDI trustees, there will still be more than three covered workers for each OASDI beneficiary; by 2025, this ratio is projected to be down to 2¼. This dramatic demographic change is certain to place enormous demands on our nation's resources—demands we almost surely will be unable to meet unless action is taken. For a variety of reasons, that action is better taken as soon as possible."

—Federal Reserve Board Chairman Alan Greenspan, testimony to U.S. Congress (2004)

"These long-run budget projections show clearly that the budget is on an unsustainable path . . . As the baby-boomers reach retirement age in large numbers, the deficit is projected to rise steadily as a share of GDP. Under most scenarios, well before the end of the projection period for this chapter rising deficits would drive debt to levels several times the size of GDP."

—U.S. Office of Management and Budget, *Analytical Perspectives on the Budget* (2003)

"If you look ahead in the federal budget, the combined Social Security or OASDI program together with the rapidly growing health programs (Medicare and Medicaid) will dominate the federal government's future fiscal outlook . . . Absent reform, the nation will ultimately have to choose between persistent, escalating budget deficits, significant tax increases, and/or dramatic budget cuts . . . Taken together, Social Security, Medicare, and Medicaid represent an unsustainable burden on future generations."

—Comptroller General of the United States, Statement to the Special Committee on Aging of the U.S. Senate (2003)

These are government agencies. I could have made the list much longer by adding similar warnings from think tanks and policy academics—left, right, and center, from the Progressive Policy Institute to the Cato Institute to the Urban Institute. True, today's Congress and White House are in the hands of Republicans. But the warnings were very much the same back in the mid-nineties, when Democrats were largely in charge. In 1994 I served on President Clinton's Bipartisan Commission on Entitlement and Tax Reform, whose interim report flatly declared: "In 2030, unless appropriate policy changes are made in the interim, projected spending for Medicare, Medicaid, Social Security, and Federal employee retirement programs alone will consume all tax revenues collected by the federal government." Who listened? Neither party. Not in Congress or anywhere else.

The problem, in short, is not lack of knowledge. It's lack of will by elected politicians to act on this knowledge—and yes, if you like, the complicity of voters who allow them to look the other way. As in a gothic horror movie, we sense the truth but don't want to wake up fully and act on it. Most politicians are happy to let the facts lie undiscussed. In fact, the best politicians are so good at separating political practice from policy knowledge that they are hardly aware they do it. It becomes a sort of practiced cognitive dissonance, where two sides of the brain seem to function independently.

I've had several conversations about deficits with Bill Clinton, who by all accounts (including my own) is a superbly informed policy maestro as well as a consummate politician. Once during his presidency, after hearing that he had told a recent Renaissance Weekend gathering that our "trust funds" would take care of Social Security until 2037, I asked him, "Mr. President, you're not buying this trust-fund story on Social Security, are you?" Without hesitation, he answered: "Oh my, no, Pete. You and I know that this is a pure cash-in, cash-out program and that it will be draining revenue from the Treasury decades before the formal bankruptcy date. We have to act soon." Alan Greenspan could not have done better. Reassured, I assumed that the person who had told me about the president must have been mistaken. Shortly thereafter, the president addressed one of a series of White House meetings on Social Security jointly sponsored by the AARP and The Concord

Coalition. I switched on CNN to watch him praise the audience for wanting to become better educated on this daunting policy issue—and then lo and behold saw him hold up a chart showing how our "trust funds" would "totally safeguard" Social Security until 2037.

Few politicians do it as well as Bill Clinton. But nearly all politicians do it. And they do it because they are allowed to do it. The saga of Enron should remind us that it's not enough to properly account for future liabilities. Something must compel decision-makers to translate knowledge about where current policy will lead us tomorrow into corrective action today. With Enron, that meant bankruptcy, which allowed the firm's remaining assets to be reallocated to productive purposes. With the federal government—facing a future of ever-rising deficits driven by ever-rising entitlement costs—it ought to mean immediate and fundamental reform. But it doesn't. That's where the political circuit is broken.

Why Structural Deficits Matter

Growing structural deficits are deficits that will keep widening no matter how well the economy performs. They are a cause for grave concern—and not just because, if left to grow unchecked, they must ultimately shatter the economy. Long before that happens, growing structural deficits can slow and even halt the steady growth in material living standards that has always nourished the American Dream. When such deficits are incurred in order to fund a rising transfer of resources from young to old, they also constitute an injustice against future generations.

Economically, the problem with deficits is that they absorb national savings and crowd out productive investment. They do so by raising real interest rates (that is, interest rates after expected inflation), by around one-quarter to one-half of a percent for each 1 percent increase in the long-term federal deficit as a share of GDP. The former figure appears in a just-released study by the Federal Reserve Board; the latter figure was cited in a recent report by the Committee for Economic Development. Many other studies have confirmed a response of at least this magnitude.

I should emphasize that there is widespread agreement within the economics profession on this matter. Indeed, I am able to invoke the full support of none other than Harvard economist Gregory Mankiw, the author of America's best-selling economics textbook (thus, the Paul Samuelson of his generation) and not incidentally President Bush's recent choice as chairman of his Council of Economic Advisers. He writes in his textbook: "When the government reduces national saving by running a budget deficit, the interest rate rises and investment falls. Because investment is important for long-run economic growth, government budget deficits reduce the economy's growth rate." Pretty clear, isn't it?

Most economists who study this issue conclude, in general, that the strongest connection is between *long-term* real interest rates and *long-term* deficit expectations. A single deficit year doesn't matter much; indeed, a deficit during a recession is usually good policy. What matters is what markets believe about the deficit trend over the next decade or more.

So does that mean large long-term deficits always translate into a predictably high real interest rate? Not always—economists always have their provisos. In the near term, interest rates can be hugely influenced by temporary swings in the demand for investment and in the supply of savings. Such swings explain why the interest rates have remained very low over the last few years despite the dramatic shift in deficit projections.

Consider the demand for investment. Although the U.S. economy has recovered from its recent recession, it continues to function well below capacity, with businesses reluctant either to hire new workers or add to their plant and equipment. As the economy continues to grow and investment necessarily rekindles, real interest rates will surely rise—and nearly all economists agree that they will rise faster and further with large deficits than without. Now consider the supply of savings. The rest of the developed world is currently awash in excess savings, in part due to stubbornly slow business conditions in Japan and much of western Europe. In unprecedented volume, much of that savings is now flowing into the U.S. economy, buying our stocks and bonds. This also helps to keep interest rates low. Yet like the slow recovery, the surging inflow of savings from abroad can only be of limited duration. When it slows down, the impact on interest rates is likely to be dramatic. Indeed, if it suddenly stops or reverses, the impact could be catastrophic.

Defenders of today's careless fiscal policy feel these concerns are overblown. They don't disagree that U.S. business investment remains weak. But many don't see anything wrong with plenty of foreign borrowing. After all, if the rest of the world offers their savings, why not use it to run big deficits and still maintain our investment at low interest rates? That's what we did in the 1980s. Is that bad? Maybe the rest of the world just thinks we're a great place to put their money, like back in the 1870s, when Europeans snapped up our bonds so that we could build our railroads.

This is a reassuring, even swashbuckling explanation (our internet is like yesteryear's railroads!). And it is true that both then and now productivity growth in the United States did rank and does rank number one in the world. Unfortunately, the historical parallel fails in two critical areas. First, in the 1870s our national investment rate was higher than that of our creditors. Not so today. And second, in the 1870s our economy was growing faster than our foreign liabilities were accumulating. Definitely not so today. In fact, the speed at which the United States is accumulating net financial liabilities to foreigners ("net" here means us to them minus them to us) is downright alarming—from roughly zero twenty years ago to $2.6 trillion at the end of 2002.

Clearly this tide cannot rise indefinitely. With our annual net borrowing from abroad now running at about 5 percent of GDP, the highest rate in our history, an urgent question (which I will return to in Chapter 4) is how suddenly, or even ruinously, this massive foreign lending will stop. The potential for financial crisis aside, whatever America borrows it will have to pay back—or else fork over a permanent debt-service charge. Either way, future living standards will suffer. Yes, America is clearly better off with these foreign-financed investments than with no extra investments at all; but America is clearly worse off than if we were financing these investments ourselves. Like everyone else, foreign investors expect a return on their capital. To say that it doesn't matter if Americans own their own economy is like saying that there is no difference between being a landlord and being a sharecropper.

The bottom line is simple: deficits drain critically needed national savings, regardless of their effect on interest rates. The only source of investment that America doesn't have to pay for is the net savings generated by its own households and businesses. Some economists believe that private savings rises to "offset" some of the impact of higher federal deficits. Few economists, however, believe that this offset is any larger than 33 cents for every dollar of extra federal borrowing. It follows that for each dollar of those savings that gets diverted to finance budget deficits, there must be one dollar less, or (let's say) at least 67 cents less, to invest productively. The debate over how interest rates regulate this dynamic is largely a sideshow.

Another question sometimes raised is whether there aren't plenty of other things that determine productivity and wage growth other than the quantity of our investment. My answer: of course there are, from entrepreneurship and labor mobility to managerial skills and a strong work ethic. America possesses these sorts of intangibles in abundance—and if we lacked them, we wouldn't prosper as well no matter how much we invested. Yet even if strong investment is not a *sufficient* condition for rising living standards, it is surely a *necessary* condition. It is, moreover, the one condition that public policy can directly control. We cannot legislate technological breakthroughs—nor even a habit of personal thrift. But we can legislate a budget surplus, and surpluses add to national savings just as surely as deficits subtract from them. It may not matter to private savers whether their dollars end up building a machine, training a worker, or purchasing a Treasury bond. But it matters a great deal to the economy. New machines or trained workers are likely to raise the economy's productivity and income. A Treasury bond that enables a government to subsidize someone's consumption is not.

This brings us to history's bottom line, as insisted on by one economic luminary after another, from Adam Smith to Karl Marx to Alfred Marshall to John Maynard Keynes: no nation can enjoy sustained living-standard growth without investing, no nation can sustain high investment for long without saving, and no nation can save for long without fiscal responsibility. Though many of today's supply-siders praise the "classical political economists" as their inspiration, the founders of this school regarded few national policies as dangerous as the issuing of large public debts. It is a "practice," wrote Adam Smith, that causes "the waste or removal of capital stock" and "always tends to enfeeble states."

Keeping Pumped: An Economy on Steroids

More than other nations, the United States has a special reason to be concerned about growing federal deficits. A century ago, America's net national savings rate was the highest in the developed world. Fifty years ago, it was somewhere in the middle. Today, it is the lowest. The U.S. Bureau of Economic Analysis measures this rate by taking the savings of each sector, "net" of depreciation on assets like houses or equipment, and then adding them all up. In the 1960s the net U.S. savings rate averaged 11.0 percent of GDP. That rate has fallen ever since, not in a straight line perhaps, but the decade averages tell a clear story—to 8.7 percent in the seventies, to 6.2 percent in the eighties, and to 4.5 percent in the nineties. By 2002 the net national savings rate had sunk all the way to 1.7 percent, a record postwar low. It may even drop below zero within the next few years—meaning that depreciation actually exceeds new capital purchases. The last time this happened was during the depths of the Great Depression.

One big reason this rate keeps dropping, of course, is the rising trend in federal deficits. A rising negative number in the federal sector essentially wipes out a growing share of the positive savings of all the nonfederal sectors—households, businesses, and state and local governments. That's what we mean by "fiscal crowding out." But that's not the only reason. Nonfederal savings has itself declined over time, from roughly 12 percent in the 1960s to only around 5 or 6 percent in recent years. In other words, we're launching more frequent raids on a larder that's getting stocked with fewer goods to begin with.

Why the declining trend in savings outside the federal budget? One recent culprit has been the appearance of large deficits in the budgets of state and local governments (most notoriously, the multibillion-dollar shortfall in California). A more important reason is the steady, decades-long decline in savings by households, spurred on by the so-called democratization of debt. Every year, it seems, access to credit gets easier—with no-money-down mortgages, daily credit card solicitations (the average household now has 6.5 credit cards with an average balance of $8,000), and the erosion of any stigma attached to personal bankruptcy (which now occurs at a record rate).

Yet if easier forms of credit are the instruments that enable the decline in our household savings—that is, our boom in household consumption—what motivates households to use these instruments is less obvious. Some observers of our culture point to a growing post-modern aversion to the whole concept of planning or preparing for the future—an aversion which may have gotten a "let's live it up now" boost in the wake of 9/11. Another reason, many economists suspect, may be the very growth in the retirement and health care benefits that is fueling our rising deficit projections. Most working-age Americans expect to receive a wide variety of government benefits during their retirement. To the extent people believe that these future benefits are both generous and certain, they are relieved of the need to save as much on their own. (Many believe their "contributions" are equivalent to savings, but of course they are not.) Here's another way to look at it. What is an unfunded liability to the government is an unfunded asset to families. And if families view these unfunded assets as cash in the bank, they will probably feel less need to accumulate genuine assets of their own. This is precisely where the platitudes of politicians about "trust funds" do real harm to people's lives.

So far, like any good Republican, I've only been focusing on what drives private-sector investment. I can imagine some readers thinking: OK, Pete, but what about public investment in areas like the infrastructure, the environment, basic research, or public health? Why can't we spend more there? Let's look again at rising benefit outlays: as they grow steadily as a share of all federal spending, they crowd out investment *within* the federal budget itself. Back in the late 1960s and early 1970s, total federal spending on physical capital, research and development, and education and training averaged over 6 percent of GDP; by the late 1990s it weighed in at under 3 percent of GDP. The decline occurred both in defense- and nondefense-related programs. Between 1965 and 2000, these kinds of future-oriented investment outlays shrank from 32 to 14 percent of total federal spending. Benefits to individuals meanwhile grew from 25 to

59 percent. The decline of federal investment also has an impact on our nation's economic future.

Thirty or forty years ago, in the imagination of youth, government spending was all about monorails and spaceships—the future. Today, it's all about benefit checks to retirees—the past. Back then, we read announcements of brand-new waterways and cyclotrons. Today, we hear mere proposals, like a trillion-dollar Mars mission, that everyone knows are unaffordable unless we send the entire bill to our kids. Or we read dreary reports about crumbling bridges, rat-infested federal warehouses, and (according to a recent GAO release) "many federal assets in an alarming state of deterioration," with repair needs estimated "to be in the tens of billions of dollars." We all know that you only get what you pay for. So long as we avoid paying for a better future, we have no right to be surprised at the logical consequences.

President Bush closed his 2004 State of the Union address with a plea to get our nation's athletes to stop using steroids when playing sports. A better plea might have been to get our nation's leaders to stop using steroids when managing the economy. For decades they have pushed and heaved to tilt the economy ever more steeply toward debt and consumption and away from saving and investment. Over the last four years they have let loose such an unprecedented flood of fiscal and monetary stimulus that (with some complicity by our trading partners) they have turned America into a no-savings economy and left behind a global wake of liquidity that will be washing around for years after the recession it was meant to "cure" has been forgotten.

When people ask me how these domestic and global economic imbalances will unwind in the near term, I tell them honestly that I do not know. When I consider the magnitude of the stimulus and the unflagging "propensity to consume" of the American people, I could easily imagine it could all surge back on us in a wave of inflation, or the printing-money option, as the experts put it. When I look at the lingering slow growth of many of the other developed economies, I suppose deflation is still a possibility. With a hundred million Chinese workers scheduled to enter the global marketplace at dollar-per-day wages over the next decade, the world economy certainly has major structural changes in store. If we're very lucky, we'll steam past many of these challenges.

But as I look further into the future, deep into the era of retiring boomers, the more certain I am that luck and stimulus cannot substitute for real leadership and farsighted choices. You never know if the next dose of steroids will keep you pumped up. Maybe it will, maybe it won't. But what you know for sure is that cumulative doses will gradually wear down your body, shorten your life, and render you unfit for the long haul. And for a nation, it's only the long haul that counts.

Tough Times Ahead for Elder Boomers?

In 2008 the first boomer will be able to retire on Social Security at age sixty-two. In 2039 the youngest boomer will turn age seventy-five. The intervening era from roughly 2010 to 2040 promises to be a fateful one for America's prospects, at least fiscally if not in other respects as well. Which way this fate turns will depend in part on how this large generation exercises its electoral power and how leaders exercise power on its behalf.

If boomers insist on clinging to every benefit and tax promise extended to today's elderly, they might find a way to succeed—but only at terrible cost to their own children and grandchildren. A "winning" strategy would require Congress to squeeze all nonbenefit federal spending into an ever smaller box. It would require pushing the allocation of government benefits, already steeply tilted toward retired Americans, even more in that direction. To avoid runaway deficits and complete fiscal meltdown, some taxes would have to be raised. But a we-first boomer strategy would ensure that any new tax burden would fall mainly on working-age adults, either by focusing mainly on payroll tax hikes or by exempting retirees from general income tax hikes. The creation of special tax favors for seniors (on real estate taxes and on the taxation of pension income and investment accounts) already has ample precedent, especially at the state and local level.

At best, this course would ensure that younger generations end up giving even more and receiving even less from government than they now expect—a "deal" which has already gotten a lot less sweet over the years. Let me offer some examples. A single male with average earnings who retired in 1965 received lifetime Social Security benefits that were worth an 8.5 percent annual real return on his lifetime payroll taxes. A single male who retired in 2000 is projected to receive a 1.6 percent return. A single male who will retire in 2030 is projected to receive a return of just 1.0 percent. These numbers assume no changes in taxes or benefits. If payroll taxes are raised to ensure that boomers get all their promised benefits, a growing share of today's younger workers will end up with a return of less than zero, meaning they will actually get back less than the real value of their contributions. If the whole projected federal deficit were to be closed entirely through extra taxes on working-age adults, these younger couples could wind up experiencing no rise or even a lifetime decline in their real after-tax wages—an outcome without precedent for any prior generation in American history.

At worst, this course would end in unforeseen disaster even before the boomer retirement is complete. A nation that expects progress and plays a dominant role in world affairs cannot suddenly turn away from the future without inviting a crisis—perhaps economic or military or political—that would rudely interrupt even the best-laid plans. In this case, all generations would end up losers.

Fortunately, most boomers don't want this future. They are mortified to learn that their kids might be heavily burdened by their own retirement. Get boomers in focus groups, and they talk passionately about "stewardship" and a commitment to "future generations." Poll them, and most will say that current policy is unsustainable. According to one recent survey, nearly nine in ten agree that "government has made financial promises to [their] generation that it will not be able to keep." According to several surveys, large majorities agree that senior entitlement programs are in need of major reform—and soon. As many as 70 percent of boomers are fully prepared, at least in concept, to remain employed in some fashion beyond the traditional retirement age. The majority concede that the main motivator will be financial necessity.

But here's the paradox: although boomers seem to have some abstract understanding of what lies ahead and what's at stake, most are unable or unwilling to take concrete steps to prepare for this future. They certainly are doing little to organize politically and to change public policy. Nor are they doing much to prepare their lives and to boost their household finances. This widespread negligence could itself have major political consequences.

Dozens of studies have appeared on the boomers' retirement prospects, and they make for dreary reading. The good news, according to most of them, is that boomers on average are projected to have somewhat higher real incomes than their parents had in retirement. The bad news is that they will experience larger drops from their preretirement incomes and will have to spend much of their retirement gains on health care. Very few boomers are preparing for the extra cost of infirmity in old age—for example, by purchasing long-term care insurance. Few understand that Medicare doesn't pay for this, and many aren't aware that one in three of them will someday enter a nursing home. According to one gerontology professor, "Much less is said about what happens when the postwar baby boomers become not golf-playing sixty-five-year-olds sipping chardonnay at the nineteenth hole, but wheelchair-bound eighty-five-year-olds being fed Ensure through a straw."

Another bit of bad news is that few of these projections assume any cuts in government benefits. Surprisingly few boomers realize that on their watch, Social Security benefits are already starting to become less generous (as a share of their preretirement earnings)—for example, that the normal retirement age is already rising from age sixty-five to sixty-seven and a growing share of benefits is subject to taxation. Even fewer fully grasp that this generosity is likely to be cut still further.

The income averages beloved by researchers, moreover, hide a widening distribution of boomer incomes. Though the top 10 percent will be much better off than their parents, the bottom 40 or 50 percent are likely to be worse off in retirement by every measure. And though the more affluent half of today's retirees are doing very well, the less affluent half remains dependent on government benefits, especially Social Security, for four-fifths of their money income and nearly all of their health care. That dependence is on track to grow, setting up tens of millions of boomers for genuine hardship if benefits are suddenly cut across the board. One researcher sums up the overall situation as follows: the top third of boomers don't have to worry, the middle third had better start worrying, and the bottom third should seriously rethink their life expectations—starting with their retirement age.

The raw numbers are sobering enough. As of 2000, according to Census Bureau data, only 50 percent of all workers (60 percent of full-time workers) aged twenty-five to sixty-five participate in *any* kind of retirement plan other than Social Security, and most of these are voluntary defined-contribution accounts that are liable to be cashed out well before retirement. Incredibly, a survey by Hewitt Associates shows that over 40 percent of workers who change jobs cash out their plans rather than roll them over into new accounts. As of 2001, according to the Fed's Survey of Consumer Finances, half of all households aged forty-five to fifty-four possess total financial assets (everything from bank accounts to insurance policies to 401(k)s) of less than $46,000.

Take this $46,000 figure and place it next to another figure we met earlier in this chapter—$200,000. That is what each household would need in its savings account today in order to pay for growing structural deficits in the federal budget over the next seventy-five years. The mismatch is painful to behold. And it gets worse. Even the $46,000 figure is in some ways an overestimate. It does not include the 7 percent of households with no financial assets of any type. And it is not netted against the extensive personal debts of today's midlife households (remember all those credit cards).

One out of three families has earned rights to some sort of defined-benefit company plan, whose assets are not reported to households. But this brightens the picture only slightly, since most of these families already reside in the "top half" of the Fed's asset distribution. Also, the reliability of these defined-benefit plans has recently been called into question. Many boomer workers are seeing their expected company payouts shaved by the move to "cash balance" formulas (which penalize today's older workers who have spent their careers with one company). Underfunding is another problem—with promises now exceeding assets of company plans by about $400 billion. In July 2003 the General Accounting Office put the U.S. Pension Benefit Guarantee Corporation, which insures these plans, on its list of "high-risk" agencies. Pension plans covering 17 million state and local government workers are in even deeper trouble. An estimated four in five are underfunded; many have already engaged in desperate borrowing ploys. States in chronic fiscal distress may have no choice but to cut benefits across the board to pay their bills.

During the 1990s many boomer families figured they could make up lost ground by investing in an endlessly rising stock market. That hope has faded. Some still expect to receive an inheritance bonanza with the death of their last surviving parent, though this hope too is running aground. A small number of families are indeed inheriting large estates. But according to the Fed, only 27 percent of boomers say they either have received *or ever expect to receive* an inheritance. Of the 17 percent who have already received an inheritance by 2001, the median amount reported was $48,000—which, after settling the parents' estate, is not enough to make a large impact on retirement.

Yet another unpleasant surprise that may rough up the affluent edge of this generation is the impact of raw demographics on financial markets. When they reach retirement age and the time comes to sell off their mutual funds, where will all these boomers find enough willing buyers? At home, among the smaller and economically troubled Generation X following behind them? Overseas, in developed economies where younger households will be even scarcer? Or, in the emerging market and developing economies, like China and India—which will themselves be aging rapidly in the 2030s and which will in any case remain much poorer than America for several decades? Some financial analysts go so far as to predict that a "great depreciation" in financial assets is likely to accompany the boomer retirement.

One needn't subscribe to any dire financial outlook to be genuinely concerned about how most boomers will fare, especially if old-age entitlements are suddenly and belatedly slashed. Many ex-yuppies could become what retirement expert Craig Karpel calls "Dumpies" (Destitute Unprepared Mature People) carrying signs reading "Will Work for Medicine."

No one wants this future for any generation. Yet to plan for a better outcome, it's not enough simply to wait until boomers change their savings behavior on their own. Very soon elected leaders in both parties must exercise real leadership on this issue. At the very minimum, they should educate boomers about the nation's fiscal future and explain what kinds of limitations must ultimately be placed on which future benefits and who would be most affected. Ideally, they should go further and immediately frame legislation that would both increase future tax revenue and reduce the projected growth in benefit outlays—while phasing in all reductions gradually and protecting benefits (in some cases, perhaps even increasing benefits) to those who are least able to fend for themselves. I would offer families new opportunities to provide for their own future and indeed *require* them to put aside some minimum savings for their retirement. Setting clearer expectations about what government can afford would itself encourage more household savings, which would further strengthen our economic prospects.

When President Bush recently remarked that our deficits are "just numbers on paper," he missed a great chance to explain to Americans what's at stake. America's vast prospective gap between outlays and revenue—measurable in the trillions of dollars—is more than just a number. It is more than just a potential fiscal or even economic disaster. It is a colossal mismatch between what Americans expect to give to their nation and what they expect to receive from it. As such, it is a civic tragedy which arose through a dysfunction of political leadership and which threatens to cause serious hardship measurable in tens of millions of American families.

Left uncorrected, this fiscal gap will force our nation to make an odious choice, between our obligations to our children and our obligations to our elders. It will permit us to be either a forward-looking society or a humane society—but not both. Again, no one wants to arrive at this impasse. Yet to avoid it America must change course, decisively and soon. The only other way to avoid it—for now—is to pretend that it won't happen and that the official fiscal projections, like many other long-term projections, are highly uncertain. Some supporters of the fiscal status quo even dismiss them as guesswork.

We hardly know what the economy will do next year, they say. How can we possibly make fiscal projections forty years out?

That would be a mistake. Even if the size and timing of ocean *waves* cannot be predicted, the size and timing of ocean *tides* can be. Budget experts inside and outside of government agree with remarkable unanimity on the magnitude of the cost growth in federal entitlement payments. This agreement, in turn, rests on demographic forces that can in fact be more reliably forecast than nearly any other trend monitored by policy experts. Remember: tomorrow's retirees have already been born and can be counted. The aging of America is about as close as social science ever comes to a certain forecast. Absent a Hollywood catastrophe—a colliding comet or an alien invasion—it will surely happen. To these projections we now turn.

Chapter 3

THE CHALLENGE AT HOME: THE AGING OF AMERICA

Thirty-five years ago, uncontrollable population growth seemed to pose a grave threat to America's future. Paul Ehrlich's best-seller *The Population Bomb* envisioned a teeming, youthful humanity falling off the edges of the continent. The Club of Rome predicted that we would soon eat our way locust-like to the bottom of every natural resource.

More recently, in a little-noticed shift of expert opinion, demographers now project a dramatic deceleration in U.S. population growth and an equally dramatic rise in the U.S. median age. According to the official projections of the Social Security actuaries, the population will slow to a crawl two or three decades from now and—if it weren't for immigration—it would thereafter start declining. Meanwhile, between now and 2040 the number of "elderly" Americans (aged sixty-five and over—or so convention has it) will more than double while the nonelder population will grow by just 10 percent. Thirty-five years ago, the future was crowded with babies. Today, it's crowded with seniors.

Oscar Wilde once remarked that "youth is America's oldest

tradition." Much of our nation's history, before and even after the closing of the frontier, has been a saga of large families and rowdy young settlements. As recently as 1940 college-age youths (eighteen to twenty-one years old) outnumbered the elderly in the United States by 9.6 to 9.0 million. Yet by 2040 the Census Bureau projects the number of college-age youths will grow to only 20.3 million while the number of elderly will swell to 77.2 million. When the nursing-home crowd outnumbers the dorm room crowd by nearly four to one, America's youth tradition may be little more than a memory.

Most young people have difficulty contemplating their own old age, much less preparing for the discomfort and dependency that often accompany it. Likewise, America today finds it hard to confront its collective aging, much less the difficult political and economic choices that an aging society will have to make. Yet we can no longer afford denial. It's time we took a hard look at the shape of things to come.

The Shape of Things to Come

For nearly all of human history, until the industrial revolution, people aged sixty-five and over never amounted to more than 2 or 3 percent of the population. In America today, they amount to 12 percent. By the year 2040 they will be reaching 20 percent and may be closing in on 25 percent. In the days of Hammurabi or Julius Caesar or (indeed) Thomas Jefferson, your odds of a random encounter with a person aged sixty-five or over were about one person in every forty. In America today, your odds are about one person in every eight. A few decades from now, they may be one person in every four.

Been to Florida lately? You may not have realized it, but as you gazed upon the vast concentration of seniors there—nearly 18 percent of the Sun State's population—you were looking at our future. By the mid-2020s at the latest, the United States as a whole will have an age structure as old as that of Florida today.

For the moment, America is still enjoying the last few years of what has been called a "demographic Indian summer." With the large postwar boom generation in the workforce and a small Depression-era generation retiring, the elder share of the U.S. population has been flat since the mid-1980s. But when boomers start turning sixty-five less than a decade from now, the demographic climate will change abruptly. Over the next ten years about two million U.S. citizens will be celebrating their sixty-fifth birthday each year—a number that will reach four million once the Woodstock retirement is in full swing. Just as boomers once overwhelmed the schools as children, the job market as they came of age, and the housing market as mature adults, so too are they on track to overwhelm America's retirement systems as they enter elderhood.

This explosion in the number of elderly Americans will place an unprecedented economic burden on working-age adults. As recently as 1960 there were 5.1 taxpaying workers for every Social Security beneficiary. This ratio, now 3.3, is officially projected to fall to 2.2 by 2030. By then each two-earner working-age couple will have to support at least one anonymous retiree.

Many people assume that the aging of America is a temporary event—a onetime challenge triggered by the retirement of the baby boom generation. This is not the case. The passage of the baby boom "pig" through the fabled "python" simply gives the story an extra twist. The last phase of the boomers' life-cycle journey is about to accelerate a demographic transformation that would have occurred anyway even if the boom had never taken place. Between 2010 and 2030, roughly the years the first and last boomers turn sixty-five, the Social Security Administration (SSA) projects that the elder share of the U.S. population will surge from 13 to 19 percent. In 2075, when the last of the boomers have passed away, it projects that the elder share will be 23 percent—that is, higher, not lower. The retirement of the boomers is thus due to usher in a permanent transformation in the age structure of the population.

To the extent that tomorrow's nonworking elders finance their retirement out of their own savings today, one might argue that they won't really constitute an economic burden. By living off the income from such savings, they are not consuming wealth that would have existed in their absence—which is another way of saying that the pennies they save (and consume in old age) are the pennies they earn. But the point is moot, since only a minority of Americans retire mostly on their own saved income. Economist Victor Fuchs estimates that, including Medicare and Medicaid benefits, 56 percent of the income of the elderly comes from government. And that figure is an average that includes the affluent. Dependence on government is higher for middle-income elders—and for lower-income elders, it is almost absolute. According to the SSA, Social Security and other government benefits accounted for 91 percent of total cash income in 2001 among elder households in the bottom fifth of the income distribution.

The graying of America therefore translates into a huge and growing bill to taxpayers for senior entitlements. Between now and 2040, Social Security outlays as a share of worker payroll are officially projected to rise from 11.1 to 17.8 percent. Both parts of Medicare will rise from 5.6 to 18.2 percent. The full gamut of federally funded entitlements, including everything from pension checks to retired military officers to nursing home care for frail elders, now amounts to 12.5 percent of GDP. By 2040, according to the GAO forecast we introduced in the last chapter, it will nearly double to 21.7 percent of GDP. That's a tenth more than *total* federal spending in 2003 and a third more than *total* federal revenue in 2003.

We sometimes hear that the growth in the number of dependent elderly doesn't really pose a major fiscal or economic challenge because it will be offset by a steep decline in the relative number of dependent children. It's hard to imagine a more wrongheaded argument. As a factual matter, the ratio of *all* dependents (children and elderly) to working-age adults will still rise sharply in the United States over the next thirty years. The public cost of supporting each elder, moreover, is far greater than the cost of supporting each child. At the federal level, each elder receives on average seven times as much in benefits as each child: $17,688 versus $2,491 in fiscal year 2000, according to the Congressional Budget Office. Even including state and local spending—and hence the nation's entire education budget—the ratio is still at least three to one in favor of the elderly.

The numbers aside, the "total dependency" argument misses a more fundamental point—namely, that money spent on seniors is mostly for today's consumption, while money spent on children is an investment in the future. Thirty years ago, when America teemed with children, working-age adults were sacrificing through families to build the future. Thirty years from now, when America will be teeming with seniors, they will be sacrificing through government to reward the past.

Driving the Projections: Longer Life Spans and Fewer Babies

There are two fundamental forces behind the aging of America, the first being that singular triumph of modern times: the unprecedented advance in human longevity. Because of stunning progress in public health and medical technology—everything from chlorinated water to miracle vaccines to heart bypass surgery—life expectancy in America has risen to age seventy-seven from around age forty-five in 1900. This is a greater gain in the last one hundred years than civilization had achieved over the previous ten thousand.

The longevity revolution is shattering long-standing personal expectations. "Most people my age are dead," declared Casey Stengel in 1964 at age seventy-three—a quip that is still funny but no longer true in today's world of zestful senior living communities. When Social Security was founded in 1935, the typical U.S. worker at age sixty-five could expect to live another 11.9 years. By the year 2040, say today's official projections, the typical worker at age sixty-five can expect to live at least another 19.7 years. If the normal retirement age had been "indexed" to longevity since Social Security was founded, today's workers would be waiting until age seventy-three to receive full benefits and tomorrow's workers even longer. In reality, Americans have been retiring earlier, not later. In 1950 the median age at which workers started collecting their Social Security retirement pensions was sixty-eight; today, it's sixty-three.

Nearly everyone agrees that lower mortality rates are a blessing. Indeed, longer and healthier life spans are probably the greatest personal advantage we moderns enjoy over our ancestors. I rejoice for myself, and for tens of millions like me, who are likely to live to ages that most people could never hope to attain a half century ago. I also celebrate the enrichment of families and communities that comes from living around more elders. But the question remains: Is America prepared for the fiscal and economic consequences of much longer life spans?

Longer lives mean not just more elderly but disproportionately more in each successive age bracket over sixty-five. From 2000 to 2040, the Census Bureau projects that the population aged sixty-five to seventy-four will grow by roughly 85 percent—but that the population aged 85 and over will grow by roughly 225 percent. Over the long run, the growth multiples for this "old-old" population are phenomenal. In 1900 U.S. residents aged eighty-five and over numbered a mere 374,000. In 2004 they number nearly 5 million, and by 2040 they will exceed 14 million. At the very oldest ages, the multiples soar. Centenarians are projected to grow from 88,000 this year to just over 1 million by 2050, a thirteenfold increase over the next half century.

This "aging of the aged" adds an extra multiplier to the economic burden of aging, since virtually every measure of disability, dependence, and health care expense rises with increasing age, even among the elderly themselves. Total per capita health spending on the "old-old" (aged eighty-five and over) is three times as much as that on the "young-old" (aged sixty-five to seventy-four). For specific types of health care, this multiple varies greatly—from twice as much for hospital spending to over twenty times as much for nursing homes. Already the medical profession is adapting to an older clientele. In the late 1990s, for the first time in history, women over age sixty-five began to outnumber men under age forty in annual hospital admissions for injuries. Meanwhile, "geriatric" medicine has become a booming specialty—and not just in retirement communities. Even prisons are adding geriatric wards to handle the new demographic.

The cost of long-term care is certain to rise explosively. According to one study, the total spending on nursing homes will grow almost fivefold by 2030. By then the United States would be spending more on nursing homes (in real dollars) than it spends on Social Security today. Understandably, the federal government and states are experimenting with home health benefits and other "aging in place" strategies that are supposed to be less expensive and more humane than standard institutional care. It remains to be seen, however, whether such reforms will restrain the growing public cost of long-term care—or, more likely in my view, accelerate it by making government benefits more appealing to millions of households who would not otherwise have applied for them.

It's easy to understand how longer life spans can raise a society's average age. But this is only part of the story. At the same time that life spans are increasing, fewer babies are being born. As recently as the early 1960s most demographers assumed that the U.S. fertility rate (that is, the average number of lifetime births per woman) would continue indefinitely at somewhere around three. Then came a behavioral revolution that took the experts by surprise. It was driven by affluence, feminism, rising female participation in the workforce, growing acceptance of new birth control technologies, and legalized abortion. The result was a precipitous fertility-rate decline. Today, the U.S. fertility rate stands at 2.0—just under the so-called 2.1 replacement rate required to maintain a stable population with no immigration.

This birth dearth is the second fundamental force behind the aging of the population. While rising life spans increase the relative number of old, falling fertility decreases the relative number of young. Together, these forces are driving down the ratio of taxpaying workers to retired beneficiaries—and driving up the burden of old-age benefit programs on public budgets. At the same time, they threaten to heap vast new costs on the American family.

Throughout history, most people who reached old age came to know personally far more of their descendants than their ancestors. In the near future, this will be reversed. It is likely you will never get to know as many of your children (and all their progeny) as your parents, your parents' parents, and so on. Already people are adjusting to an entirely new set of life-cycle expectations and family living patterns. Many elders raised in large families are surprised (and sometimes saddened) by their grown children's decision to have no or few children, while many younger adults find large families undesirable or unaffordable. Many couples have as many aging parents to care for—during as many years—as they had children. A whole new "sandwich" generation of fifty-somethings is learning how to cope simultaneously with needy seventy-five-year-olds and twenty-five-year-olds, any of whom may at some point "boomerang" back home.

In the future, the challenge will become more acute. With each passing decade, the number of family "caregivers" available to help each dependent elder will decline steadily, increasing the time and money burden on mature adults and putting extra pressure on governments to pick up the slack. Today, America's boomers are typically able to share the task of taking care of mom and dad among many siblings. But when the boomers themselves grow old, they will be much more likely to have no child or only one child (or to be never-married, widowed, divorced, or estranged from spouse or children) even as they live much longer. Since 1980 the proportion of women ending their childbearing years childless has risen from 10 percent to 19 percent.

For boomers unable to pay for at-home or institutional care on their own, a rising share will have no alternative to public programs. Much of the vast amount of unpaid caregiving given to elders within families will eventually show up in government budgets. For every elder now in a nursing home, it's estimated that there are two other elders receiving equivalent care from their families. For every elder now cared for by paid at-home nurses, ten other elders receive equivalent care from their families. With informal care networks stretched to the limit, even younger adults may find themselves forced to turn more to government to replace the assistance that extended families often provide in weathering financial emergencies. In an era of fiscal austerity, shrinking family size will create new *public needs* on practically every front.

Are the Official Projections Too Optimistic?

The coming age wave is largely locked in by demographic trends that have already been set in motion. To be sure, the exact magnitude of the age wave is still uncertain. But if the official projections miss the mark, it will almost surely be because they have *underestimated*—not overestimated—the magnitude of the challenge.

Consider longevity. Medical science is making remarkable progress on unlocking the genetic origins of illness and the biochemistry of human aging. Over the last decade entire new industries have emerged, specializing in everything from organ replacement to gene splicing. Large firms are poised to take advantage of what some entrepreneurs are calling a "golden age" of biomedical discovery. Yet incredibly, the Social Security trustees assume in their official projection that U.S. longevity at age sixty-five will grow just half as fast over the next seventy-five years as it has over the past seventy-five. If current trends are merely extrapolated, female life expectancy in the United States could reach ninety by 2075, five years more than the Social Security Administration projects.

In recent years the SSA's longevity pessimism has come under increasing criticism from demographers. In 1999 and again in 2003, the official Social Security Advisory Panel, a group of outside experts who review the SSA's projections, recommended that the trustees substantially raise their longevity assumptions—at least to bring them up to historical trend. Some biotech visionaries go much further and predict the imminent arrival of "postmortal" societies with life expectancies of 120 or more. But you don't have to agree with the visionaries to conclude that the trustees are too conservative. Accepting their projections means believing that American men will have to wait until 2040 to match the life expectancy that Japanese men *already* enjoy today; the corresponding date for American women is 2070.

To the extent that there is any justification for the SSA's pessimism, it lies in the conventional wisdom that there is a fixed limit to the human life span—and that improvements in longevity must therefore slow and eventually cease. In recent years, however, many experts have begun questioning conventional wisdom. If there's a limit to the human life span, they point out, mortality improvements for the oldest elderly age brackets should be slowing relative to those for younger elderly age brackets. At the same time, variations in life expectancy should be narrowing as more people bunch up against the "limit."

None of this appears to be happening. Life expectancy for the old-old is improving as fast or faster than for the young-old. In other words, the odds of living from eighty-five to ninety are improving at the same rate as the odds of living from sixty-five to seventy. Nor are variations in life expectancy diminishing, whether we look at the data by country, by region, by income, or by education. For many years Sweden and Japan have enjoyed a sizable longevity advantage over other developed countries—and some states like Minnesota and Utah have had a huge advantage over states like Mississippi and Louisiana. Such differences appear to be persistent. Everywhere people are living much longer. Yet everywhere some groups are living much longer than others. Demographer James Vaupel sums up the evidence this way: "The Social Security Administration would prefer it if the low-cost future were true. But . . . there does not appear to be any genetic barrier to a substantially increased life expectancy."

And what about birth rates? At first glance, the fertility assumption underlying the SSA's projections appears more reasonable. The trustees assume that over the long run, the U.S. fertility rate will be 1.95 births per woman. That's close to the current (2003) fertility rate of 2.02—and it is about what fertility has averaged over the past twenty-five years. To judge by the experience of other countries, however, the assumption may be optimistic. As far as fertility has fallen in the United States, it has fallen much further elsewhere in the developed world. With the exceptions of Iceland and New Zealand, no other developed country has babies at close to the rate Americans do.

No one knows what surprises demography may have in

store. Fertility is notoriously difficult to forecast over the short term. No one predicted the postwar baby boom in the United States, and no one predicted its end. It's worth noting, however, that apart from episodic exceptions like the baby boom, the long-term trend in fertility has been in one direction since the industrial revolution got under way two centuries ago—and that direction is down. Today's birth dearth is the result of deep-seated historical trends, most importantly rising affluence and the emancipation of women, that most of us expect will continue. Although U.S. fertility may never fall to Japanese or European levels, we cannot discount the possibility.

All of which raises an obvious question: What would the fiscal projections look like if we were a bit less sanguine in our demographic outlook? As it turns out, the SSA calculates an alternative scenario in which longevity rises at its historical pace and fertility falls to 1.7, closer to—but still significantly above—the developed-country average. Under this "high-cost" scenario, Social Security outlays rise from 11.1 percent of worker payroll today to 21.3 percent by 2040. Medicare outlays rise from 5.6 to 35.4 percent. Just to pay for these two programs we would have to tax away 56.7 percent of workers' taxable payroll.

The "Grow the Economy" Fantasy

The projections are stark. America will have to undertake fundamental reform of senior benefits or else experience a fiscal meltdown within a few decades. Given this choice, it's not surprising that many leaders of both political parties prefer denial.

The magic bullet most often extolled by Republicans (as well as some Democrats) is faster economic growth. If the economy grows faster than projected, say these GOP optimists, today's benefit promises will become affordable. As evidence of a doom-and-gloom conspiracy by official agencies, the "grow the economy" crowd point to projections showing a future slowdown in the growth rate of the U.S. GDP. It's true that the Social Security trustees project that real GDP will grow more slowly in the future than it has in the past. But this is arithmetic, not pessimism. Remember: GDP equals the number of workers times output per worker, or "productivity." GDP growth thus depends on workforce growth, and workforce growth in turn depends on demographics. From 2.1 percent growth in the number of workers per year during the 1970s and 1980s, when waves of coming-of-age boomers swelled the U.S. workforce, employment growth is due to fall to just 0.3 percent per year by the 2020s, when boomers will be retiring en masse. Given the demographics, it would fly against all logic if GDP growth did not slow.

A better question is whether the official assumptions about productivity are reasonable. From 1973 through 1995, productivity grew at the average annual rate of 1.2 percent per year, far beneath its performance during the 1950s and 1960s "American high." Since 1995, however, productivity growth has accelerated to 2.1 percent per year. The optimists say that the recent improvement heralds the advent of a "new economy" characterized by permanently higher levels of growth—and that the improvement should therefore be reflected in the projections. The CBO and GAO have recently raised their long-term productivity assumptions to about 2 percent, and so in effect assume that the entire recent improvement will be permanent. The Social Security trustees have been slower to accept the new-economy gospel. Since the late 1990s they have only raised their long-term productivity assumption from 1.3 to 1.6 percent.

In my view, the trustees are right to be cautious. The welcome acceleration of U.S. productivity growth since the mid-1990s may justify ratcheting up growth expectations. But to assume a huge and permanent departure from the historical trend seems premature. No one really knows why productivity growth slowed in the early 1970s. And no one really knows whether the recent improvement will be more than temporary.

I agree that we are witnessing the emergence of a new economy based on new information technologies and globalization. But I'm also old enough to be more than a bit skeptical about the claims of permanently higher growth. This is not the first time self-appointed prophets have proclaimed the arrival of a new era of endless prosperity, only to be proved laughably wrong. In my boyhood memories of the 1930s, I still recall the disappointment among adults who had been assured by experts in the late 1920s (to quote the immortal words of economist Irving Fisher) that "stock prices have reached what looks like a permanently high plateau." But we don't need to look back that far. Most adult Americans can recall how the go-go expectations of the late 1960s were betrayed by the turbulent stagflation of the 1970s.

Even if the optimists are right, the bottom line remains: given current policies, faster economic growth cannot overcome the resource challenge of an aging society. Faster growth boosts tax revenue, and this improves the budget outlook. But on the outlay side, it also boosts spending, largely canceling out the gain. Most economists assume that over the long run, discretionary spending will keep pace with the growth in the economy. Health-benefit spending, in the absence of clear policy intervention, has always grown faster than the wages of the highly skilled professionals who deliver it. The most lockstep relationship of all is with Social Security, since benefits are directly indexed to wages. Yes, when productivity goes up, average wages go up, and this adds to long-term tax revenues. But when average wages go up, average benefit awards also go up, and this adds to long-term outlays. So long as the link is retained, higher productivity growth cannot possibly save today's pay-as-you-go retirement systems. As Fed chairman Alan

Greenspan cautions, "Favorable productivity developments, of course, can help to alleviate the impending budgetary strains, but no one should expect that productivity growth will be sufficient to bail us out."

None of this is to say that faster economic growth—and the resulting rise in living standards—wouldn't bring vast benefits to society as a whole. It could even be argued that a more affluent society may be willing to allocate, through higher taxes, a much larger share of its income to old-age benefits. But this is a shaky case, and one that few new-economy enthusiasts are eager to make.

Aside from raising productivity, the other way to increase GDP growth is to raise employment—that is, to add more working bodies to the economy. Increased immigration is often billed as an easy fiscal fix for our aging society. Because most immigrants are young, the initial effect of more immigration is to expand the Social Security payroll tax base. It is important to remember, however, that in addition to paying taxes, immigrants consume government services, from education to welfare—and this offsets some of the revenue gain. Moreover, immigrants eventually grow old, too, and thus enlarge the Social Security benefit rolls. As a result, only a massive and sustained increase in immigration can make a real difference.

And that's the problem: Americans would never tolerate—politically or socially—the levels of increased immigration required to prop up our aging welfare state. The Social Security trustees assume that annual net immigration will total 900,000 in the future, about the average over the past decade. To close Social Security's long-term cash deficit through immigration alone, American voters would have to accept roughly five million immigrants annually, quintuple the recent historical average. Relative to the size of the population, our rate of immigration would be more than twice the all-time historic high reached during Teddy Roosevelt's presidency.

Not only is this massive inflow unlikely, the post-9/11 drift in public opinion seems to be heading the other way—toward raising, not lowering, the fence at our borders. At least one-third of today's immigrant inflow is illegal; thus, even current levels of immigration are considerably greater than what the law allows. Ironically, the U.S. Social Security projections assume an indefinite continuation of this "other-than-legal" immigrant stream (to use the actuaries' delicate phrase), even as other federal agencies are urgently trying to shut it down.

If we can't grow our way out of the cost problem, some say there's another option: inflating our way out of it. Printing money has been the last recourse of governments throughout history. From Revolutionary France in the 1790s to Weimar Germany in the 1920s, regimes under duress have made their ends meet by inflating their spending power ahead of their fixed obligations. Although no one, Democrat or Republican, today advocates a policy of deliberate inflation, many suppose that if all else fails the government could someday resort to inflation to reduce its long-term entitlement obligations.

Is this a realistic option? Probably not. Inflation usually ends up destroying social trust and ruining the economy. Furthermore, it's a "fix" that can only be used once—indeed, can only be seriously discussed once. The mere expectation of inflation will cause interest rates to leap upward to compensate creditors for the anticipated erosion of their real claims. Even as a short-term palliative, moreover, inflation may not have the desired effect. Social Security benefits are by law indexed to the price level—and Medicare benefits are in effect indexed to it. Yes, inflation would reduce the real value of the formal public debt. But it would do little to reduce the value of our unfunded entitlement promises, which as we have seen are many times larger. In the end, deliberate inflation would act like a perverse chemotherapy regime that ravages the body while leaving the tumor untouched.

The "Cut Health Care Waste" Fantasy

Democrats are less likely to count on faster growth to avoid the difficult trade-offs. But Democrats (as well as some Republicans) often argue for another painless strategy to roll back the cost of the age wave. The problem isn't the aging of the population, they say. The problem is runaway health care costs—and with a few simple changes in our health care system, we can easily ratchet down the long-term projections. Simply get rid of all the waste, fraud, and abuse, they insist, and cost control will be within reach.

The optimists are right that health care is much of the long-term cost problem. From now to 2040, the GAO projects that Medicare and Medicaid will account for 55 percent of the total growth in entitlement spending. They are deluded, however, in thinking that there are painless solutions. Let's be honest. Health care spending is not growing so fast due to the proliferation of obviously useless medical services. It is growing because of the continual introduction of new technologies and treatments that are beneficial—or at least deemed to be beneficial by providers or patients. In a survey of fifty leading health economists in 1995, more than four out of five agreed with the statement, "The primary reason for the increase in the health sector's share of GDP over the past thirty years is technological change in medicine."

America—indeed, the world—is in the midst of a medical revolution that shows no signs of abating. One of my earliest childhood Nebraska memories is of good old Dr. Edwards carrying a black bag filled with all the tools of his trade. If he couldn't help us with his stethoscope and hypodermic needle, my family made a rare visit to a community hospital, which may have boasted an X-ray machine. There wasn't much that medicine could do, and most of that wasn't very expensive. Dr. Edwards would never have comprehended what has happened since—the growth of a U.S. medical-industrial complex that now spends more than $110 billion in research and construction each year. The pharmaceutical industry alone now runs neck and neck with the Pentagon for total R&D outlays.

Medical miracles unimagined only a decade or two ago are now commonplace. Some of these technologies screen for low-probability risks (from space-age imaging devices to genetic testing). Others improve the odds for low-probability cures (from organ transplants to powerful new AIDS therapies). Others help alleviate debilitating chronic conditions (from insulin-pump implants to microchip hearing and seeing devices). Still others simply enhance our quality of life (from sports medicine to the Viagra vogue). And the pace of innovation may be accelerating. Pointing to an enormous bow wave of biomedical research now on the horizon, health technology expert William Schwartz insists that few governments have any idea what's about to hit them. "Everything that's happened up until now in medicine is a prelude," he reports. "What's really ahead is stunning. It's going to be . . . very expensive."

There's no doubt that America's technology-intensive style of medicine—there are more MRI units in Greater Atlanta than in all of Canada—is the single most important reason we spend so much more on health care than other nations do. But technology isn't the only reason costs keep growing. There's also society's expanding definition of health itself. In recent decades we have broadened the definition of insurable health care to include whole new realms of social life, from psychiatric counseling for troubled youths to home care for the frail elderly. "Health," moreover, is not a fixed target. It is a subjective standard that has risen over time as society has become more affluent, less tolerant of risk and discomfort, and more secular—that is, more apt to see happiness in the here and now as life's ultimate goal. As this rising standard interacts with medical advances, it is transforming the practice of medicine. While once health care meant an occasional visit to the doctor, it is fast becoming a lifelong process of diagnostics, monitoring, and intervention in which any extra dollar spent is likely to confer *some* benefit.

These underlying cost drivers are given an extra push by open-ended benefit and insurance systems that shield most Americans from the need to make tradeoffs between health care and competing priorities. Dan Yankelovich, the dean of American pollsters, says that our spare-no-costs attitude is explained by our "maximum right" view of health care. With most public goods, we agree that government should guarantee minimum access—or what Yankelovich calls a "minimum right." It is generally agreed, for instance, that every American should be able to get a decent meal or, if qualified, an affordable education at a state university. But it is not generally agreed that everybody should be able to dine free at the Four Seasons or be guaranteed a subsidized education at Yale. With health care, however, we are uncomfortable with these distinctions. We believe that every citizen should have unlimited access to the very best that modern medicine can devise.

Over the postwar era we have witnessed occasional interruptions in health-care spending growth. Yet when these pauses are the result of limitations on access, public opinion and the political system react vehemently. In the mid-1990s, for example, the "managed care" revolution plus strict spending caps set by Congress were briefly successful in putting the reins on health care cost growth. The restrictions do not appear to have compromised "quality." Despite the horror stories, surveys consistently show that patients of HMOs rank their providers higher in quality of care than do patients of fee-for-service medicine. Nonetheless, heated complaints about loss of "choice" quickly led to looser cost control—and the renewal of spending growth since the late 1990s.

In just the five years from 1997 to 2003, total U.S. health care spending surged from 13.1 to 15.3 percent of GDP. In per capita dollars, we now spend 55 percent more than the next runner-up, Switzerland. Public health care spending is setting new records as well. In 2003 spending on Medicare, Medicaid, and other government health benefit programs reached 7 percent of GDP, more than some developed countries spend on universal health-care systems covering everyone. New demands, moreover, are creating new cost pressures on every front. As of 2002 the number of uninsured Americans stood at 44 million. Most of the uninsured are low-income working families who cannot afford coverage of their own—but must pay first-dollar payroll taxes to finance the Medicare benefits of retired stockbrokers. Sooner or later some public assistance for the uninsured is inevitable—and desirable. But it will necessarily add to the total fiscal burden.

Meanwhile, the age wave and its special cost multipliers loom just over the horizon. On average, each older American consumes about four times as much in medical services as a younger adult and about seven times as much as a child. Although the elderly now make up just 13 percent of the U.S. population, they account for roughly 40 percent of U.S. medical bills. Assuming these patterns hold true, the growth in the number of elderly will inevitably drive up total spending as a share of employer payrolls, government budgets, and the national economy.

True, some aging experts believe that tomorrow's elderly will be healthier, and hence less costly, than today's. According to what is often called the "compression of morbidity" thesis, we can expect health spans to rise along with life spans—and should eventually see the ills of old age relegated to a brief period of declining vigor at the very end of life. There are other experts, however, who argue that much of what modern medicine does, especially at older ages, is to prolong life without restoring people to full health. According to this rival "failure of success" thesis, aging societies can expect to see a rising incidence of chronic morbidity at every age—more diabetes, more hypertension, and more Alzheimer's.

A number of recent studies have shown that disability rates

among the elderly have declined dramatically over the past two decades, which at first glance seems to lend some hopeful support to the compression of morbidity theory. A lower incidence of disability, however, doesn't necessarily mean that the elderly are in better health. Even as the share of elderly with limitations on "activities of daily living" such as dressing, cooking, and walking declines, the share with serious medical conditions could be constant or rising. In other words, grandma may be getting around better but still be seeing the doctor as often or more often than before.

If the decline in disability really did portend slower future cost growth, we might expect it to have moderated past cost growth as well. But it is difficult to find any evidence of this in the historical data. Since Medicare was founded in the mid-1960s, real spending per beneficiary has risen at the blistering average annual rate of 5 percent. Although this growth has occasionally slowed, every period of slower growth has been followed by a renewed spending surge. Clearly any saving from declining disability has been overwhelmed by other factors, from the introduction of new medical technologies to rising social expectations about care and cure.

Still, let's be generous and grant that dramatic and effortless savings are possible. This still might not deflate the official health care cost projections. Why? Because the official projections *already* build in a dramatic cost slowdown. The trustees assume that the growth in real per capita Medicare spending will decelerate from its historical rate of 5 percent per year to just 2 percent per year by the 2020s. The trustees fail to point to any change in medical technology, or health status, or social expectations that might account for the slowdown. The only justification they offer is that if Medicare spending did not slow down by then, it would rapidly take over our entire economy. Let us all take a collective gulp: *The unsustainable official cost projections already assume tough, perhaps even draconian cost-control measures that today we do not even contemplate.*

The sheer growth in U.S. health care spending is, alas, a fiscal and economic malignancy for which the scientists at the National Institutes of Health cannot possibly discover a cure. We the people must design the cure—and implement it.

Never the Right Time for Reform

The long-term Medicare projections raise an important issue. Like the long-term fiscal projections for the entire budget, they tell us where we are heading, not necessarily where we will end up. After all, they are projections, not *predictions.* They will only happen if the underlying demographic drivers and current public policies remain unchanged.

As far as the demographic drivers are concerned, no change is a safe bet. The aging of America is not a strange historical accident. It is the by-product of a trend toward affluence and individualism that the vast majority of Americans welcome. Many demographers believe that as it develops every society sooner or later moves from high fertility and high mortality (the traditional norm) to low fertility and low mortality (the modern norm). They even have a name for it: the "demographic transition." It is modernization's defining rite of passage, and thus far it appears to be irreversible.

That leaves public policies, which will surely have to change. And this is exactly why we must look closely at the projections, even if we reasonably conclude that they are unsustainable and cannot come to pass. They tell us the magnitude of the policy changes that will be required to put senior entitlements and the overall budget back on a sustainable trajectory. And they focus our attention on the paramount question: How and when will we change our policy course? Will we do so sooner, when we still have time to control our destiny? Or later, after economic damage and political and social trauma lead to a wrenching and involuntary upheaval?

What's most remarkable about the historical growth in senior benefits is that it has continued with only an occasional pause for four decades, no matter what the party in power and no matter what the fiscal and economic outlook. Somehow it's never been the right time for reform. When economic times are bad, the argument in favor of spending more on the elderly is that they are vulnerable and dependent. When times are good, the argument is that younger adults are going to be so affluent that it would be criminal not to share their wealth with the old.

Neither argument withstands scrutiny. The elderly, for one thing, aren't as vulnerable as they used to be. Over the past twenty-five years the real median income of households aged sixty-five and over has risen by over one-third, while that of households under age forty-five has remained virtually stationary. The premise of the second argument—that the young can finance current-law senior benefits and still enjoy big gains in after-tax living standards—is equally mistaken. In fact, hiking taxes to pay for the projected growth in senior benefits would, under the SSA's official scenario, erase most of all growth in pretax worker earnings over the next fifty years. And this projection may be optimistic. Under the high-cost scenario, after-tax earnings would actually decline.

Defenders of the status quo sometimes argue that Social Security and Medicare are "separate deals"—and that, while runaway health care costs may be pushing Medicare toward a major overhaul, this shouldn't influence the debate over Social Security. It's as though the bleak future of one program were a reason not to worry about the other. This logic is backwards. Both Social Security and Medicare tax the same people (mostly workers) to pay benefits to the same people (mostly retirees). Indeed, because cost savings in Medicare is bound to be so difficult, it is even more urgent to save what we can in Social Security. The defenders of the status quo seem to think that tomorrow's workers won't mind paying a stupefying total tax burden so long as different federal agencies are spending the money.

The public resources we have available to pay for elder dependency are not unlimited. In the long run they cannot exceed what can be raised from taxpayers. They must also leave room for other important national agendas—one of which, national security, is also likely to consume a growing share of our economy over the first half of the new century. It is to this agenda that we now turn.

Chapter 4

•

THE CHALLENGE ABROAD: A DANGEROUS WORLD

Long before September 11, 2001, Americans already had ample reason to worry about terrorism. Several blue-ribbon panels had issued reports detailing our vulnerability to weapons of mass destruction (WMDs)—including the Richards-Rindskopf Report in 1995, the Brown Commission in 1996, the Marsh Commission in 1997, the Deutsch Commission in 1999, and the Bremer and Gilmore Commissions in 2000. In the spring of 2001, just months before Al Qaeda hit the twin towers, the U.S. Commission on National Security, chaired by Gary Hart and Warren Rudman, released its astonishingly prescient recommendation that the president move quickly to create a new "Department of Homeland Security."

And then there were the grimly realistic war-game simulations designed to test America's preparedness, using real public agencies and hospitals. In Operation TopOff, run in May of 2000, an airborne release of plague killed one thousand Denver residents in three days and mustard gas injured hundreds in Portsmouth, New Hampshire. In an exercise called "Dark Winter," run at Andrews Air Force Base in June of 2001, terrorists released smallpox virus at several shopping malls in Oklahoma City. On December 9 the first patients began reporting symptoms at hospitals. Eight weeks later, by February 6, three million Americans had contracted the disease, one million were dead, and civil disorder was widespread despite a call-up of the National Guard and declarations of martial law. Most of those who took part in the "Dark Winter" simulation, even veteran policy leaders, reported being shaken by the experience.

Yet no report or simulation could match the impact of reality on that terrible 9/11 morning, instantly likened by the media and the public to Pearl Harbor Sunday, when all Americans awoke to discover that we do in fact face mortal enemies who threaten our nation with as much destruction as they can muster. Between 80 and 90 percent of Americans now agree that preventing future acts of international terrorism and the spread of WMDs should be "among the most important goals of U.S. foreign policy." President George Bush has called terrorism America's greatest national security threat since World War II and has declared that America's "war on terrorism" must be waged "for years and decades, not weeks and months." Most Americans agree with this assessment—and with the need to pay whatever price is necessary to wage this war.

But what is that price? And how will we pay it? It now seems nearly certain that the aging of America, which was due to pose a great fiscal challenge over the next few decades in any case, will unfold in an era of large additional commitments to our national security agenda. Clearly, there are long-term fiscal trade-offs to be faced—between retirement security and national security, or between today's taxpayers and tomorrow's taxpayers. As yet, however, the leadership of neither party has even mentioned these trade-offs, much less discussed them seriously.

The purpose of this chapter is to examine America's fiscal future from a global perspective. This means looking at the likely cost of America's post-9/11 security agenda. It also means paying attention to two other issues having profound connections both to our national security and to our fiscal and economic performance: America's growing net indebtedness to foreigners, and the extreme aging that is overtaking the rest of the developed world.

In a book dealing mainly with America's own national future, I hope this global excursus does not seem beside the point. No man is an island, wrote John Donne. No nation is an island, either—least of all a superpower with such manifest responsibilities in a newly dangerous world. Americans are not imperialists, and few are eager to manage a global "Pax Americana." But to commit ourselves to a broader role while remaining blindly ignorant of the ultimate cost is sheer folly. When it comes to fiscal consequences, our parties and leaders are mute not only on our domestic challenges but on our global challenges as well.

First Global Challenge—the War on Terror

In September of 2003, with bombs still flying in Baghdad, the president made an emergency war-spending request for $87 billion. It was the largest such request since the opening months of World War II. And that's when the bombast started flying in Congress. One instant analysis showed that this rate of spending exceeded, in real (inflation-adjusted) dollars, the cost of U.S. participation in World War I. Another showed that $87 billion could pay for a decade's worth of foreign aid to the rest of the world. Still another pointed to bridges and electricity grids in the midwestern United States that go unfixed while infrastructure in Iraq gets repaired.

The cost details arriving from the battlefield were riveting. For patrolling the Sunni Triangle, the army wanted 595 extra Humvees, at a fully equipped price tag of $250,000 each. Another 60,000 troops needed three-piece body-armor suits, at

$5,000 each. Every day the logistical needs of the Iraqi forces required dozens of thirty-truck convoys from Kuwait and Turkey, carrying everything from half a million bottles of spring water to countless electronic modules, all provided by 6,000 civilian contractors. Sun and sand, meanwhile, did more damage to the equipment than ambushes by insurgents. Each Bradley in Iraq needed new tracks every sixty days, at $22,576 per vehicle. Apache attack helicopters, in perpetual need of maintenance, single-handedly devoured an amazing $1.3 billion in spare parts in fiscal year 2003. Engineering and construction costs were (and still are) billions over their original estimates.

"Fiscal shock and awe," announced Senator Robert Byrd, an outraged Democratic leader. "I have no doubt that some people will be angry," admitted Representative James Greenwood, a defensive Republican.

We all had better get used to it. The armed forces of superpower America are amazingly effective. Their personnel are the best trained and best led in the world, and their technology—now featuring precision-guided munitions and integrated communications over a digitized battlespace—clearly has no equal. As one Iraqi colonel put it after firsthand experience, "U.S. military technology is beyond belief." In a conventional war, America can swiftly defeat most likely adversaries with minimal casualties either to itself or to civilians.

Yet alongside this amazing capability comes an equally amazing price tag. For most of U.S. history, going to war was like organizing a large federal jobs program, with most of the work done by inexpensive, quickly trained recruits. Today, it is more like a NASA moon launch, entailing a massive logistical tail supporting a professionally managed and swiftly depreciating stock of high-tech physical capital. Just keeping two divisions engaged in "stability operations" in Iraq for one week costs $1 billion; keeping them engaged for a full year would cost the entire GDP of New Zealand.

Since 9/11, moreover, the military is planning to invest even more in this machine to overcome some of its remaining weaknesses: slow reaction time to crises in remote regions and inexperience in dealing with unconventional (so-called asymmetrical) threats such as terrorism, guerrilla war, or the use of WMDs, including nukes. Even after the scrapping of certain old weapons plans (like the Crusader artillery system) and the paring back of some other purchases, the total net cost of this "military transformation" will be impressive. Weapons procurement, which fell to a post-Cold War low of about $50 billion yearly in the mid-1990s, is scheduled to rise to over $100 billion yearly by 2010, more than its previous (real-dollar) peak in the mid-Reagan years. On the drawing board are lightweight "Stryker Brigades," DD(X) stealth warships, superfast low-profile watercraft for coastline combat, and all the science-fiction paraphernalia of the army's next-generation "Objective Force." These weapons will include non-line-of-sight cannons, electromagnetic "rail guns," robotic mules and assault vehicles, long-endurance unmanned tactical aircraft, loitering attack missiles, and total digital integration of fire and sensor systems.

Although the Bush administration incorporates an estimate of these new costs into its projections for defense outlays, most budget experts believe these projections seriously underestimate the total future cost of the war on terror. To begin with, the administration refuses to make any projections for future military operations; it plans to procure all such funds through emergency appropriations. Also, much of the new technology is still under development and thus sure to experience cost overruns.

The CBO recently reran these projections assuming, first, ongoing but diminishing operations in Iraq, Afghanistan, and elsewhere, and, second, a historical rate of cost overruns for all new procurement. The results are eye-opening: total defense outlays over the next decade would cost 18 percent more than the official projection. Including interest costs, this excess amounts to $1.1 trillion in new spending—a price tag that competes with the cost of the new Medicare drug benefit.

Even this number does not reflect the cost of any new military operation abroad, which (says Gallup) three of every four Americans believe is very likely in "the next few years." Nor does it reflect any permanent increase in active-force troop strength, which Congress may insist upon even over administration resistance. With ongoing peacekeeping missions around the world, not even help from (worn-out) reserve and National Guard units can prevent the armed forces from being stretched dangerously thin should a new threat emerge. In December of 2003, only two of the army's ten divisions were both uncommitted and in a high state of readiness. That same month, fifty-four of the sixty-one members of the House Armed Services Committee, joined by the top Republican and Democrat on the House Intelligence Committee, signed a letter to President Bush urging him to enlist more troops.

In the war on terror, most Americans agree with the president's premise that the best defense is a good offense and forward deployment. Along with augmenting the capabilities of its armed forces, America is sharing intelligence with friendly governments around the world and training and equipping their antiterrorist forces as needed. Sea- and land-based ballistic missile defenses, long under development, are now being deployed at a growing cost ($10.3 billion in the FY 2005 budget). No matter how effective we are at global preemption and deterrence, however, we must also take effective measures to prevent terrorism within our borders—"homeland security," as we now call it. Here too we face a large gap between the resources we need to commit and those we now allocate in our official projections.

Let me begin with the obvious, as stated in the 2002 National Strategy for Homeland Security: "Our society presents an almost infinite array of potential targets that can be attacked through a variety of methods." America is a large country, with 7,514 miles of land borders and 95,000 miles of shoreline and navigable waterways. America is also a free society that is fully integrated into the global economy. Each year more than 500 million people (including 330 noncitizens, many of them commuters) legally enter our country. Each working day $9.4 billion in imports and exports cross our borders. There is no conceivable price at which America could make itself totally secure against a major terrorist attack.

Yet it is possible, at a reasonable price, to take extra steps that would make us significantly less vulnerable than we are now to attacks that would cause catastrophic human or economic losses. Thus far, we have not taken many of these extra steps, nor do we have any plans to take them. The final (Gilmore) report of the Homeland Security Commission warned in December of 2003 that "the momentum appears to have waned" in the drive to reduce national risks. A month later a study by the Institute of Medicine and the National Research Council concluded that biodefense programs were underfunded and offer "dismal prospects for successful results." I believe it is only a matter of time before American voters insist that we do more—and, indeed, I believe this insistence will crystallize overnight come the next serious terrorist scare.

Doing more of course will cost money. Here are just a few of the areas needing action:

- FIRST RESPONDERS. Although fire, police, and other emergency personnel are America's "first responders" to any act of domestic terrorism, they remain so underequipped and undertrained for this task that (declared Warren Rudman, who recently chaired a task force on first responders) we would never consider sending such troops into combat. For example, only one-tenth of all fire departments have the capacity to respond to a building collapse. Only a third of all firefighters on a shift are equipped with breathing apparatuses, only half with radios (a deficiency that directly contributed to the high fatality among New York City firefighters on 9/11). Biochemical and radiation sensors are lacking. Urban search and rescue is spotty. The 911 phone system is still not national. Emergency communications are not interoperable. *Estimated cost to prepare first responders for a nonnuclear attack: $62 billion over five years.*

- HEALTH CARE SYSTEM. During last winter's flu outbreak, health clinics had to turn away patients and vaccines ran out—not a good sign that our health care system is ready to handle a major terrorist attack. Acute-care hospitals have few quarantine or decontamination facilities and very little "surge capacity" in beds. Vaccines for major biological threats (most notably, smallpox) remain understocked. National Guard and reserve personnel and even many professionals in our public health network have little or no training in responding to a nuclear or biological emergency. *Minimal estimated cost to remedy: $36 billion over five years.*
- CARGO CONTAINERS. Half of all U.S. imports arrive each year in 16 million cargo containers—roughly 20,000 arriving each working day at 300 commercial ports of entry before being loaded onto intermodal trains or trucks. The sealing and labeling of these containers is entirely unregulated, and only 2 percent of them (at most) are ever inspected by federal authorities. According to John Meredith, CEO of Hutchison Port Holdings, one of the world's largest cargo firms, smuggling a WMD through containers is "a question of when, not if." One recent study concludes that the current odds of detecting a shielded nuke inside a container are only about 10 percent. Closing all U.S. ports for more than a month, in response to the mere threat of a smuggled WMD, would throw the U.S. economy into recession. *Minimal estimated*

cost to remedy, including globally monitored packing, tamperproof seals, and satellite tracking: up front $20 billion, ongoing yearly unknown.

- IMMIGRATION CONTROL. The fact that six of the 9/11 terrorists had expired or fraudulent visas points to the manifest inability of federal agencies to prevent illegal entry, to locate illegals once here, or to monitor noncitizens who enter legally. There are currently 8 to 12 million illegal aliens in the United States, including nearly 300,000 fugitives fleeing official orders of deportation. The FBI cannot possibly handle this caseload, and local authorities have historically been excluded from any data on illegals. Few terrorism experts believe we can attain an adequate margin of safety without total overhaul of our immigration system, a reform that may ultimately include biometric national ID cards. *Minimal estimated cost to remedy: unknown but very large.*
- CRITICAL INFRASTRUCTURE. America's infrastructure includes nodes of great vulnerability which, if disabled, could trigger widespread public terror and serious economic loss. Few water reservoirs or grain silos are any better guarded now than before 9/11. A large share of our consumable energy flows through a relatively small number of pipelines and refineries in remote, unguarded locations. A well-placed blow at electronic communications could bring financial trading to a stop. Transportation lines also have bottlenecks: for example, five bridges and one tunnel entering New York State account for 70 percent of all trade with Canada, the largest U.S. trading partner. *Minimal estimated cost to remedy: unknown but very large.*

To be sure, any effort to "cost out" America's homeland security agenda must be hedged with the language of probability. In my mind, most of the wild-card surprises (say, another major terrorist strike) clearly lie on the side of higher costs. Yet even absent such dreadful news, it seems very probable that America will be spending progressively more on homeland security over the next decade or two. No one can foretell exactly which areas of spending will rise fastest. Much will depend on our assessment of emerging threats as the war on terror wears on. Much will also depend on whether homeland security mutates into home-district pork. Regrettably, Congress is allocating much of the early spending on a politics-as-usual formula (each state receives according to its population) rather than on an objective assessment of need.

At a prudent minimum, let's say that this extra homeland spending prevents domestic discretionary outlays from shrinking, as a share of GDP, after 2004. (Recall that "discretionary" refers to programs that Congress actually votes on each year, unlike most benefits, which are deemed "entitlements.") In other words, this kind of spending will rise as fast as GDP, an assumption many budget analysts make even with no consideration of homeland security. Let's also assume that the CBO is correct in its "high cost" reassessment of projected defense spending. The result will be future outlays that are more expensive than the (already grim) do-nothing projections by at least another 1 percent of GDP. Keep in mind that this implies no troop-level increases nor any new military campaigns. It also says nothing about other new domestic initiatives that may carry sizable price tags—from education reform and health insurance to more college and job-training aid.

Let me put this into a larger historical context. Throughout the postwar era, the federal budget has been able to accommodate steady growth in benefit spending in part by cutting back on all other domestic spending—including investment, as we have seen, but most of all by cutting back on defense. From 1960 to 2000, federal benefits grew from 4.7 to 10.8 percent of GDP. Meanwhile, defense outlays fell from 9.3 to 3.0 percent of GDP—with only temporary backtracking during the Reagan rearmament of the mid-1980s. After the end of the Cold War, President Bill Clinton's budgeteers published long-term projections that cushioned at least some of the future growth in retirement benefits by assuming a steady "withering away" of all other federal spending. The FY 1999 budget includes one amazing table that shows, by the year 2070, *total* federal discretionary spending (domestic *and* defense) shrinking to a mere 2.2 percent of GDP. Aside from Social Security, Medicare, and Medicaid, Clinton's numbers really did reflect the expectation that "the era of big government" would ultimately disappear.

This sort of benign optimism is now officially dead. For the first time in the postwar era, we face a future that will call upon every major category of federal spending to grow as fast as or faster than our economy for many years to come. The Bush administration has adjusted its long-term discretionary spending projections upward from where they were in the Clinton era, but not sufficiently in my view. In a post-9/11 world, we should not be banking on any reduction in our level of discretionary spending—at least not until we have some assurance that the danger is past.

Second Global Challenge—the Danger of a Hard Landing

In the classic novel by Charles Dickens, Mr. Micawber instructs David Copperfield that if his annual income exceeds his annual expenses by a mere sixpence, the result is "happiness"; the other way around, "misery." This was good advice for any young Victorian who wished to prosper as he grew older. It is also good advice for any nation that wishes to prosper as it enters the twenty-first century—especially if, instead of sixpence per year, we're talking about $540 billion per year.

That's how much the United States is now borrowing from the rest of the world. Economists call this figure our "current account" deficit, because this net inflow of capital is what pays for our overall deficit on goods, services, and foreign aid transfers that are "currently" consumed. Along with direct lending, our current-account deficit is paid for through the net sales of U.S. assets to foreign businesses or persons, everything from stocks and bonds to corporations and real estate. America imports roughly $4 billion of foreign capital each day, half of that to cover our current-account deficit and the other half to finance our own investments abroad.

In Chapter 2 I explained how the rise in our current-account deficit over the past thirty years is linked to the decline in our national savings and the deepening of our federal deficits. Over time, our chronic borrowing from other countries has accumulated into large liabilities to other countries. U.S. citizens must pay for these growing liabilities with a growing annual debt-service charge, consisting mainly of interest and dividend payments. The annual debt-service charge is very sensitive to interest rates—it goes up when interest rates go up—and its growth over time will itself widen the current-account deficit.

If nothing else changes, the borrowing will continue until foreigners accumulate all the U.S. assets they care to own, at which time a rise in interest rates (choking off investment) and a decline in the dollar (choking off imports and stimulating exports) will gradually close the current-account deficit. It may not entirely disappear, but it will close enough to stabilize foreign holdings as a share of the U.S. economy. Afterward, Americans will cease to borrow as much from the rest of the world. Absent any rise in our national savings rate, we will just have to get by with less investment in our own economy. Debt-service payments will no longer rise. Instead, Americans will simply make do with less capital, slower growth in GDP, and of course slower growth in living standards.

One thing I did not mention about this scenario. Dreary as it is, this sort of "soft landing" is *the very best outcome* we can hope for so long as America's future fiscal path and national savings rate remain unchanged. It is quite possible, in the opinion of many economists, that the dynamic of gradual adjustment will at some point be short-circuited by market psychology—triggering a sudden loss of confidence, followed by a financial and economic crisis. According to a joint paper by Bob Rubin, Allen Sinai, and Peter Orszag (a formidable combination of policy, forecasting, and academic expertise): "The adverse consequences of sustained large budget deficits may well be far larger and occur more suddenly than traditional analysis suggests." In a recent paper on widening U.S. deficits, the International Monetary Fund staff conclude: "The possible global risks of a disorderly exchange rate adjustment, especially to financial markets, cannot be ignored." The Congressional Budget Office agrees, noting that "such a path could result in an economic crisis."

These risks are yet another cost posed by our fiscal profligacy and may, in time, translate into entirely new global challenges that few of our political leaders have even considered. Keep in mind that a global trauma that rocks our own economy can easily swamp other economies. With his customary flamboyance, Lester Thurow explains: "A sharply falling dollar is a comet crash where the point of impact is located in the United States but where the greatest economic damage is done elsewhere in the world."

How might this crisis unfold? Well, let's assume that global investors gradually lose faith that the United States will ever rein in its federal deficit. This will make it ever more certain, in their eyes, that the value of their dollar assets will sooner or later be eroded by rising inflation, higher interest rates, and a stock market decline. As they begin shuffling their portfolio away from dollar assets, they will soon realize that once other investors start moving the same way, the exchange rate of the dollar will fall at an accelerating pace, producing a large and sudden decline in the value of their assets. This can easily lead to a get-out-the-door-first mentality—in short, to a run on the dollar. (We have already experienced such dollar runs four times over the last thirty years, with far less daunting projections than those that confront us today: 1971–73; 1978–79; 1985–87; and 1994–95; they typically begin after the dollar has already been declining gently for some time.) Once the dollar "overshoots" in a large and sudden plunge, inflation and interest rates may jump and financial markets may ratchet downward.

Reverberations in the "real" economy could then follow, including a loss of consumer and investor confidence, a severe contraction, and ultimately global recession. Soaring interest rates will cause the federal deficit to jump, as Treasury bond buyers demand much higher returns. (If short-term Treasury rates were to jump back to the 4 to 5 percent range, federal interest outlays would climb by $30 billion in the first year, $50 billion in the second.) Rather than improve the prospect of fiscal reform, gloomy economic conditions may delay it further. According to Rubin, Sinai, and Orszag: "These various effects can feed on each other to create a mutually reinforcing cycle; for example, increased interest rates and diminished activity may further worsen the fiscal imbalance, which can then cause a further loss of confidence and potentially spark another round of negative feedback effects."

How likely is this scenario? No one knows. But in my own interviews with a wide range of policy leaders, financial traders, and economists, I've found that few believe the U.S. current-account deficit is sustainable at current levels much longer than five more years and many worry that the inevitable readjustment may be a "hard" rather than a "soft" landing. Most say there is a real risk of a crisis. Ex-Fed chairman Paul Volcker tells me the odds are something like 75 percent. Ex-Treasury secretary Bob Rubin talks of "a day of serious reckoning."

What might trigger the crisis? Almost anything might push currency markets over the tipping point—an act of terror, a bad day on Wall Street, a disappointing employment report, or even a testy remark by a central banker. Before that happens, it is likely that global investors will feel they already hold about as much in dollar assets as they care to own. Since most investors instinctively resist diversifying very much outside their own countries (a tendency known as "home bias"), the point of dollar satiation may arrive long before economic theory might predict. Morris Goldstein, senior fellow at the Institute for International Economics (IIE) and former deputy research director at the IMF, puts it this way: "Even if home bias declines some over time, the level of it is likely to remain high enough in many creditor countries to make problematic the dollar accumulation associated with 'large' (5 percent of GDP or more) U.S. current-account deficits."

Fred Bergsten, head of the IIE, points out another possible trigger. Over the postwar era, he says, serious readjustment typically begins only after large trade deficits have ignited protectionist fires, compelling our own leaders to act—and then tempting foreign leaders to retaliate. So far, the world has managed to avoid an all-out 1930s-style trade war. But with the rhetoric of "fair trade" and "America first" again on the rise, especially among Democratic politicians, many of the wiser heads are holding their breath. Fed chairman Alan Greenspan has said repeatedly that nothing worries him more than "the clouds of emerging protectionism that have become increasingly visible on today's horizon."

Again, no one knows what will happen. Everyone hopes for a soft landing. "The history of financial markets suggests, however, that the shifts in investor confidence can be sudden, with the timing driven by self-fulfilling expectations," explain Laurence Ball and Gregory Mankiw. "Hard landings are hard to think about because things can go wrong in such a rich variety of ways."

There are, to be sure, many skeptics who explain why we don't need to worry about a hard landing. I think their reassurances are unpersuasive.

To begin with, these skeptics say that the United States has never before experienced a full-blown financial crisis triggered by exchange rates. True enough. But there's much else that's never happened before. Never before has our own current-account deficit (now at 5.1 percent of GDP) been nearly so large. It's not reassuring that the closest we have ever come to hard landings in the past correspond to the previous peaks in our current-account deficit—0.7 percent of GDP in 1978 and 3.5 percent of GDP in 1987, when the dollar fell by a third and the stock market took its "Black Monday" plunge. Never before has our net indebtedness to other countries (now close to 30 percent of GDP) been anywhere near so large. Never before has the global economic system allowed nations with floating currencies to trade such a large share of their production and savings across borders. Perhaps "system" is too strong a word, since it has become perversely warped, like a billiard ball on a featherbed, around U.S. demands for plentiful credit and foreign demands for plentiful exports. Incredibly, the U.S. current-account deficit now absorbs, directly or indirectly, two-thirds of the total reported current-account surpluses run by every other nation on the planet.

If the skeptics looked more closely at these numbers, they might find plenty to worry about. Most economists who've examined the historical record say that nations typically get into trouble when their current-account deficit exceeds 5 percent of GDP (that's where we are now, and the New York Fed predicts we'll soon be moving higher). They also say that nations get into trouble when their net indebtedness exceeds 40 percent of GDP (that's where we'll be by 2006 on our current path). "The United States is on course to increase its net liabilities to around 40 percent of GDP within the next few years," observe the IMF staff, "an unprecedented level of external debt for a large industrial country."

But wait, say the skeptics, none of this matters. America is in a privileged position. Global investors have *no choice* but to invest in dollar assets. In the short run, this is clearly untrue. In the midst of a crisis, global investors will turn to anything—Siberian peanut oil, if necessary—rather than lose their shirts by riding the dollar down. Yet even in the longer term, there are plausible alternatives. Global investors currently hold a much smaller share of their assets in euros or yen than the European or Japanese share of world GDP. If confidence in the stability of the dollar is shaken, investors could opt to increase this percentage—or switch to gold. Indeed, some market experts tell me that the recent 40 percent rise of the euro can be partially explained by a shift in asset preferences away from the dollar. Central bankers in East Asia are talking openly about a move in this direction; some Asian traders go so far as to predict that the Chinese yuan will be the world's dominant reserve currency by the mid-twenty-first century.

Finally, the skeptics tell us not to worry because governments around the world would never allow a crisis to happen. They would intervene massively to support the dollar by buying dollars. Well, they might try. But foreign governments might lose their nerve before investing vast sums of their taxpayers' money into declining dollar-denominated assets. And once the mood of global investors changes decisively, there is really not much that governments can do even if they had nerves of steel. The magnitude of tradable assets around the world (global stock markets alone are now capitalized at over $30 trillion) would overwhelm the efforts of even the most dedicated band of central bankers or treasurers. King Canute had better odds of turning back the tide with the wave of his hand.

The skeptics are right about one thing: most governments have no great desire to correct the current imbalance of global trade and finance. Foreign leaders are as eager to stimulate their economies with a bustling export sector as U.S. political leaders are to keep running budget deficits at low interest rates. It's an ugly but politically convenient arrangement.

Yet this does pose another troubling question. Let's assume, as nearly all economists do, that some sort of readjustment is inevitable. As Warren Buffett puts it: "Our national credit card allows us to charge truly breathtaking amounts. But that card's credit line is not limitless." Let's also suppose the readjustment begins for reasons that are either good (major fiscal reform) or bad (a gathering loss of investor confidence). What happens, at this juncture, if some major governments try to prevent the readjustment? For the United States to export more and import less, it follows by arithmetic that the rest of the world must do the reverse. But what if the rest of the world refuses? In a deflationary era of slack demand, some world leaders may feel compelled to maintain their trade surpluses by whatever means available—buying dollars, cutting interest rates, subsidizing exports, or resorting to outright protectionism and capital controls. Such policies may for a time succeed in delaying the readjustment, but only at the cost of throwing the global economy further out of kilter and worsening Robert Rubin's "day of serious reckoning" when it arrives.

The question is not just hypothetical. With the substantial fall in the exchange value of the dollar since the beginning of 2002, global investors may be telling markets that a partial readjustment of the U.S. current-account deficit is overdue. Yet while this dollar fall has mostly been accepted by some countries (members of the Eurozone and Canada, for example), it has mostly been rejected by others (most notably Japan, Taiwan, South Korea—and China, whose currency is pegged to the dollar). The resulting regional asymmetry means that those who follow the "euro" path get hammered, while those who follow the "Asian" path get off easy by resisting the readjustment. In time, without better global cooperation, those following the euro path may throw in the towel and resort to a variety of surplus-preservation measures, for example, subtle import restrictions ("de facto" protectionism).

Although no one can predict how the current imbalance in

the global economy will play out, trade economists marvel at just how many ways this lopsided flywheel can spin off the axle. In the long term, for the world to readjust to a balanced growth path, they all agree that America must export more and save more, and that the rest of the world must import more and consume more. This will require major shifts of labor and capital within all these economies. Yet if moving there too fast (a dollar plunge) is full of peril, so is moving there too slowly (keeping adjustment on hold). And so too, for that matter, would be a scenario in which different regions work at cross-purposes. All of these risks will have to be borne, moreover, during an era in which a major act of terrorism or war can send shock waves through global financial markets at any moment.

The United States will try, of course, to exercise its global leadership and get every major region to cooperate. But leadership requires trust, which may be difficult enough for a superpower whose conduct is so often resented around the world—and even more so for a debtor nation that keeps urging everyone else to save on its behalf. Foreign residents currently own or are owed nearly $10 trillion in U.S. assets. About $1.5 trillion of that consists of U.S. federal debt, which now accounts for 37 percent of *all* publicly held federal debt (thus, we can no longer say we "owe it to ourselves"). And over $800 billion of these U.S. Treasury securities consist of official dollar holdings that sit in government accounts around the world, from Tokyo and Beijing to Berlin and Mexico City. During 2003 official dollar holdings grew by over $10 billion per month.

What happens to the dollar and the global economy will depend as much on what foreign political leaders do with these accounts as on any policy we can pursue alone. If that fact pains us, we should have given it more thought when we first embarked, several decades ago, on a long-term path of falling national savings and rising federal deficits. Given that path, the birth of a large current-account "twin" was practically inevitable. Twenty-five years ago, our nation was still the largest net lender on earth. Twenty years ago, our global assets still exceeded our liabilities. Today, as our net investment position sinks below negative $3 trillion, it's time we grab the wheel and check our seat belts. We may hope that the rest of the world will go on lending us unlimited funds forever. That, however, cannot be.

Third Global Challenge— the First World Becomes the Gray World

"Where are you, Lafayette?" lampooned several American editorials in the wake of France's refusal to join the U.S. campaign to depose Saddam Hussein. However barbed the headline, the message bore the expectation that, down deep, we developed countries of the "first world" (often defined as Europe, the English-speaking nations, and Japan) are somehow all in this together. It's a natural assumption. Throughout much of its history, the United States has worked alongside most of these now-prospering countries to defend democracy against tyrants, to preserve the peace, to explore the universe, to conquer nature with new technologies, and to help (in our own clumsy fashion) bring a better life to less fortunate societies. The United States was created out of immigrants from these countries and still shares many of their deepest values—such as democracy, individualism, progress, and due process.

To this very day, America continues to rely on the assistance of the developed countries—not least in meeting both of the global challenges we've just looked at: the war on terror and the financing of our fiscal deficits. Along with donating large sums to improve the education, infrastructure, and security of terror-prone societies, most of the first world has joined America's efforts to contain or defeat rogue regimes in the Balkans, the Middle East, and Asia. And it's the first world that has fueled the U.S. economy over the past decade by financing most of the $3 trillion in current-account deficits that the United States has run since 1990. From time to time Americans may engage in unilateralist bravado about how we'd just as soon "go it alone" in the world. But can we really imagine bearing the full burden and full cost?

Well, perhaps we had better start. The hard truth is, America in the future will not be able to rely materially on the other members of the first world as it has in the past. The reason is not pique or unwillingness. It has nothing to do with tiffs over the color of George W. Bush's cowboy boots or the shape of Dominique de Villepin's tie. The reason is sheer incapacity—caused by the dramatic aging and (ultimately) the accelerating population decline projected to occur in nearly all of these societies over the next several decades. This is the third global challenge facing America's long-term fiscal strategy. It will burden us by increasing the cost of the first two challenges and by forcing us to assume global leadership on problems we once relegated to others.

The primary cause of this demographic revolution is falling fertility. Since the 1960s birth rates have declined steadily throughout the developed world (indeed, in most of the developing world as well). But whereas in America fertility has stabilized at just under 2.1 births per woman (which, as we have seen, roughly assures a stationary population), it has continued to fall much further in the other countries—all the way to 1.5 in western Europe overall, to 1.4 in Japan, and to 1.2 in certain southern European nations like Spain and Italy. In most of these countries, people live at least as long as in America and immigration is much lower.

The result: very rapid aging. Between now and 2040 in America, the median age is projected to rise from thirty-five to thirty-nine, already an unprecedented climb. But compare that to what will happen abroad—assuming that fertility in every country stays where it is (and doesn't sink further). In France, the median age will rise from thirty-eight to forty-six. In Japan, thanks to very high longevity and low immigration, it will rise to fifty-four. And in Italy it will rise all the way to fifty-five. By the year 2040 there will be more Italians in their eighties than in their twenties. "While the 20th century was the century of population growth," comments Austrian demographer Wolfgang Lutz, "we can already say from a demographic perspective that the 21st century will go down in the history books as the century of aging."

Superimpose these dramatic demographics on extravagant pay-as-you-go retirement systems, and you have the fiscal equivalent of a perfect storm. Monthly public pension benefit levels in most of these countries are considerably higher (relative to worker wages) than in the United States, and their retirement ages have been dropping even faster. Quitting work in your late fifties, often on special disability or unemployment arrangements, is very common. In France, only 39 percent of men aged fifty-five to sixty-four are today still employed—down from 65 percent as recently as 1980. These super-aging societies will also consume more health care (though here is one area where U.S. cost projections remain the world's scariest). The long-term projections are more than sobering. Over the next forty years, according to the Center for Strategic and International Studies, total public benefit spending on the elderly in Japan, France, Germany, and Italy will (on average) climb from 15 to 28 percent of GDP. That latter figure is more than the *total* revenues collected at *all* levels of government in the United States today.

How will these countries come anywhere near paying for these costs? They can try raising taxes, but many of them already have tax burdens of over 45 percent of GDP—and payroll tax rates of over 35 percent of wages. At these lofty rates, many mainstream economists warn that the "supply side" argument may indeed have merit—and that further tax hikes may slow the economy more than they will raise new revenue.

Political leaders can propose trimming benefits, but here they will encounter enormous resistance because the elderly in these countries are so dependent on public benefits, which in turn are vigorously defended by powerful trade unions. In continental Europe, employers do little on behalf of workers. According to Merrill Lynch, only 7 percent of workers are covered by corporate pensions and only 1 percent by 401(k)-type savings plans. Household savings rates are higher in Europe than in the United States, but the savings are heavily skewed by income. Most median-earning households have nothing to count on except the promise of a government check. Thus, whether in Paris, Berlin, or Rome, the political leader who suggests even minor benefit reductions is typically greeted by general strikes and mass demonstrations.

In the end, these governments will patch together some fiscal expedient to tide them over. But of one thing I am quite sure: they will be subjected to viselike pressure to slash other spending and run larger budget deficits. The cuts will probably include defense, security, and international aid; leaders will grow even more reluctant than they already are to commit public resources to U.S.-led military actions or nation-building. Meanwhile, private-sector savings rates are almost sure to fall as the number of retired households rise and the number of working-age households decline. Combine larger budget deficits with declining private savings and we will soon see a cessation, perhaps even a reversal, of the large current-account surpluses that these countries have historically generated over the postwar era.

Haruhiko Kuroda, special adviser to Japanese Prime Minister Junichiro Koizumi and former vice finance minister for international affairs, is a world-class financial expert. My recent conversation with him on this issue was most illuminating. "Mr. Kuroda," I asked, "is the aging society and your low birth rates still a big problem in Japan's future?" "Ah so, Mr. Peterson," he replied. "Mr. Kuroda, with your longevity at the world's highest levels and with your low birth rates leading to a drop of 25 percent in the number of workers under the age of thirty in the next decade, you are going to face unprecedented deficits in the future, is that correct?" "Ah so, Mr. Peterson." "Mr. Kuroda, how do you plan to finance those deficits?" "Mr. Peterson, as you know, we have a big savings rate and a big capital-account surplus. For some period we can use those resources." "Mr. Kuroda, you are now financing about a quarter of America's current-account deficit. Can you really spend the same money twice?" "Ah so, Mr. Peterson. Very difficult problem."

Very difficult, indeed. If nothing else forces a rebalancing of the global economy, demography will be the clincher. Like the inching descent of a trillion-ton glacier, its impact is slow but inexorable.

Longer term, low fertility will mean not just a vicious fiscal squeeze but also an accelerating population decline. This too will have profound global consequences. Outside the United States, the population of the developed world is now peaking. By the early 2010s, assuming (again) no change in fertility, it will be declining at about one million per year; by the late 2020s, at about three million per year; by the 2040s, at over five million per year. In Japan and southern Europe, where each generation of parents is giving birth to a generation of children barely half as large, the descent will be exceptionally rapid. By the year 2100 Italy is on track to lose two-thirds of its current population. Japan's Ministry of the Interior has drafted several major reports on the issue, one of which includes a (somewhat sardonic) calculation of the date at which there would be only one Japanese citizen left alive. Russia too is slipping into a population decline, prompting President Vladimir Putin to warn the Duma recently that the "serious crisis threatening Russia's survival" is not the economy, not Chechnya, but "babies."

The United Nations periodically publishes a list of the twelve most populous nations. Back in 1950 this list included six nations from the "first world" (United States, Japan, Germany, Britain, Italy, and France) and one from the "second world" (Russia). By 2000 only four of these nations remained on the list. In the UN projection for 2050, only one "first world" country remains—the United States, still in third place. Demography is destiny, says the old adage. As we look toward the future, we need to think about what this list implies about America's first-world partners and what we can count on from their economies, financial markets, infrastructures, and defense capabilities.

Several years ago, I wrote a book on global aging (*Gray Dawn*) and was surprised to discover how little attention had been given to the global consequences of this impending demographic decline. Economists typically assume young populations and growing economies. Few have given much thought to economies whose workforces are shrinking from one decade to the next. If workforces shrink faster than productivity rises, many of these economies may actually experience shrinking markets and shrinking real GDP from one decade to the next.

The issues aren't just economic. Can such economies remain innovative and competitive? Sociologists typically look at immigrant communities as sideshows. Yet perhaps the hottest debate among Europeans right now is over the projected rapid growth of its 25 million Muslims—driven both by immigration and by a fertility rate that is three times higher than the European average. (Muslims make up just under 10 percent of the population of France, but an estimated 20 to 30 percent of all French under age twenty-five.) The cultural implications of demographic aging and decline also remain unexplored. How might it alter the social mood? Will it dull the passion for individual risk-taking and collective progress that we have for so long associated with the first world?

Diverging demographic trends often lead, with a lag, to dramatic changes in the balance of power between societies. As Europe and Japan grow less important as sources of global savings, some observers speculate that China may soon become the world's premier capital exporter. The jury is still out: although its GDP is growing very rapidly, China has an imposing domestic investment agenda and will remain a relatively low-income society at least until the middle of the century—at which time it too will be aging rapidly. Yet just to ask the question is to marvel at the speed with which national reputations and resources can rise and fall.

According to political scientist Samuel Huntington, "The juxtaposition of a rapidly growing people of one culture and a slowly growing or stagnant people of another culture generates pressure for economic and/or political adjustments in both societies." Over the next few decades Americans will be asking just how these "adjustments" may reshape the geopolitical contours of tomorrow's global order.

America, the Shoestring Superpower

When President Bush announced that America "has no ambitions of empire" in his 2004 State of the Union address, he was no doubt echoing the feelings of most of his fellow citizens. Americans have traditionally been hostile to "empire." And yet there's an irony here. No other president in living memory has shifted his strategic vision so much in an imperial direction since entering the White House. George Bush began his term tacking toward isolationism and assailing "nation-building" and "open-ended intervention" abroad. He will end his term having launched two full-scale invasions, initiated new security and assistance operations in dozens of nations, and conceived a strategic doctrine of preemption that gives unprecedented breadth to America's global responsibilities.

We still don't like the word "empire," and that probably reflects an honest preference for republican ideals. But maybe our aversion also reflects something else—an effort to hide from ourselves the large and rising cost of America's enlarged role in the world.

More to the point, maybe it says something about our political leaders, who are perfectly content to let us imagine that our vaunted superpower status comes with few long-term costs or responsibilities. They will have us believe we can wage a "war" without a war budget. They will allow us to hope against all evidence that great debtors can be great leaders. (According to Harvard economist Benjamin Friedman, "World power and influence have historically accrued to creditor countries.") Most critically, they say nothing to prepare us for the emerging demographic reality of the twenty-first century, which is this: no one else can substitute for America's global role.

The perspective of America's British friends is worth hearing. Michael Ignatieff, journalist for the BBC, characterizes the U.S. rush to set up a carnival-tent democracy in Iraq as "Empire Lite." Niall Ferguson, a British-American historian who has examined in some detail America's global aspirations in light of the British imperial experience, calls it "a foreign policy based on the Wal-Mart motto: Always low prices." Ferguson explains that it doesn't matter what you call your policy—you don't have to use the E word ("empire")—but if the object is to transform another society or stabilize an entire region of the world, you'd better give your policy the time and resources it deserves. Otherwise you could just end up making matters worse.

Chapter 5

•

HOW THE DEMOCRATS GOT US INTO THIS MESS (WITH REPUBLICAN HELP)

It is a fact that in February of 1972 Senator Wilbur Mills, powerful Democratic chairman of the House Ways and Means Committee, abruptly announced he would support a 20 percent across-the-board hike in Social Security benefits. No one can be certain why he did it. Some say it had to do with a midlife crisis involving women and booze. More likely he wanted to be elected as that year's Democratic presidential nominee over Senators George McGovern and Frank Church, who had already urged a 20 percent benefit hike. Whatever the explanation, the announcement was in keeping with the prevailing mood of America—an expectation of endless "go-go" affluence and a growing urge to flush redundant savings out of the "establishment" (as government was then called) and allow everyone to live a bit more "for today."

Whatever the reason, the support of this famous fiscal conservative guaranteed that the benefit hike would be overwhelmingly approved (with plenty of Republicans joining in) by a Democratic Congress later that year. It made no difference that Congress had *already* jacked up new Social Security benefits 25 percent faster than wages since 1967. Or that Congress was preparing to undertake other major benefit expansions that same year—including the enactment of Medicaid, Medicare for the disabled, a liberalized "earnings test," and automatic annual 100 percent cost-of-living adjustments (COLAs) for all Social Security benefits henceforth. President Richard Nixon saw that nothing could stop what was coming. In one of his signature outflanking maneuvers, he suddenly declared his own support for the benefit hike while saying not a word about its cost. I was serving in the White House when Nixon signed the bill. Afterward, I recall chief of staff Bob Haldeman asking everyone what they thought of inserting the American flag (at that time, a "Nixon" symbol) into the envelopes holding the bigger new benefit checks. The flags were inserted and the checks were mailed just days before the fall elections—much to the Democrats' consternation.

That year would prove to be the climax of a long era of legislated expansions in federal benefits. (Indeed, another thirty-one years would pass before America witnessed another such expansion—the 2003 prescription drug addition to Medicare.) If you had asked the Democrats in Congress what they were doing by voting yes in 1972, many would have told you they were trying to complete the "Great Society" initiated by President Lyndon Johnson. And if you had asked Johnson what he was doing, he would have said he was completing the "New Deal" vision of President Franklin Roosevelt, the leader whom Johnson (along with many of his peers) had personally worshipped in early adulthood.

Any honest account of how America has fallen into today's deficit hole—our catastrophic mismatch between expectation and reality—must acknowledge that both parties have helped take us there. Early on, from the New Deal through the mid-1970s, it was mainly the Democrats who set the fiscal agenda and took us down the road to unsustainable promises. Their strategy: persuade voters there is no limit to how much they can take from government. Over the last twenty-odd years, it's been the Republicans who have taken us yet further. Their strategy: persuade voters there is no limit to how little they can give to government.

In this chapter, we begin with the Democrats.

The New Deal and the Entitlements Legacy

Franklin Roosevelt entered the White House at a time of unparalleled economic deprivation and insecurity. The Great Depression struck a society largely without economic cushions, public or private. From 1932 to 1935 a quarter of the workforce was unemployed. From peak to trough, the Dow Jones Industrial Average fell by 89 percent. Tens of thousands of businesses were driven into bankruptcy, hundreds of thousands of home mortgages were foreclosed, and the financial crash shattered the life savings of even the most prudent families. Bread lines, vagrant armies, hungry migrants, helpless mothers, soapbox Communists—all these gritty images defined America in those years.

Roosevelt conceived the New Deal as a way to mobilize the nation and get Americans to believe once again in their collective future. And despite its many bureaucratic fiascos, the New Deal achieved its central purpose by the end of the 1930s. Banks were saved, industry was restarted, farms were reclaimed, youth were put to work, and giant public works were built.

As the legislative cornerstone of the New Deal, Roosevelt's brain trust designed the Social Security Act, which Congress approved in 1935. The eleven titles of this act authorized the federal government (often with the partnership of the states) to disburse social welfare assistance to a wide variety of needy persons—including unemployed workers, fatherless and disabled children, and destitute old people. The act relieved the suffering of millions in short order because it sent immediate, targeted relief to Americans who had nowhere else to turn. The act also defined the policy agenda of the modern Democratic Party and has given structure and form to much of the federal government's activity ever since.

Yet this very triumph contained within itself at least two vulnerabilities that would, decades later, grow into major forces behind uncontrollable benefit growth and fiscal imbalance.

First is the notion that government can and should "insure" citizens against life's risks—which quickly raises such questions as: Every citizen? Any risk? No matter how small? No matter how foreseeable? No matter how avoidable? Today, it has spawned a gigantic federal benefit system that is 50 percent larger, as a share of today's (vastly larger) GDP, than the *entire federal government* was at the height of the New Deal. Citizens at every age can and do get a piece of the action. It is a system that pays off veterans "disabled" by smoking at age thirty; pays off the owners of agribusiness and energy corporations turning large profits at age fifty; pays off healthy workers choosing to retire at age sixty-two, pays off the routine medical bills of affluent Americans at age sixty-five, and preserves the ample estates of seniors by reimbursing the cost of their nursing home care at age eighty. When Roosevelt cautioned in 1935 that government could "never insure 100 percent of the population against 100 percent of the hazards and vicissitudes of life," America's image of a beneficiary was Ma and Pa Joad facing catastrophic hardship. Today, our image is, literally, every American facing mostly foreseeable life events.

Second is the notion that government can pay for these benefits through "trust funds" that would not actually "save" the money from "contributors" (deceptive advertising practiced then and now by the Social Security Administration), but rather through promises to tax the next generation for today's benefits. The adoption of this Ponzi-like financing method did not happen overnight. Contributory FICA-funded retirement actually remained a rather tiny part of federal benefit spending until the mid-1950s, and "pay-as-you-go" accounting was not officially adopted for both Medicare and Social Security (as the contributory program is now called) until the early 1970s. Only in recent years has the total size of America's implicit lien on future generations reached gargantuan dimensions.

Yet even during his lifetime, there is evidence that Roosevelt knew just what he was doing. When asked about the inability of his trust funds to effect genuine savings, he once answered, "Those taxes were never part of economics. They are politics all the way through. We put those payroll taxes there so as to give the contributors a legal, moral, and political right to collect their pensions . . . With those taxes there, no damn politician can ever scrap my social security program." Not only will it be much harder to cut these benefits, he might have added, but it will be much easier to expand them, since the extra cost of a *new* benefit won't have to be faced until the *next* generation comes along.

How large, exactly, is the sum total of federal benefit spending today? In fiscal year 2003, this spending amounted to $1.349 trillion, or fully 12.5 percent of GDP. Next to this benefit Amazon, the defense budget (at $0.376 trillion) looks like a mere rivulet. And even this figure does not include the cost of program administration, nor the cost of benefits (like the earned income tax credit) distributed through the tax code, nor additional spending on benefits (like Medicaid) by state and local authorities.

Roughly half of all U.S. households include at least one person who receives a federal benefit; and virtually every American can expect to receive significant benefit income over the course of his or her life. By race or region or even household income, the average annual benefits received per household shows remarkably little variation. By age, however, it shows a vast gap. As we have seen, the average elder receives seven times as much in benefits as the average child (and this includes all child-related outlays, even nonbenefits like education). Adults under age sixty-five receive even less than children.

This gap in benefits by age is what gives rise to the time lag between benefit promises and benefit payouts. And it's this lag that in turn has created the enormous benefit liabilities that threaten to oppress the next generation of young workers or, alternatively, to immiserate boomers in their old age if they are suddenly repudiated. These liabilities, if incurred by a financial corporation, would scream out from the balance sheet. But in the federal government they remain hidden because traditional cash-in, cash-out accounting does not acknowledge them. As Treasury Undersecretary Peter Fisher aptly puts it, "Think of the federal government as a gigantic insurance company—with a sideline business in national defense and homeland security." With accounting appropriate to insurance, he warns, the federal fiscal outlook looks dire indeed.

That's the fiscal legacy of America's entitlement expansions. The political legacy is a network of powerful lobbies, mostly headquartered in Washington, that are nearly as extensive as the benefits they defend. First and foremost is the retirement lobby, headed by the massive AARP (with over 35 million members) but including many others, such as the National Association of Retired Federal Employees, the Retired Officers Association, and the National Retired Teachers Association. Then there is the health care lobby, including the American Medical Association and the American Hospital Association. And the veterans' lobby (the American Legion and Amvets), the pork and cotton lobbies, the medical equipment and nursing home lobbies, the ethanol and peanut lobbies, and so on. Finally, to furnish this network with an overall policy vision, there are the Democrat-affiliated think tanks like the Century Fund, the Economic Policy Institute, the National Academy of Social Insurance—and grassroots activist groups like Families USA and the National Committee to Preserve Social Security and Medicare.

Along with the programs and the lobbies, many legislators have observed as well the emergence of what budget scholar James Payne calls "a culture of spending." In visits, letters, e-mails, telegrams, and from witnesses before committee hearings, the typical congressman hears annually from thousands of people, nearly all of whom want some special benefit for some special reason. They rarely hear from young taxpayers, and they never hear from posterity. Like all the rest of us, congressmen like to be liked—and they care most about the opinions of those they see or hear from regularly.

I recall back in the mid-1980s visiting the office of Congressman Kent Hance to chat with him about trimming the annual 100 percent cost-of-living adjustment (COLA) for Social Security and federal civil service pensions. I told him I knew of no private-sector pension plans, large or small, that offer them. I told him they add significantly to federal spending each year—and no doubt add more than Congress would otherwise choose, especially when federal deficits are large and growing. (They still do. In 2003 at least $150 billion, or 30 percent of Social Security's total benefit outlays that year, consisted of accumulated COLA hikes to current beneficiaries.)

Congressman Hance agreed with me and said my arguments all made sense. But then, while explaining what I was up against, he turned to his office assistant and asked her to bring in all the letters opposing any change in the COLA. "All of them?" the assistant gasped. She came staggering back into the room with a huge stack of paper. Hance then said with a smile, "OK, now get the letters from people who favor COLA reform." "But Congressman," said the assistant, looking perplexed, "you know we never get letters like that!" Indeed, congressmen don't. And because they don't, future generations remain unrepresented in politics except to the extent that others of us speak up on their behalf.

The Great Society Heyday of Benefit Expansion

The modern era of benefit expansion got under way in the early 1950s. Finally free from their preoccupation with the Depression and total war, Congress was at last able to carry out Roosevelt's intention to make payroll-financed "Social Security" a cornerstone of postwar middle-class life. In 1950, 1952, and 1954 (all election years—this timing soon became a ritual), Congress voted to more than double the benefit level and get rid of the remaining tie between each worker's benefit and the number of years he or she had been paying into the system. In just six years, 1949 to 1955, the number of families receiving Social Security tripled and the total cost grew sevenfold. The last vote was especially important because, for the first time, a benefit expansion was approved by a Republican Congress and was signed by the Republican president (Eisenhower). Many in the opposition party might complain about the benefits juggernaut, but it was beyond their power to stop.

More benefit expansions soon followed. As the Democratic majorities in Congress grew wider in the late 1950s, prominent intellectuals began pointing out how our "affluent society" lacked an adequate public-sector counterweight. According to Robert Myers, chief actuary for Social Security during the 1960s, there was at that time a coterie of Democratic policy experts and legislators who believed "with almost a religious zeal" in benefit expansion: "The ink is scarcely dry on a newly enacted amendment before plans are being developed for the next legislative effort." In 1958 it was the enactment of disability insurance and an earlier retirement (at age sixty-two) for women. In 1961 it was earlier retirement for men. Thereafter, legislative flames began burning for a whole new program of doctor and hospital benefits on behalf of retirees who were beginning to go by the name of "senior citizens." And those flames were about to grow into a firestorm.

Just two months after the Democrats crushed the Republicans in the 1964 election, newly inaugurated President Lyndon Johnson called for the creation of a "Great Society." In the passionate years that followed, vast new initiatives—some stillborn and others ultimately enacted—rose up in spectacular variety: model cities, Volunteers in Service to America (VISTA), Community Action, the Comprehensive Employment and Training Act (CETA), the Older Americans Act, the negative income tax, the Department of Housing and Urban Development (HUD), food stamps, and family assistance. The benefit expansion was moving into a higher gear.

It was the founding of Medicare, however, that towered above all of these other efforts in terms of its ultimate impact on federal spending. In order to get the program approved and accepted, Democrats had to assuage the doctor and hospital lobbies by giving them what they wanted—fee-for-service billing and little effective cost regulation. In practical terms, this became a sort of cost-plus system: the bigger the cost, the bigger the plus. Although Congress routinely underestimates the future cost of new benefits, here the forecasting error was in a class of its own. When President Johnson signed the Medicare act in 1965, he reassured voters by saying that "an extra $500 million" (that's right, *million*) of new spending would pose "no problem." Today, thirty-nine years later, Medicare spends $294 billion per year—that is, *more than five hundred times* that original estimate.

After Medicare was enacted, reports Myers, a mood of "What's next?" arose among Democrats generally and the Great Society expansionists in particular. Their answer soon became clear: higher Social Security benefit levels. Congress agreed by enacting four steep benefit hikes between 1967 and 1972. The last year, which also featured COLAs, Medicaid, and talk of family "demogrants," marked the high tide of benefit expansion—and, not coincidentally, the last year of the great sixties economic boom. In 1974 the consolidation of several poverty and disability programs into Supplemental Security Income (SSI) marked the last major initiative. The expansion was exhausted, at least for the time being. Yet the resulting growth in total federal benefit spending during its final decade was impressive indeed. From 1966 to 1976 benefits more than doubled (4.9 to 10.4 percent) as a share of GDP and nearly doubled (27 to 49 percent) as a share of federal spending. The Vietnam "peace dividend" disappeared without a trace.

Explaining this era of expansion is no simple task. One essential precondition was the swelling mood of economic optimism that first arose during the "affluent society" of the 1950s, gathered steam during LBJ's "guns and butter" years, and reached an apogee during Nixon's first term. Prominent academics celebrated, in all seriousness, the arrival of pleasure-palace America. According to sociologist David Riesman, "the problem of production had been solved" and we were "moving into the frontiers of consumption." Economist Stuart Chase advised us to "cash in on the triumph of our thrift." William Baumol wrote that "in our economy, by and large, the future can be left to take care of itself."

High "baby boom" birth rates, meanwhile, were now assumed to be an enduring fact of American life. Combine economic and demographic abundance with the prevailing Keynesian view that economic savings was an overrated virtue (stimulating consumption was deemed to be a bigger challenge) and the expansionists found many willing listeners. Get the government to pass out more benefits, even at the expense of giant liabilities, and everyone will be better off. Administrators at Social Security and Medicare began making "dynamic" fiscal projections which reflected this optimism and enabled congressional leaders (like Wilbur Mills) to abandon their customary prudence about future tax revenue.

The buoyant mood of these times is summed up in a now classic *Newsweek* column by economist Paul Samuelson, who cheerfully predicted in 1967 that Social Security could pay generation after generation of retirees huge returns above and beyond their contributions:

> The beauty about social insurance is that it is actuarially unsound. Everyone who reaches retirement age is given benefit privileges that far exceed anything he has paid in . . . How is this possible? It stems from the fact that the national product is growing at compound interest and can be expected to do so as far ahead as the eye cannot see. Always there are more youths than old folks in a growing population. More important, with real incomes growing at some 3 percent per year, the taxable base upon which benefits rest in any period are [*sic*] much greater than the taxes paid historically by the generation now retired . . . A growing nation is the greatest Ponzi game ever contrived. And that is a fact, not a paradox.

Deeper cultural forces were also at work. After the civil rights "freedom riders" and best-sellers like Michael Harrington's *The Other America* gained national attention in 1962, younger generations began speaking up about the hidden poverty and injustice that persisted beneath America's growing affluence. These groups needed more—poor Americans, nonwhite Americans, elder Americans—and one way they could get more was through federal "income transfers," soon to be called "entitlements" (meaning you could sue the government if you were eligible yet denied). By the end of the decade passionate benefits lobbies like the Gray Panthers and the National Welfare Rights Organization were organizing sit-down strikes on Capitol Hill.

Older generations listened, and their national leaders, Democrats especially, responded with an innocent trust in the Promethean powers of government to solve any problem. Could eradicating social injustice be any more difficult than inventing miracle vaccines or putting a man on the moon? This was a job for superpower America—for a nation, announced John Kennedy, prepared to "pay any price, bear any burden, meet any hardship." A few years later, the very appearance of fiscal caution (along with the now reviled "puritan ethic") was regarded with a sort of contempt. When Secretary of Health, Education, and Welfare (HEW) Wilbur Cohen came to President Johnson in 1967 to recommend a Social Security benefit hike of 10 percent, Johnson reportedly glared at him and said, "Come on, Wilbur, you can do better than that." And so Wilbur did (he came back with 13 percent).

Era of Fiscal Paralysis: Entitlements on Autopilot

America ultimately awoke from its benefit binge with a horrendous fiscal hangover. During the Ford and Carter presidencies, the economic boom of the sixties and early seventies ended with gas lines, stagflation, and severe back-to-back recessions. In just a few short years nearly every premise that had justified the era of expansion lay in wreckage. The first premise had been buoyant real-wage growth. That came to an end. In fact, real-wage growth turned negative during much of the decade for the first time anyone could remember. The second premise had been low unemployment and low inflation. That was no more. High inflation accompanied by high unemployment spelled the end of Keynesian demand management and focused new attention on the importance of capital formation. The third premise had been high birth rates. But big families—indeed, the very idea of any family at all—was going out of fashion among young adults. Unprecedented declines in the birth rate meant that the "baby boom" was over and a new "baby bust" had started.

And then there was that thing called the "credibility gap." Watergate marked the beginning of a severe erosion of the public's confidence in government. It wasn't just that leaders sometimes misbehaved. More generally, as the 1970s wore on, voters had second thoughts about the crime, social disorder, and rapid cultural change that seemed to accompany all the ambitious civic energy of the prior decade. More Americans turned inward to answer life's problems. You can't solve social problems "just by throwing money at them" became a common refrain.

Every year in Congress, worried budgeteers watched benefit outlays leap upward—and projections for future outlays fly upward even faster. Social Security outlays rose with a special vengeance due to a "double indexing" flaw in the new COLA that caused new benefits, in the presence of high inflation, to ratchet upward much faster than wages. (President Nixon later told me that signing this faulty COLA legislation in 1972 was the worst fiscal policy decision of his presidency.) Spurred into action by the imminent threat of bankruptcy, Congress went to work on two Social Security rescue packages in a row. The first, enacted in 1977, fixed the flaw in benefit-indexing. The second, enacted in 1983, restored the program's long-term fiscal balance—though only on paper and only temporarily.

During the 1970s the expansionists' volcano turned from still-molten to stone-cold. The decade began with dazzling predictions about how government would soon create a future of unimaginable affluence for younger generations (some small share of which they could easily share with older generations). The decade closed with gloomy talk of "diminished expectations" and "limits to growth"—and with Joe Califano, President Carter's secretary of HEW, offering long-term fiscal projections that stunned his audiences. "When the senior boom hits in 2025," he announced, the share of the federal budget consumed by seniors "will hit about 65 percent."

Califano was perhaps the first public figure to understand that in the future, federal benefits would continue to grow faster than the economy even if Congress didn't raise a finger. Benefit awards in most of the large cash programs were by now indexed to wages; and per capita benefits from health care programs typically rose much faster than wages. That was enough. The growing demographic tilt from young to old would do the rest. And as it happens, Congress really didn't lift many fingers for the next three decades. From 1974 until 2003 Congress neither created nor eliminated a single major benefit program, nor—other than its two Social Security rescue plans (when it really had no choice)—did Congress legislate a single major structural reform in such a program. Federal benefits were subject to forecast and projections, but no longer to hands-on legislative control.

That didn't mean, of course, that no one tried. Democrats attempted and failed to push through two major expansions. In 1988 Democratic majorities in the House and Senate agreed to a "Catastrophic Coverage" addition to Medicare and persuaded President Reagan to sign it into law. But only months later senior lobbies were so upset that affluent seniors themselves would have to bear the cost (through means-tested premiums) that they forced Congress to rescind the plan the next year. In 1993 the Clinton administration sent to Congress a "Health Security Act." Originally, a central purpose of Clinton's project was to control the growth of health care spending both in the private and the public sector. But by the time the final 1,342-page document was shipped to legislators, it had become a colossal, highly intricate, and very expensive effort to restructure U.S. health care in a way that would insure more Americans at a modest out-of-pocket cost. Republicans in Congress not only shot the plan down but used the "Clinton Plan" as an effective war cry to rally voters in 1994. Once again, the threat of higher taxes proved to be a decisive argument.

Meanwhile, Republicans tried several times to enact major benefit cuts. But they weren't any more successful than the Democrats. There was "Schweiker's Folly" in 1981, the abortive attempt by President Reagan's secretary of health and human services to chop Social Security's early retirement benefits with virtually no advance notice. A political firestorm arose, Reagan quickly distanced himself, and Secretary Dick Schweiker resigned a year and a half later. By the end of his first term Reagan made it clear to his staff that, yes, he wanted to eradicate "waste, fraud, and abuse," but that, no, nearly all veterans, pension, and health care benefits (to say nothing of defense) were off limits.

There was Senators Bob Dole and Pete Domenici's vast spending cut package in 1985, which included a politically incendiary one-year Social Security COLA freeze. The package barely squeaked by in the Senate after Republican senator Pete Wilson, hours after an appendectomy, was wheeled onto the Senate floor to cast the tying vote, allowing Vice President George Bush to cast the deciding vote. Shortly afterward, alas, the package was sunk in the House after President Reagan cut a secret deal with Democratic House Speaker Tip O'Neill behind the backs of the Senate Republicans. (Reagan proposed to give up the COLA freeze if O'Neill would go along with a large defense spending request. O'Neill agreed.) Exactly ten years later there was Republican House Speaker Newt Gingrich's ambitious "Contract with America" spending cut package, which included an equally incendiary overall cap on Medicare spending. Gingrich went one-on-one against President Clinton, and he lost. Even in the flush of their stunning 1994 victory at the voting booth, the GOP House leaders could not even keep all of their own members behind the cuts—much less persuade the opposition.

Thirty years of policy paralysis can thus be described as the outcome of an unending legislative impasse. Each time a legislated benefit expansion was proposed, some Democrats defected to the Republican side amid complaints about "higher taxes," and the proposal was defeated. Each time a legislated benefit reduction was proposed, some Republicans defected to the Democratic side amid complaints about "slashing" and "burning" of widows and orphans, and the proposal was defeated.

Yet there was one obvious asymmetry in this paralysis. Doing nothing meant that the total cost of federal benefit programs as a share of the economy, though rising during recessions and falling during business-cycle expansions, always rose a bit more than it fell—keeping the long-term trend sloping upward. In the recession year of 1976, the OMB's measure of federal "benefits to individuals" peaked at 10.4 percent of GDP, which seemed unthinkable at the time. It next peaked in 1983 at 11.5 percent; then in 1995 at 12.0 percent; and most recently in 2003 at 12.5 percent of GDP. Even the so-called pay-go budget rules of the 1990s did little to stop the rise. The dirty little secret of these rules was that they only applied to *new* programs, not growth in *old* programs—because, of course, no "promise" must ever be broken to those of us who are old and influential enough to get an early seat at the table.

Since the late 1980s, moreover, the pace of growth has been restrained substantially by a favorable though entirely temporary demographic development: a small (Depression baby) generation has been retiring and a large (boomer) generation of taxpayers has been hitting its peak income-earning and tax-paying years. But that restraint is deceptive—like the long-retreating surf just before the tidal wave hits. Around 2010 the demographic imbalance will swing the other way and the pace of spending growth will surge for decades yet to come.

Though it should have been possible in concept to gather a group of leaders from government and the private sector and focus on these longer-term challenges, such "commissions" in practice never compelled legislators to make fundamental reforms. The 1983 Greenspan Commission did achieve significant long-term savings, but they proved to be insufficient. What's worse, the Greenspan package (which mainly raised taxes and cut future benefits for boomers and all younger generations) asked for no sizable sacrifice from anyone who would retire for another twenty years.

More often the commissions didn't achieve anything at all. President Bill Clinton appointed two, the Kerrey-Danforth Commission on Entitlement and Tax Reform (on which I served) and the Breaux Commission on the Future of Medicare. Both issued eloquent statements on the magnitude of the cost challenge, both gridlocked hopelessly over policy recommendations, and both were flushed by the president who appointed them. More recently President George W. Bush appointed a bipartisan Commission on Social Security Reform. He has yet to act on any of its findings. Along the way, these commissions were racked by political firestorms ignited for partisan advantage. Only months before Clinton appointed the Breaux Medicare Commission, for example, the Democratic Party ran a demagogic "Mediscare" campaign to vilify any candidate who proposed touching Medicare—an effort that no doubt cast a shadow over any commission member up for reelection.

My experience with the Kerrey-Danforth Commission was eye-opening. After studying the demographic projections and their cost implications in the summer of 1994, we issued an interim report in August that was endorsed unanimously by the commission's twenty Democratic and Republican congressional members and by thirty of its thirty-one total members. (The sole dissenter was the president of the United Mine Workers.) The report concluded that if we did not reform tax and spending policies, the benefit outlays for just five programs—Social Security, Medicare, Medicaid, and federal civilian and military pensions—would exceed total federal revenues by the year 2030. This would leave zero tax revenue for any other purpose—not even for interest payments, nor for national defense, nor for education, nor for child health, nor for the federal payroll.

America's political leadership thanked us for the report,

shook our hands, and walked away. Then something amazing happened: we received roughly 350,000 preformatted "outraged" postcards from seniors *even before we had discussed a single reform*. By the time our discussion of possible reforms began, many of the members visibly lost interest. In the end, the commission expired without agreeing on any proposal to reform a system it had in its own report called "unsustainable."

During my commission tenure I learned how much the tone of benefit advocacy had shifted from activism to mere reaction. Back in the 1960s, benefits crusaders had tried to argue that new benefits were both just and affordable. By the 1990s established lobbies were arguing that existing benefits were unchangeable regardless of their justice or affordability. Back then, Democrats argued (with some good evidence) that retired and elderly beneficiaries were on average much poorer than working Americans. By the 1990s their main argument was that the only way to help the poor among the beneficiaries was by bribing all the affluent to support the program as well. Agreeing with David Stockman that "Congress rewards the strongest claimants, not the strongest claims," their (utterly unaffordable) solution was to make sure to include plenty of strong claimants to protect the strong claims.

The Approaching Age Wave and Medicare's Last Hurrah

Let's set the stage. A new century dawns. The Republican Party, long the home of frustrated benefit cost-controllers, at last ascends to the presidency and takes control of both houses of Congress for the first time in fifty years. The media begin to run feature stories on the boomers' approaching retirement, giving rise to a broad public awareness that America's favorable demographic window is closing—and that the time to prepare fiscally will soon be over. Pushed into war by a horrific act of terrorism, America feels its national sense of purpose grow more sober, more focused on the long term. In the fall of 2003, nearly three years after the Republicans take over, Congress passes the most sweeping legislative change to Medicare in thirty years.

If you had explained this scenario to Washington hands back in 2000, they would have assumed that the stars were at last aligned for a far-reaching cost-control package. They would have been wrong, of course. The shocking surprise of the George W. Bush presidency is not just the absence of any serious effort to confront the entitlement cost challenge but the largest benefit expansion by far since the glory days of Presidents Johnson and Nixon.

Why did it happen? Quite simply because the rising partisanship of both parties conspired to make it happen. For years the Democrats had cultivated the issue of prescription drugs for seniors, and many GOP leaders (especially in the Bush White House) were convinced that the Democratic Party was preparing to launch vicious attacks during the next election over their failure to do anything about it. Given the Democrats' growing success at running "Mediscare" campaigns, the GOP had good reason to be anxious. This time, because they were out of power, the Democratic rhetoric was expected to be especially ferocious. And then, when the GOP unexpectedly came forward with a broad and expensive benefit package, the Democrats played their role perfectly by savaging the Republicans at every turn for their "stinginess" and lack of generosity. Even while bearing gifts, the Republicans were painted by the Democrats as that old Uncle Scrooge again.

As for the Republicans, their leadership had changed—in part due to generational turnover. A generally older club of fiscal conservatives no longer occupied many of the top leadership spots. A new cadre of supply-side tax cutters did, and though few if any of them actively pushed for a major entitlement expansion, their fiscal agenda of permanent and unilateral tax reduction fatally undermined any good argument they could make against it. After all, if they could freely add to federal deficits in 2010 and beyond for something they thought was important, why couldn't the Democrats do the same? In practice, starve-the-beast ended up delivering a three-course meal to the monster.

Some say that the tax cuts trapped the Republicans. Others say that President Bush, like President Nixon with his COLA hike, outfoxed himself while trying to outfox the other party. Either way, the final result was a big step in the wrong direction.

What leaders on both sides should have done was to acknowledge that, yes, there are some seniors in trouble and that a rationally designed Medicare system should at least provide backstop coverage for large out-of-pocket drug costs. But they also should have observed that for most seniors drug costs were not a problem. In 2003 fully three-quarters of the elderly already had prescription drug coverage, about half through employer retiree health plans or through Medicaid and another quarter through Medicare HMOs or private Medigap policies. According to a 2002 government survey, 86.4 percent said getting the prescription drug they needed in the last six months was "not a problem." Another 9.4 percent said "a small problem," and 4.2 percent said "a big problem."

In designing their new benefit, leaders could have kept costs in check by focusing on the "problem" groups—especially, the heavy users of drugs among lower-income households. Since the costs projections for Medicare were already out of control, they also could have coupled the new benefit to a serious overall reform package that restrained total Medicare costs and reined in the unlimited fee-for-any-service outlook of so many physicians and hospitals. Indeed, one issue entirely overlooked in the recent debate is the rampant *overconsumption* of drugs among seniors. An estimated 40 percent of seniors take five or more prescription drugs per week; 12 percent take ten or more. According to a 2003 study published in the *Journal of the American Medical Association*, roughly 200,000 seniors suffer fatal or life-threatening "adverse drug events" every year due to improper drug use or drug interaction.

That's what leaders could have done. What they in fact did was to enact a universal benefit with an absurdly low out-of-pocket deductible ($250 per year) for the express political purpose of maximizing the number of seniors who take advantage of it. To keep the initial cost estimates deceptively low, leaders designed the benefit with a gap or "doughnut hole" in the coverage. The benefit pays for 75 percent of an enrollee's drug costs from $250 to $2,250 per year. But above $2,250, the benefit pays nothing until the enrollee's drug costs exceed $3,600 per year, at which point the government begins to cover 95 percent of the bill. Members of Congress fully expected this gap to be filled by later expansions. Though Republicans included in the bill some language about "demonstration projects" for managed competition, this was widely regarded as a reform fig leaf.

With great fanfare, President George W. Bush signed the Medicare Prescription Drug, Improvement, and Modernization Act in December of 2003. Even after concealing costs, the final act weighed in at $400 billion in projected outlays (net of enrollee premiums) over the next ten years. Amazingly, a full $71 billion of this is projected to go to businesses, mainly large corporations with aging workforces, in return for keeping their own prescription drug plans in operation. Though the provision was criticized as "Rust Belt welfare" by members of both parties, most of these businesses now say they will probably cut back their plans anyway and let their retirees join the Medicare plan. If this happens, outlays will rise still further.

Only weeks after the signing, the OMB raised the CBO's original cost estimate from $400 to $535 billion. (Top administration officials had apparently known for months that its own cost estimates were higher than CBO's, but they twisted the arms of Medicare's actuaries not to divulge the higher numbers until Congress had voted.) Thus did a "conservative" White House force-feed a new entitlement to its own party and to the nation. During its second decade, this new "Medicare Part D" benefit is now expected to add over $2 trillion to the deficit. By the year 2030, incredibly, the federal government will be spending as much on prescription drugs for Medicare enrollees (as a share of GDP) as everything it now spends on nonhealth benefits for needy working-age Americans—including means-tested cash welfare, food stamps, unemployment compensation, child nutrition, foster care, and the refundable portions of the earned income tax credit and child tax credit. When Congress first convened in January of 2003, Medicare loomed as the single largest source of federal unfunded liabilities hanging over the American taxpayer. Congress went to work. By the time it last adjourned in December, Congress had enacted a new benefit that raised these liabilities by another $8 trillion over the next seventy-five years (according to the Medicare trustees)—without reducing the liabilities of any other program.

It would be wrong to suppose that the politicians and lobbyists who pushed hardest for this new act were blind to the huge fiscal cost crunch of the approaching age wave. To the contrary, many of them could see clearly what's ahead—and for that very reason regarded this bill as their last best chance to get any deal at all. AARP president Bill Novelli, while defending to his members the AARP's support of what he called an "imperfect" bill (meaning, we didn't get all we wanted), added some perceptive reflections on what was on his mind. "We also had to grapple with the reality that, as tight as the federal budget is today, it may well be much tighter in coming years—so that $400 billion might not appear on the bargaining table again."

No, it won't appear again. Not anytime soon. Maybe not

for decades. Like a dying bulb that flares brightly just before going out, America's postwar infatuation with benefit expansions may have experienced its last big moment for a long while to come. Over the foreseeable future, America will be grappling with a much harder task: how to cope with the fiscal consequences of what it has already put in place.

Chapter 6

•

HOW THE REPUBLICANS GOT US MUCH DEEPER (WITH DEMOCRATIC HELP)

Nobody in the White House saw it coming. When the long-awaited tax bill came up before Congress in June of 1981, President Reagan's newly appointed advisers figured they would only have to pass out a few odd favors to line up the necessary votes. No one imagined, before all the politicians and lobbyists began bidding, that this tax bill would grow into the biggest tax-reduction free-for-all in history—a giant midsummer Christmas tree adorned with favors of every imaginable shape and size.

Yes, there had to be income tax cuts *and* accelerated depreciation *and* an investment tax credit extension. And there had to be tax-free savings certificates, special write-offs for trucking companies, and bigger pension plan write-offs for the affluent (Keoghs). And there had to be tax benefits to farmers, tax breaks for mass transit systems, and tax exemptions for citizens living overseas. And there had to be major exemptions of estates from federal inheritance taxes and employee stock ownership plans (ESOPs). By the time it was enacted, the Emergency

Recovery Tax Act was hundreds of pages long. Some of the tax favors may have been good policy; others were just bribes. But whatever they were, any distinction was lost in the frenzy to hand them out.

"Once the bidding war started," recalls David Stockman, then the young and idealistic chief of Reagan's Office of Management and Budget, "we became ensnared in its logic. If it was logic, it was that of the alcoholic: One more couldn't hurt, given all that had gone down already." Stockman then goes on to describe how "everyone was accusing everyone else of greed, and in the same breath shouting 'What's in it for me?'" At a White House strategy meeting, minority whip Trent Lott summed up the mood: "Everybody else is getting theirs, it's time we got ours." By the time the getting was over, a trillion dollars of future revenue had been legislated away over and above White House expectations. One liberal Democratic congressman, David Obey, wryly observed that "it would probably be cheaper if we gave everyone in the country three wishes"—though even he could see that plenty of his fellow Democrats were voting for the cuts.

With the stroke of Reagan's pen a few weeks later, a whole new breed of American Republican—the tax cut conservative—made history. At first the GOP vanguard were jittery, even panicky about the vast deficits these massive tax cuts would trigger. Then they gradually learned to enjoy their newfound popularity. All their lives, most of them had delivered stern lectures about why government shouldn't hand out favors. And few voters loved them. Now they had discovered a "conservative" way to hand out tons of government favors. And now it seemed that most voters loved them. It was intoxicating. By Reagan's second term, the conservative makeover even picked up a catchy theme song: "Don't worry, be happy."

The Reagan Revolution and the Cutting of Taxes

Like Franklin Roosevelt, Ronald Reagan won the presidency at a time of perceived national crisis. Inflation was racing out of control, the prime interest rate hit 21 percent, joblessness remained high, and real wages foundered. Having just weathered back-to-back energy shortages and suffering post-Vietnam doubts about their "hollowed-out" military, Americans turned on their TVs each night to see Iranian radicals taunting captured U.S. hostages. Attitudes about family, children, and gender roles seemed to be changing at a dizzying pace. In no year since the Great Depression, according to polls, have Americans expressed such trepidation about their nation's future as they did in 1980.

Like Roosevelt, Reagan went on to lead America in overcoming most of these challenges and fears. On three major fronts, his successes have gained almost prophetic stature, since they flew in the face of the despairing predictions of most experts. He put an end to double-digit inflation by giving unwavering support to Fed chairman Paul Volcker and by facing down the air traffic controllers union. He brought the Cold War to a peaceful and victorious conclusion, in part by showing resolve on defense and foreign policy. And he persuaded the nation to abandon the worst vices of regulation in industries like airlines, banking, and energy. Overall, his optimistic outlook energized America and, by the time he left office in 1989, seemed to reflect a more hopeful public outlook. Even as Roosevelt signaled a decades-long trend toward greater trust in government planning, so Reagan signaled a decades-long trend toward greater trust in individualism and markets. This too will remain part of his legacy.

Yet the Reagan Revolution paralleled the New Deal in another, less positive respect. Hidden within its near-term successes were a number of long-term costs, the most fateful of which was the invention of a tax-chopping strategy by which political leaders could promise more in future benefits than anyone expected (or could even afford) to pay for. To be sure, America needed tax reform in 1981. Many economists, especially my old University of Chicago professors, had been saying for years that very high (70 percent) marginal tax rates on income were wasteful and pointless. Also, high inflation was unfairly pushing middle-class families into ever higher tax brackets (so-called bracket creep). Lopping off these lofty rates and indexing the tax brackets was good policy.

But the rest of the Reagan tax strategy was akin to flooding an entire city to extinguish a single burning house. Over the next twelve years—those of his presidency and of his successor, George Bush, Sr.—it caused our publicly held national debt to expand by 25 percent of GDP, an achievement with no peacetime precedent in U.S. history except for the Depression decade of the 1930s. Longer term, this strategy continues to foster chronic federal deficits, to divert serious attention from either the objectives or the distribution of federal spending, and to lock both parties into a partisan gridlock over fiscal policy.

Today, the young Reagan-era tax cut movement has grown up, and it imposes its mature orthodoxy on Republicans with a D.C.-based organization, discipline, and funding that rivals what the entitlement establishment does for Democrats. There's the Cato Institute and the Heritage Foundation, providing the libertarian worldview and doing all the number-crunching policy work. There's Citizens for a Sound Economy and the National Taxpayers Union, mobilizing thousands of activists nationwide. There's Americans for Tax Reform (ATR), led by Grover Norquist (variously known as "the field marshal" or "Grand Central Station" of the tax cut movement), which coordinates the national leadership. Rewarding the good votes and punishing the bad, ATR is best known for its "Taxpayer Protection Pledge," which "asks all candidates for federal and state office to commit themselves in writing to oppose all tax increases." And then there's Stephen Moore's Club for Growth, whose chosen mission is to use creative media to humiliate if not defeat any heretical "Republican in Name Only" who while in office dares let a tax go up.

One might expect that most Republican tax cut champions would care a lot about how government taxes people. Curiously, most don't, so long as it's less instead of more—in the same way that most Democratic entitlement advocates don't really care about where government benefits go, so long as it's more instead of less.

It would be unfair to say that Republican tax reform is to blame for the growing inequality of household income in America over the past quarter century. Yes, inequality has grown, but clearly for reasons much broader than taxes. Inequality has grown for pretax as well as posttax income and during the Clinton years as well as the Bush and Reagan years. (It has also grown in most of the other developed countries.) Yet even if the GOP tax reformers are not responsible for initiating this trend, it is fair to point out that they have done precious little to redress it or to improve the situation of America's average-earning workers. When all is said and done, the aggregate impact of their tax reforms has been to shift the total tax burden away from income and property taxes, which are more progressive and usually pay for "general-purpose" public programs; and to shift the burden toward payroll taxes, sales taxes, and user fees, which are less progressive and more often dedicated to some special purpose ("get your money back") fund. This can't possibly work to the advantage of ordinary families, either in the near term or in the long term.

The new GOP activists seem averse to getting rid of special tax deductions or exemptions even when these "loopholes" function exactly like a benefit outlay. Consider the tax provision that allows mainly higher-income employees working for large corporations or the public sector to take advantage of gold-plated health insurance plans tax-free while most lower-income workers working elsewhere don't have that option. Or consider the home mortgage deduction, whose dollar worth generally rises (up to the million-dollar cap) with the value of one's primary residence. The end result is the same as if there were no such tax provisions and the U.S. Treasury sent checks to the higher-income workers or the high-end homeowners. Tax activists turn purple when they hear this logic. As Ronald Reagan once put it to his advisers, "That implies government owns all your income and has the right to decide what you can keep. We won't have that kind of thinking around here." In other words, whatever money "you keep" is rightfully yours—no matter why or for what absurd reason you get to keep it. One need not travel much further to the conclusion that all taxation is somehow illegitimate.

In a way, Reagan's tax revolution has turned FDR's New Deal exactly on its head. Instead of promising more benefits and staying mostly mum on taxes, now the strategy is: Let's cut taxes and stay mostly mum on benefits. The new revolutionaries do not say to the average American, You're getting more from government than you're prepared to pay for; you ought to get less. They say instead, Whatever you're getting from government, you're paying too much for it; you deserve to pay less. Today's Republicans often pride themselves on having "reversed" the cultural tide of narcissism and irresponsibility that supposedly favored Democrats during the 1960s and 1970s. But when it comes to government's fiscal bottom line, they merely invented a new way to surf the tide.

The 1980s: From Grand Experiment to Read-My-Lips Orthodoxy

When they tell the story today, supply-side tax cutters like to say that a massive tax reduction was intended to be the centerpiece of the Reagan economic plan from the very moment he came to office. They say that huge deficits were expected in the first several years, but over time the "supply side" incentives triggered by lower tax rates would "grow" the economy in such a volcanic fashion that everything would end up in surplus. And it would have worked, if only faint-of-heart tax hikers and backsliders had kept the faith, "stayed the course," let "Reagan be Reagan," and so on.

All of this is false. According to the original White House plan, in fact, a carefully calibrated tax cut package was supposed to *follow* a large spending cut package—so that the entire budget would reach balance in just two years (by 1984). What went wrong? First, the tax cut turned out to be anything but calibrated. Not only did it get massively overlarded with political freebies, but its hastily designed income tax and depreciation provisions wrongly bet that inflation and "bracket creep" would continue at a brisk pace. When inflation fell faster than expected, revenue dropped out of sight (and investment tax shelters promising government rebates sprang up like mushrooms across the country). As with the notorious "double indexing" of Social Security during the 1970s, this was an error whose unintended consequences no one was in a hurry to fix. The OMB soon projected that by 1986 *annual* revenues would be *$660 billion less* than under the original plan.

The second thing to go wrong: the large spending cuts never happened. When the Reagan team arrived, there were plans to get rid of the Department of Education and the Department of Energy, the Small Business Administration and the farm credit system, peanut subsidies and needless veterans benefits. None of it ever happened. Arguably, the only major program that was cut was CETA (a scandal-ridden urban youth jobs program)—but it was quickly replaced. What really sank the spending cut plans, however, was the team's failure even to attempt serious cuts where most of the big money was: Social Security and Medicare. As early as 1982 it was obvious to the executive budget experts that the combination of huge revenue losses, few serious cuts in domestic social programs, and (as planned) large increases in defense spending could only mean one thing: spectacular deficits.

The Reagan vanguard's first instinct was to hide the bad news. White House insiders began joking about their "rosy scenario." A $47 billion hunk of the OMB's planned savings went by the name of "magic asterisk" (explanation: "savings to be identified later"). Democrats recalled John Anderson's caustic how-to remark about Reaganomics: "You do it with mirrors."

Then, when the truth couldn't be hidden any longer, the GOP had to accept a seemingly endless string of grudging tax hikes. There was a tax hike in 1982, another in 1983 (featuring huge payroll tax hikes), another in 1984, another in 1986, and yet another in 1990 during the term of George Bush, Sr. By 1991 most tax rates were right back where they were at the end of Jimmy Carter's presidency—proving that if spending keeps rising, taxes do ultimately catch up. The main enduring legacy of the tax cut decade was a veritable mountain of publicly held federal debt.

By the middle of the decade Reagan's slow retreat-from-Moscow on taxes proved to have a lasting impact on the politics of the Republican Party. Thwarted by the obvious need to shrink the budget deficit (amid collateral headlines about a record trade deficit and a falling dollar), the tax cut diehards turned inward. If they couldn't change history now, they would change it later. They began to define a new nucleus of GOP purity by "litmus-testing" Republicans according to how easily they "gave in" to tax hikes. Some of the faithful (like Jack Kemp, Art Laffer, or Paul Craig Roberts) truly did believe that deficits would cure themselves. For others (especially the neoconservatives, led by Irving Kristol), it was politics through and through. Deficits didn't really matter. So long as "conservatives" made sure America stood tall in the world, while spending on programs that favored a high-voting "civic" base of seniors and investors and intact affluent families, they would continue to trump the liberals. Keep tax rates low, and let deficits look after themselves.

The supply-siders' fetish about "optimistic psychology" fed this dogmatism, since even expressing a negative thought about tax cuts could in itself undermine the "market expectations" on which everything rested. Disagreement thus became tantamount to disloyalty. When conservatives of manifest intelligence and ability (like OMB head David Stockman or CEA chief Martin Feldstein) resigned from the administration over their disagreements about deficits, the diehards vilified them. I recall Pete Domenici, GOP chairman of the Senate Budget Committee, telling me about his efforts to explain the deficit danger to the president and his advisers. He pleaded with them to scale back the defense increases and to kill the third year of the tax cut. He was told, curtly, to "get back on the team."

When George Bush, Sr., campaigned in 1988 to consolidate conservative support as the logical "caretaker" of the Reagan achievement, the tax cut radicals played hard to get. Bush, Sr., was the 1980 candidate who had accused Reagan of "voodoo economics." He had a well-known reputation as a technocrat, a realist, a constructive compromiser—in short, as a tax cut skeptic. Could he be trusted? Bush, Sr., delivered his famous answer during his August nomination acceptance speech in New Orleans. "The Congress will push me to raise taxes, and I'll say no," he declared. "They'll push me again, and I'll say no," he continued, building momentum. "And they'll push again and I'll say to them"—pause—*"Read my lips: no new taxes!"* The slogan became an instant hit, and that fall candidate Bush could hardly resist leading crowds with this chant nearly everywhere he went.

The diehards were delighted. Sure, they would campaign to help him get elected. With the pledge, they knew they would be winners no matter what Bush did in office. And elected he was. But only a year after taking office, President Bush felt the other half of a trap begin to close behind him. In the spring of

1990 the CBO began reporting rising deficit projections—brought about, in part, by an explosion of red ink from runaway Medicaid spending and an S&L crisis that neither party had done anything to avoid during the 1980s. Hemmed in by a Gramm-Rudman deficit target that threatened to slash spending across the board if he did not reduce the deficit, Bush convened a series of meetings with the leaders of both parties looking for some basis for compromise. As the summer wore on, the economy slipped into recession and the budget projections worsened. Then, on August 2, Saddam Hussein invaded Kuwait with his Iraqi Republican Guard. A distracted president prepared for (what was then predicted to be) a brutal and expensive conflict halfway around the world amid widening uncertainty about the economy.

Bush felt he had no choice. He agreed to raise taxes ("tax revenue increases" was the delicate term floated by chief of staff John Sununu) in order to reach an agreement with Democrats on a legislative package that would reduce the deficit by $500 billion over the next five years. After several false starts, the package was delivered and signed before the end of October.

Fiscally, the deal was a brave act of statesmanship. While managing to gain roughly two-thirds of these savings through spending cuts, Bush brought both parties together at an urgent moment in our nation's history and persuaded them to agree to significant sacrifices. He also managed to forge new budget rules (the Budget Enforcement Act of 1990) that would help control deficits during the rest of the decade. Politically, however, the deal was a disaster. Partisan Democrats attacked their own leaders for having agreed to any cuts in social spending and hikes in the gas tax. Far more viciously, partisan Republicans tore into Bush for recanting on his pledge. Both sides blamed the deal for triggering the recession (though the recession had already started before the deal took shape). Both sides blamed the deal for failing to keep the deficit from rising (though the deficit, now driven by a renewed surge in health care benefit spending, would have grown much faster without it). And both sides said they hated the "elitist" and "secretive" manner in which the deal was reached.

From that moment on, Bush's chances for reelection were doomed. Not even the epic victory of Desert Storm could save him. Vice President Dan Quayle later wrote that when he learned of the deal, he saw the administration's future "go down the drain." According to Peggy Noonan, the White House speechwriter who had originally authored the read-my-lips line, "When Bush rescinded his tax pledge, that day Bush was over." Leading a vanguard of younger compatriots, rising star Newt Gingrich, minority whip in the House, forged his political image to represent everything that George Bush, Sr., was not—vision rather than achievement, assertion rather than consensus. As House leader, Gingrich would later famously ban anyone from using the S-word ("summit") during the budget process.

Tax Cutters Return to Power: Reagan's Third Term?

The tax cut radicals did not really mind Bill Clinton's subsequent victory over Bush, Sr. Their logic was akin to that of the Bolshevik underground during the czarist twilight: it was better, in the end, to punish an apostate and strengthen the orthodoxy than to allow a moderate to dilute (or pollute) their ranks.

Nor were they bothered by the further tax hikes contained in Bill Clinton's major deficit reduction package in 1993. To the contrary, they were proud that not a single Republican in Congress voted for any version of it. The movement was gaining discipline. Ever since the infamous Bush retraction, Grover Norquist still brags today, not a single Republican has yet voted in Congress for a major tax increase. After helping to expose unpopular missteps by Clinton (including a proposal for a "BTU energy tax" and new taxes for a national health care plan), the tax cutters ably assisted Newt Gingrich in his triumphant "Contract with America" campaign, which in the fall of 1994 took back both houses of Congress for the GOP for the first time in forty years.

The next year, as the GOP's resurgent conservative wing put together its ambitious seven-year "zero-deficit plan," the radicals enthusiastically offered to help—just so long as the package included a big fat $350 billion tax cut. It was like inviting a hippo to come aboard and steer your rowboat. The radicals knew the cut would never fit into the agreement, but they didn't particularly care. For them, the purpose was to humiliate President Bill Clinton and prove to the nation that the Democrats could no longer govern the country. Overwhelmed by the size of these tax cut demands and threatened by budgetary "train wrecks," the deal fell apart and the plan capsized. Clinton survived looking stronger than ever. Gingrich's reputation never recovered.

The tax cutters didn't really mind this failure, nor even, a year later, the defeat of Bob Dole in 1996 to Bill Clinton. Before his defeat, they had at last gotten Dole to sign the "tax pledge." They had even managed to get one of their own leaders, Jack Kemp, to be his running mate. They were redefining the party.

But as Bill Clinton's presidency wore on, there was something that did rankle them: a steady yet noninflationary acceleration in job growth and in productivity growth—and a similar takeoff in the stock market indexes, especially the entrepreneurial NASDAQ. For many years supply-side gurus had been teaching that "the markets" are an infallible judge of Washington leadership. They had often cited the Dow revival after 1982 as a sure sign that Reagan was on track. Now, mysteriously, a liberal president who had said no to capital gains cuts and who had hiked the top marginal income tax rate from 31 to 40 percent was presiding over the most spectacular equities boom in

American history. As the Dow shot past 7,000, then 8,000, then 9,000, and more, and as the federal deficit narrowed and finally turned into a surplus, the Whitewater-obsessed *Wall Street Journal* ceased entirely to run its customary editorials on the connection between fiscal policy and the stock market. A few of the faithful tried to argue that Reagan's tax cut incentives were "just now kicking in" (this was in 1996, *fifteen years after* 1981). But this didn't pass the smile test. Mostly they just gritted their teeth and fumed.

Once again, the tax cut fundamentalists turned inward to regain strength, where a new cadre of boomer leaders were gradually overhauling the movement's collective mood and purpose. Back in the Reagan years, the movement's leaders exuded optimism and tended to argue that tax cuts would somehow raise revenue and "cure" the deficit, or at least that the deficit didn't really matter much. During the Clinton years, the emotional tone darkened and the message grew passionate, even apocalyptic. A new argument gained favor: more revenue was not the object, and large deficits were actually a good thing—because they would starve and strangle and therefore kill the government "beast." The new generation of tax radicals did not especially care to be regarded as cooperative citizens; many were happy to follow Norquist's lead and call themselves the "Leave Us Alone Coalition."

Back in the mid-eighties, Stockman once remarked how deficits might serve as a "battering ram" against federal spending. But the remark was unusual—and was made in private. By the mid-nineties, tax cut leaders were making such remarks frequently and publicly. Their very definition of an apostate was a Republican who cared more about deficits than about the size of government and who therefore wished to become "a tax collector for the liberal welfare state." All issues were perceived through a polarizing and Manichaean lens. "If we had a little teeny government and a big deficit," declared Grover Norquist, "I wouldn't care. It's the size of the government we're focused on. It's also the size of the government the left is focused on." More recently, on National Public Radio, Norquist compared the estate tax (known to movement conservatives as the "death tax") to apartheid in South Africa, to East German Communism, and even to the Holocaust. Daniel Mitchell of the Heritage Foundation has compared offshore tax evaders to champions of American civil disobedience, even to "Rosa Parks sitting in the back of that bus." The new message seemed unmistakable. For the sake of ridding ourselves of "unjust" taxes, virtually any act of personal defiance—or risk of national catastrophe—would not be too high a price to pay.

Whatever their motives and arguments, the tax cut champions knew they needed a friend to get back into power and press their agenda. He had to be a leader upbeat enough to get elected, a regular guy, yet also with a reserve of principle on which to draw to "stay the course." What they needed—and got—was George W. Bush, whom Congress declared president on January 5, 2001, after the most closely contested election in our nation's history.

Thus far, every year of his presidency, Bush has pushed for and signed a major tax cut. Thus far as well, his intentions to cut have been unmoved by worsening fiscal projections. From January of 2001 to January of 2002, the CBO's official projection of the ten-year federal budget balance fell by $3.3 trillion. Over the next twelve months it fell by another $1.0 trillion. Over the next twelve months, to January of 2004, it fell yet again, by $3.2 trillion. And if the inevitable next phase of the president's budget plans (especially all of his tax plans) are enacted, and if discretionary spending keeps growing as fast as the economy, the CBO now says we can subtract another $4.1 trillion.

To be sure, this fiscal swan dive—greater as a share of GDP than even during the first Reagan term—was driven by more than just tax cuts. There was the recession, the bust of the Dow, 9/11, the Medicare expansion, and mobilization for war.

Yet tax cuts were the centerpiece. Not only did they shrink revenue directly by reducing tax rates and expanding exemptions, but the extremist rhetoric accompanying them may also have encouraged less tax compliance and thus contributed to a revenue decline that the CBO says it can't yet fully explain.

According to the IRS, the federal government misses about $250 billion in revenue per year, a figure that has risen steeply in recent years. One explanation is that the IRS has experienced a fifteen-year decline in staffing and face-to-face audit rates. Another may be a shift in taxpayer attitudes. In 2003, 17 percent of Americans said it's OK to cheat on your taxes, up from 11 percent in 1999. The link between tax cutting and tax evasion is of course circumstantial. But given the fevered emotional climate set by the tax cut radicals—likening a tax cheat to a civil rights martyr—would such a link really surprise anyone?

The diehards have been duly impressed by Bush's determination to "stay the course." They have also been impressed by the dexterous flexibility of the arguments offered by the White House. In 2001 we needed tax cuts to give our temporary surplus "back to the taxpayers." In 2002 we needed them to stimulate the economy. In 2003 we needed them to provide long-term growth incentives. Even war, typically a good time to offer up at least a gesture of sacrifice, was cited as a good reason to cut taxes—as though all of those millions of rebate checks were somehow going to spook Osama bin Laden out of his caves. For three years in a row, GOP leaders argued that these tax cuts were affordable under congressional budget rules because most of them were due to expire before the end of ten years. Now they argue that any effort to block extending these cuts should be opposed as an outrageous and unexpected tax increase.

In his heart, Bush may wish to make significant and structural spending cuts. But as a practical matter he and his advisers must know that large tax cuts have greatly constrained his room to maneuver on the spending side. His failure here has badly tarnished his reputation with many GOP radicals, who mistakenly believe that tax cuts should have strengthened the president's leverage of spending. Clearly they have not. "Republicans chop checks to widows so CEOs can get tax-free golden parachutes" is a claim that, if the Democrats could ever make it stick, would be a free ticket to electoral victory. And the GOP knows it. So can Republicans ever bring themselves to make a virtue out of necessity and embrace a high-spending government? Possibly. "Mr. Bush seems to have no real problem with big government," observes the *Economist*. "It's just big Democratic government he can't take."

The supply-side faithful believe the first term of George W. invites comparison with the first term of Ronald Reagan. "Reagan's third term has arrived," announced Club for Growth's Stephen Moore in 2001. Many parallels are obvious. Early in their terms, both presidents had to respond to an economic recession and rising alarm over a more dangerous world. Both cut taxes aggressively for an undefined amalgam of reasons—some related to short-term demand stimulus, others connected to long-term ideological goals (with the latter accounting for most of the cost). Both raised defense spending in an effort to "revive" the U.S. armed forces after a recent era of Democratic "decline." Both cultivated the culture-warrior image of a president who would lead to a renewal in sound American virtues and values. Both talked incessantly about the need to cut nondefense federal spending—and both presided over sizable increases in such spending.

What supply-siders may find less welcome is how the parallel may continue on past their first terms. After Reagan's 1981 huge tax-cutting spree, the White House and Congress spent years wrangling over how to design the inevitable tax hikes so that revenues might once again catch up with outlays—which they finally did seventeen years later. It would depress supply-siders to imagine that a similar fate may be in store for their own recent cuts. It might also depress them to realize that whereas the "Reagan Revolution" at least succeeded in cutting punitive marginal tax rates that everyone today realizes were counterproductive, the Bush, Jr., cuts are likely to leave behind no such positive legacy. In time, they may vanish with few traces.

It should alarm all Americans, moreover, that this time around we don't have the luxury of waiting another seventeen years. The demographic window is shutting much too rapidly. Perhaps the biggest difference between the Reagan and George W. Bush tax cuts is that, with Reagan, history gave us plenty of time to clean up the mess. With George W., history may not be so indulgent.

When ideas triumph in politics, they often do so only after disguising themselves as something they are not. "The New Dealers used to describe their government as Hamiltonian means to Jeffersonian ends," explains political columnist David Frum. "Supply-side economics might be thought of as adapting Franklin Roosevelt's means to Goldwater's ends." Each party, in other words, has managed to prevail only after driving a sort of Faustian bargain with the enemy. Democrats push benefit hikes while pretending that they're unrelated to a government that collects taxes. And Republicans push tax cuts while pretending that they're unrelated to a government that disburses benefits. Yet while each party warns the public about the catastrophe posed by the other side, the nation seems to have no clear path ahead. We cannot budge on spending. We cannot budge on taxes. And the debts and projected liabilities keep widening. As Ronald Reagan used to say, "You ain't seen nothing yet!" I agree. There's much I haven't seen yet. But sometimes I'm less than eager to look.

Chapter 7

TEN PARTISAN MYTHS

"I am not a politician," announced the legendary humorist Artemis Ward in a 1859 July Fourth oration. "And my other habits are good also." Americans have always made fun of their elected leaders. The yawning gap between the high art of governing and the low art of getting elected is just too ridiculous to pass over. The high art of governing is all about strong principles, practical wisdom, and making tough choices. The low art of getting elected is all about spinning, denial, pandering, playacting, deal-making, and creative accommodation—when it's not about outright deception and fraud. "A politician is an acrobat," Lillian Hellman once wrote, "He keeps his balance by saying the opposite of what he does." Here's H. L. Mencken: "A politician is an animal which can sit on a fence and yet keep both ears to the ground."

Good politicians are able to savor the humor of their own situation. George W. Bush once quipped that "my political philosophy is based on the premise that you can fool some of the people all the time—and I intend to concentrate on those people." Hearing about this, I recalled the more complex bit of levity delivered by his father when, as president, he came under fire for retracting his earlier line on "voodoo" economics. "I know there are people in this audience who, in view of my changed positions on various subjects, doubt that I have the courage of my convictions. Of course I have the courage of my convictions," he declared, pounding the lectern before then adding, "I just don't happen to agree with them."

My own initiation into the fun-house world of politics occurred some thirty-five years ago when I was CEO of Bell & Howell and went to Congress seeking help on some legislative issue. I managed to talk it over with Senator Everett Dirksen, the venerable GOP leader, who agreed to support me on this legislation. Later, when the situation became urgent, I went to visit the senator and discovered that he had totally reversed his position. Before I could say anything, he looked at me, smiled broadly, and said, "Pete, you are probably wondering if I'm a man of high principle. Well, I want you to know I am a man of principle. And my first principle is total flexibility."

In recent years, the low art of "flexible" politics has adapted to America's growing partisanship by organizing itself around two lopsided and mutually exclusive worldviews, each with its own set of self-justifying "myths." This chapter is about those myths—what they are, why they're wrong, and how they enable politicians to offer Americans an endless stream of freebies. I identify ten of them. Doubtless there are more, but these are enough to give you a good idea of what they're all about. Is buy-now, pay-later not good enough for you? Well then, what about buy-now, pay-never?

On the Democratic side, these myths describe a gleaming social democracy in which every American owes his happiness to a government conveyor belt crowded with pension, health care, housing, food, and welfare benefits. If the pace of delivery does not accelerate each year, millions will sink into abject misery. The future resources needed to pay for this cornucopia will bubble up spontaneously from some magic mountain. On the Republican side, these myths depict an invigorating libertarian paradise in which every American would be Horatio Alger if not for the ball and chain of punitive taxation. To break out of this bondage, any means are justified—including borrowing massively from our kids (who will thank us later). Meanwhile, the cost of government can be reduced to almost nothing by "privatizing" all benefits except those that serve vital national interests, which of course include my benefit and your benefit.

On balance, these myths have made it harder to laugh at low politics today. By shielding elected leaders from shame, they also shield them from humor. There was a time, for example, when congressmen who advocated an unfunded tax cut or unfunded benefit hike needed some special pleading or subterfuge—which often made them the target of farcical comedy. Today, armed with partisan myths, Republican or Democratic leaders can advocate such measures brazenly and without apology. These myths have also made it harder for talented and civic-minded Americans to get involved in public affairs. Anyone who enters the world of politics will sooner or later face a character-testing choice between principle and pragmatism: How much foolishness will you abide in your own party in order to accomplish what you believe is some greater good? Increasingly, the foolishness goes beyond what is tolerable.

More seriously, these myths have polarized the two parties by stigmatizing each in the eyes of the other and by ruling out the sort of bipartisan consensus that could avert fiscal catastrophe. What's worse, elected leaders use and abuse these myths with such casual abandon that they poison the well of our democracy. They inflame voters who would otherwise be perfectly willing to split the difference.

Charles de Gaulle once remarked, with some justice, that "since a politician never believes what he says, he is surprised when others believe him." It's time for politicians to be more than surprised. They need to rouse themselves and start saying what they know to be the truth.

Five Democratic Myths About Entitlements

Myth One. *Because federal benefits go to the poor, reform will amount to a shredding of our social safety net.*

We should never forget the critical role that federal benefits have played—and continue to play—in protecting Americans against the worst hardships of poverty. "I see one third of a nation ill-housed, ill-clad, and ill-nourished," announced President Roosevelt in 1937. Most of the benefits originally paid out through his New Deal programs were directly targeted at alleviating this misery. Ever since, federal benefit programs have provided a vital "floor of protection" (to use another Roosevelt term) to millions of Americans who have no alternative means of support in the event of unemployment, disability, sudden retirement, or the death of a parent or spouse. This year federal benefits prevent some 20 million Americans (half of them elderly) from falling into poverty.

Alleviating poverty is all to the good. Clearly, however, this is no longer the purpose toward which most federal benefits are directed. Here's one clue. Since the end of the Great Depression in 1940, real (inflation-adjusted) GDP per capita in the United States has more than quintupled, and real government benefit spending per capita has grown *more than twenty-five-fold.* In a nation with strongly rising living standards, does it make sense to suppose that all of these new benefits go only to the poor? Here's another clue. Only about one out of four federal benefit dollars flows through programs that use any measure of financial need as a criterion for eligibility. These so-called means-tested programs (like food stamps, Medicaid, rental subsidies, SSI, TANF, the earned income tax credit, and the like) are the mainstay of our social safety net. But they constitute only a corner of our benefit budget.

So how much of total benefits actually go to the poor? We don't have to guess. The Census Bureau calculates the number each year. In 2002, out of $1.2 trillion in federal, state, and local benefits, roughly $140 billion served to lift people all or part of the way out of poverty. That's about 12 cents to the poor out of every full benefit dollar. Again, these 12 cents are vital. They prevent great suffering. But they do not define the role of most benefit spending—any more than quenching thirst can be said to define the function of a municipal water system.

A number of years ago, I proposed that some share of any savings gained from overall entitlement reform be earmarked toward targeted benefits for the truly needy. (At a relatively modest cost, for example, we could raise the SSI cash benefit level so that no elderly person need fall beneath the poverty line.) To my surprise, the benefit lobbies peremptorily rejected my proposal as a "threat" that would undermine the "legitimacy" of middle-class entitlements like Social Security. Richard Titmuss, British social democrat and renowned scholar of the welfare state, wrote many years ago that "programs for the poor are poor programs." That slogan has ever since served as a rallying cry for political leaders and their advisers who believe that only "universal" programs that give benefits to everyone, including the entire middle class, can ever hope to gain lasting political support.

Most Democrats in Congress did vote in support of the 2003 prescription drug addition to Medicare, which includes a provision to reduce the government's subsidy (that is, raise the Part B premium) for wealthy retired households. But I suspect that many voted under duress—they wanted the new benefits, after all—and took comfort that the measure will affect so few people (less than 2 percent of Medicare beneficiaries, and these on a sliding scale) that it seemed less like assisting only the poor than like penalizing only the rich. The Democratic credo still stands: as a group, well-off Americans need to be bribed with benefits before they will support a program that does anything for the poor. This credo ensures that the cost of benefits for everyone keeps growing and keeps crowding out any other agenda, including helping the poor themselves.

Myth Two. Even if they don't go mostly to the poor, federal benefits foster equality by going mostly to lower-income households.

Few axioms of American political life find such uncritical acceptance as the belief that social welfare programs effect a dramatic redistribution of wealth in favor of low-income households. It apparently makes little difference that few budget experts, liberal or conservative, have ever subscribed to this axiom—and that recent data repudiate it altogether.

Back in the sixties the Nobel laureate economist Milton Friedman used to shock audiences by asserting that Social Security was actually a regressive program. In more recent decades this no-longer-shocking thesis has been seriously debated and often defended in academic papers sponsored by the National Bureau of Economic Research. When the celebrated political economist Mancur Olson examined closely the panoply of federal benefit programs, he was surprised by what he saw. He concluded: "Most of the redistribution of government is not from upper-income and middle-income people to low-income people. Most of the redistribution of income in fact is from middle-income people to other middle-income people, or from the whole of society to particular groups of rich people, or from one group to another where the groups are distinguished not by one being poor and the other being rich, but only by the fact that some groups are organized and some are not."

Income data from the Congressional Budget Office (updated here to 2003 values) back up Olson's critique. Total federal benefits to the affluent are at least as substantial as those to the needy. Among Social Security beneficiaries, for instance, households with incomes of $150,000 or more receive, on average, checks that are twice as large as those of households with incomes of less than $15,000. Even when we add in the cash and in-kind benefits disbursed by all of the other federal sources for which we have income data—including "means-tested" welfare and food stamps—we find an amazingly even distribution of benefits across all households by income. The average household in the top bracket ($150,000 and up) actually receives slightly more than the average household in the bottom bracket (under $15,000).

How does this happen? In part it's because some means-tested benefits like Medicaid go to households that are not really low-income. But mostly it's because benefits from the largest programs (especially retirement programs, including federal civil service and military pensions) are skewed to the high end of the income scale. And this metric doesn't include certain tax expenditures, benefits handed out through the tax code, which Democrats defend at least as stoutly as Republicans. These are even more skewed to the affluent. The home mortgage interest deduction, for example, is worth $72 billion annually, and 80 percent of it goes to households with incomes over $75,000. The employer-paid health insurance deduction, worth $85 billion annually, is similarly regressive.

Over the last two decades, moreover, the distribution of benefits by income has become more—not less—skewed toward upper-income brackets. One major reason: Democrats have been less interested in defending programs that target low-income Americans (like family assistance "welfare," which has been cut back, restructured, and largely converted into social services) than in defending or even enlarging programs that do not (like Social Security and Medicare).

Let me make the central point a bit more bluntly. If the federal government's sole purpose were to straighten out the national income distribution, it would do a better job if it dispensed with all the programs and agency staffs and simply mailed the checks in random amounts to random addresses—or dropped the cash from an airplane and let it scatter over major population centers.

Myth Three. Federal benefits go mostly to the elderly, whom everyone knows are much less well-off than younger Americans.

The first half of this myth is not a myth at all. Public benefits do go mostly to the elderly. At the federal level, as we have seen, per-capita benefits to elders are seven times larger than per-capita spending (of every variety) on children. Even including all state and local spending—on schools, public health, adoptions, and the like—seniors still come out on top by three or four to one. The second half of this myth, on the other hand, is indeed myth. Forty years ago, the elderly still fared worse than younger Americans according to most measures of economic well-being. But ever since, those indicators have been racing to the advantage of the elderly—thanks, in part, to all the benefit programs that were expanded on their behalf.

Which phase of life today experiences the lowest poverty rate? Answer: the elderly, of whom only 10.4 percent are officially poor. In the mid-seventies, the elder poverty rate plunged below the rate for children; and since the mid-nineties, it has been trending beneath the rate for working-age adults as well. Who has the highest homeownership rate? Answer: the elderly, 80 percent of whom own their home. Americans today are more likely to own their home at age eighty than they are at age fifty. Three-quarters of these owners have paid off their mortgages. The median net worth of elder homeowners ($245,000) now exceeds that of homeowners aged thirty-five to sixty-four ($185,000) by over 30 percent; it exceeds that of homeowners under age thirty-five ($60,000) by over 300 percent.

The pace of this improvement over the last forty years has been breathtaking. Since 1966, according to Census Bureau data, the median real income of elder men has risen by 97 percent—versus an 18 percent gain for men of all ages. According to Federal Reserve data, in the early 1960s the average seventy-year-old consumed 71 percent of what the average thirty-year-old consumed; by the late 1980s that ratio grew to 118 percent. By some measures, the overall living standards of elder households have risen above those of younger families with children. Meanwhile, seniors enjoy more leisure than ever before. Only 13 percent of the elderly are employed, the share with chronic disabilities has fallen to a record-low 20 percent, and a record-high 72 percent report that their health is either "good" or "excellent."

Some argue that entitlements for the elderly merely substitute for transfers of wealth that the young would otherwise make to their parents. They substitute all right—and then some. Before Social Security and Medicare, it was not uncommon for young families to help out their parents if and when mom and pop were in need. Today, it is more common for the help to flow in the other direction. Adults aged twenty-five to thirty-four now report receiving from their parents twenty times more support than they give to them; even for adults thirty-five to forty-four, the ratio is five to one. Social Security and Medicare sometimes embody traditional family values, but sometimes they also turn them on their head.

I'm not saying that most seniors are living it up. Like Americans in every other age bracket, many have trouble making ends meet. The less affluent half of the elderly live in modest circumstances. As I have mentioned earlier, most of these elders are hugely dependent on government benefits like Social Security, which means that any large cut in their benefits would cause many of them hardship. Avoiding such sudden and unexpected cuts is what entitlement reform is all about. But to refer to the elderly as mostly needy, as *categorically* disadvantaged, is plainly contradicted by the facts. That may have been true once. It certainly is not true any longer.

Myth Four. Social Security and Medicare are earned rights, as in a contract; beneficiaries are only getting back what they paid in.

Since the benefits from Social Security and Part A of Medicare are both paid out from special trust funds, and since these funds receive money almost exclusively from earmarked payroll taxes, it seems natural to suppose a certain justice about the arrangement. Whatever happens, these programs "live off their own revenue." You pay in and you get back. What could be unfair about that?

There are two important answers to this question: timing and demographics. First, consider timing. When you start a new pension system, full contributions from covered workers start arriving right away—but benefit payouts remain small for many years until enough workers with enough "credits" begin retiring. This gives rise to enormous early surpluses, which in an ordinary pension plan are typically saved and generate a growing return to capital until benefit outlays later catch up to revenues.

When it launched Social Security and Medicare, however, Congress cared much more about being popular than about proper accounting or building up a surplus. During the early years of both programs, Congress kept tax rates unrealistically low and awarded full benefits to new retirees who had only contributed for a year or two. As a result, early contributors experienced vast "windfall" returns. Not everyone did as well as Mrs. Ida Fuller, who received the first Social Security check in 1940 after paying $22 in contributions and went on to receive over $20,000 in benefits before she died at one hundred years of age. But nearly everyone born before the late 1920s (the "World War II generation") got exceptional returns on their taxes, several times better than they could have gotten off any type of financial asset.

This great deal, however, came at a price. It meant that the children of the World War II GIs (including the boomers, born in the 1940s and 1950s) would have to contribute at much higher tax rates over their entire working lives to pay for their own benefits as well as to keep benefits flowing to their parents. It also meant that, henceforth, the system would be pay-as-you-go. This is bad enough news for boomers, most of whom can no longer expect to do as well on their tax contributions as they could have done on low-risk financial assets. But it's even worse news for the children of boomers (including Xers born in the 1960s and 1970s, and millennials born in the 1980s and 1990s), who will also have to pay for the demographic tsunami scheduled to hit the budget when boomers retire. For these younger workers, either their taxes will be raised, their benefits cut, or both. At the end of the day, the return on their tax contributions may be effectively zero or even negative.

To say that workers only get back what they put in, then, is entirely misleading. It all depends on which workers you're talking about. Early birds often do well in a Ponzi scheme. It's the last guy out who gets slammed. And when people tell me that these programs are untouchable because they constitute a "contract" between generations, what I want to know is: When exactly did the younger generation agree to this contract? From my hazy recollection of business school law, I recall that one precondition for a "contract" is a meeting of the minds between both parties. But when I look at my grandson Peter Cary, I can't help wondering: Who ever got the consent of this thirteen-year-old? Indeed, how many of our leaders have given any thought at all to what this "deal" must look like from the perspective of kids his age? Or how it will appear to them as they grow older?

Myth Five. The future growth in the cost of senior benefits, whatever that may be, can easily be borne by younger generations.

Every year, the Social Security trustees release an annual report containing an estimate of the system's "actuarial deficit," which represents what we would need in hand today to cover Social Security's cash shortfall over the next seventy-five years. And every year, defenders of the status quo parade this figure around because it makes the long-term problem seem modest. In 2003 the actuarial deficit officially amounted to $3.5 trillion or (alternatively) an extra 1.9 percent of the U.S. worker payroll each year starting today. Yes, the defenders say, an extra 2 percent of worker pay is a significant levy, but surely we cannot regard this as a catastrophic imposition on future Americans.

Well, we can—once we get our figures straight. First of all, we need to include Medicare as well as Social Security, unless we disregard the sober judgment of nearly every policy expert and believe that health care costs will somehow miraculously turn around and head south on their own. This adds $15.6 trillion to the actuarial deficit. (All of these dollar figures are "present values," which means we would need to have that money and invest it *today*.) Next, we have to add back in the value of the mythical "trust funds," which aren't going to save the American people one nickel in future tax liabilities. This adds another $1.6 trillion to the actuarial deficit. So far we're up to $20.7 trillion. Let's round that to $21 trillion, the same number we met in an earlier chapter on Congress's penchant for "Enron" accounting.

Now we're really talking serious money. But we're not finished yet. All these figures reflect an actuarial calculation that is limited to only seventy-five years. This limit allows the system to fall off a financial cliff in the year 2078 and thus assumes that our children, come the year 2050 or 2060, will be utterly unconcerned about the fate of their *own* children. If we want to take responsibility for our own problem, and not pass the buck onto some other generation's children, we need to use an unlimited time horizon.* The Social Security trustees, in apparent

* Financial markets routinely assume infinite horizons for their present-value calculations. How else, for example, could you price a "perpetual bond" like a British consol that has an infinite maturity? Though investors don't live forever, they eventually have to sell their assets (which represent a stream of future payments) to other investors—and so on, ad infinitum.

agreement, have started publishing this unlimited-horizon figure. We'll use their number. For Medicare, we will rely on the pathbreaking research of Jagadeesh Gokhale and Kent Smetters (commissioned by the Treasury Department). Once Medicare is again added to Social Security, here is their bottom line: an unlimited time horizon will add an extra $24 trillion to the actuarial deficit, for a grand total of roughly $45 trillion in 2003. This is the *smallest* of the five estimates mentioned in Chapter 2. It does not include Medicaid or any other benefits program. And it was calculated before the drug benefit add-on to Medicare.

Nevertheless, $45 trillion is a vast sum. It amounts to $158,000 for every man, woman, and child living in the United States. It is ten times greater than our publicly held national debt ($4 trillion). It even exceeds our nation's total net worth ($42 trillion, which includes all property owned by U.S. residents—real, personal, and financial).

Paying it off would require taxing away an *extra 17 percent of workers' earnings* forever—again, *starting today*. It is, of course, unthinkable that we could or would soon enact (and save) what is in effect a doubling of our current payroll tax rate. But here's the killer: every four years we put off this tax hike, the long-term rate rises by an extra percent. According to Gokhale and Smetters, the necessary rate would rise to 18 percent by 2007, 19 percent by 2011, and so on. But couldn't we just muddle through and wait until the benefit costs rise before hiking taxes? Yes, we could. But then the ultimate tax hikes on the next generation would be much higher, enough (as we mentioned earlier) to wipe out all of their pretax wage gains. Try floating that idea with your kids at the dinner table this evening.

Five Republican Myths About Tax Cuts

Myth One. Because the American people are overtaxed, they want and deserve our tax cuts.

Let's subject this oft-heard claim to a bit of cold analysis. Are Americans really overtaxed? Compared to what? Certainly not compared to other developed countries. Of all twenty-seven developed countries (as defined by the Organization for Economic Cooperation and Development), the United States is roughly tied with Japan as the *least taxed* as a share of GDP. And compared with most of these countries, none of whom bear our global commitments, our current federal, state, and local tax revenues (at 31 percent of GDP) are quite a bit lower. The average figure for Europe, for example, is 46 percent.

Are we overtaxed relative to our past? Certainly not our recent past. Historically, we'd have to go back to President Johnson in 1968 to find a year when total government revenues were lower as a share of GDP. If we look at the federal government alone, we'd have to go back much further—in fact, all the way back to President Truman in 1951. That's over fifty years ago. Only one in every hundred of today's U.S. workers has any adult *memory* of a time when the total federal tax take was perceptibly lower than today.

Tax cutters often imply that Americans are becoming much more hostile to taxes over time. But this isn't true either. According to two Gallup polls taken in 2003, for example, the share of Americans who say that the federal income tax is "too high" is lower than in any year since 1962. In the wake of 9/11, many surveys suggest that voters agree with Oliver Wendell Holmes that "taxes are what we pay for civilized society"—and figure that civilization is something well worth paying for.

To be sure, America is not Europe, and Americans would never tolerate the high tax burdens that are routine in most other developed countries. The kind of civic vision described by both Presidents Reagan and G. W. Bush—a vision of a dynamic, entrepreneurial society in which government is smaller and less intrusive—resonates with most Americans. There are, furthermore, genuine reasons to be concerned about what we pay in taxes. First, we might worry that our taxes are no longer paying for investment-like activities which do as much for our nation's future as they did a few decades ago. And second, we might worry that our overall tax burden is certain to rise dramatically in future decades unless we reform our spending priorities.

Yet the tax-cut-now argument addresses none of these concerns. Indeed, it promises to make them worse. The fiscal bottom line, taught in every textbook on public finance, is this: the long-term tax burden is determined by the long-term spending burden, and *unless you reduce the long-term spending burden, you cannot cut taxes in any lasting way, but can only shift the burden of taxes from the present to the future.*

By the end of the 1980s, we learned this sad truth about the Reagan tax cut. Soon we will learn it about the Bush tax cut as well. As the Congressional Budget Office drily points out in its official 2003 analysis of the Bush tax cut package, "at some point in the future under the President's proposals, either taxes would have to be higher than they otherwise would have been, or spending would have to be lower." Larry Kotlikoff and Scott Burns put it this way in their fine book, *The Coming Generational Storm*: "Paying for what the government spends is a zero-sum game, and it's one we're playing against our own flesh and blood. Either we pay the government's bills, or we leave them for our kids to pay. It's that simple."

Myth Two. OK, forget the long-term tax burden. Our tax cuts are still a sensible near-term means of stimulating a weak economy back to health.

This argument certainly has much truth to it. Both the Reagan and George W. Bush tax cuts were enacted at a time when the economy was mired in a recession. Both presidents often described their tax cut in classic Keynesian terms. ("That money can cover a lot of bills," explained Bush in 2003. "That money can help families with purchases they have been delaying. That money will be in circulation, which will be good for our economy.") And in both cases, the vast majority of the economics profession agreed in principle that a tax cut could be a legitimate means to substitute for diminished consumer and investor demand.

I say in principle, because the critical issue here is timing. To be effective, the stimulus must be applied *during the near-term recession.* That is, it must put money now in the pockets of people who will spend it now. Over the entire last century, unfortunately, Congress has never been able to time this stimulus very well. The tax cuts typically aren't enacted until late in the recession and then continue long after the recession is over—overstimulating the economy and setting up the next recession. This is why many economists have grown to dislike countercyclical tax cuts in practice.

The Reagan and Bush tax cuts have redoubled the skepticism of experts for one simple reason: both of these tax cuts, in their very design, have focused overwhelmingly on long-term—not short-term—tax reduction. The 1981 Reagan tax cut, experience later proved, would have generated ever larger revenue losses forever if it hadn't been repealed by subsequent tax laws. The original 2001 tax cut by George W. contained only $5.5 billion of tax cuts in the first year. As for the 2003 tax cut, the CBO's ten-year projection (the White House projections weren't much different) showed just 17 percent of the full $1.5 trillion in lost revenues would end up in taxpayers' pockets over the *first* three years. Fifty-four percent would be distributed in the *last* three years.

So while most economists agree with the near-term stimulus rationale, most also agree that this explains only a tiny fraction of what the big GOP tax cuts were trying to accomplish. What we needed, both in 1981 and in 2003, was short-term tax stimulus and long-term tax restraint. What we got was only a bit of the first and none of the second. Some tax cutters say that you need to make a tax cut "permanent" or it won't offer much stimulus. This is not a serious argument. In the past, temporary cuts have proven to be stimulative. Besides, you can't hold the nation's entire future hostage to just one recession—unless your intent all along is to fool people by coming back later and repealing your own "permanent" cut. That would be a brazen argument indeed.

Myth Three. Even when they don't deliver near-term stimulus, our tax cuts make the tax code more efficient—which means a higher standard of living all around.

An efficient tax system can be defined as a system which raises revenue with minimal distortions in economic behavior. Economists have invented complex equations to quantify tax efficiency. Few have improved much on the explanation offered by Jean-Baptiste Colbert, finance minister to King Louis XIV: "The art of taxation consists in so plucking the goose as to achieve a maximum of feathers with the minimum of hissing." The acid test is how much the tax system itself disrupts people's work, saving, and investment choices in order to raise a given amount of revenue. An inefficient tax system causes a lot of disruption; it gets in the way of the productive process. An efficient tax system causes little disruption; it gets out of the way. But let me repeat those key words: *in order to raise a given amount of revenue.*

Over the years many tax reformers have defended their proposals—for example, to create fewer tax brackets, establish a national value-added or "flat" income tax, index the capital gains tax, or phase out the taxation of estates or dividends—by citing efficiency advantages. I've always lent a sympathetic ear to these basic arguments, many of which have been revived by the Bush administration. For decades many smart Republicans have argued that our tax treatment of corporate earnings is wasteful and that—a sore point for me—it discourages capital formation. In theory, no question: we'd be better off with a better tax code.

But if the argument itself is valid, the way today's GOP

leaders are wielding this argument in support of large tax cuts is not. By definition, a pure efficiency reform must leave revenue unchanged because less revenue *itself* imposes a new efficiency cost (by increasing the deficit and suppressing investment) and typically this cost is greater than the gain created by the tax cut. Reducing the taxation on corporate earnings, for example, may marginally raise private-sector savings—cited by some as an efficiency improvement. But even if it does, the minor extra savings will be overwhelmed by the loss in federal revenue, which adds directly to the federal debt and, in the long run, subtracts nearly dollar for dollar from national savings.

In short, if a modest efficiency reform requires large revenue losses, it probably isn't worth it. Steve Roach, chief economist for Morgan Stanley, says it well: "Who wouldn't want a more efficient tax system? But like all good things, such efforts have their time and place. Sadly, in my view, today's saving-short U.S. economy simply can't afford to indulge in the luxury of tax reform." Rudy Penner, CBO director during the Reagan years, had a similar reaction when asked about the 2003 tax cuts: "The good news is that they're doing a lot of good things with tax policy. The bad news is that we can't afford the good news."

An inefficient tax code is usually riddled with many peaks and valleys in the tax rates, meaning that some activities face a steep tax penalty and other activities are let off easy for no economic reason. So how do you get rid of the unfairly high peaks (which cause the most distortion in behavior) without losing revenue? Very simple: you fill in the unfairly low valleys by closing the loopholes and favors. This is sometimes called "base-broadening," which is what genuine efficiency reform is all about. Many "flat tax" proposals use this approach honestly. The 1986 tax act, in which both parties cooperated, reduced the highest marginal rates—without losing revenue—by eliminating some major exemptions. It was a laudable success for efficiency reform.

If President George W. Bush had really been interested in this kind of reform, he could have followed the same path. He could have argued for his cuts in the double taxation of corporate earnings or in the estate tax, but he could have paid for them by also proposing that various exemptions and deductions be closed. On the personal income side, he could have proposed capping the home mortgage deduction or the exemption for employer-paid health insurance. On the corporate earnings side, he could have urged the elimination of any number of egregious loopholes (like offshore, real estate, and life insurance tax shelters or special write-offs for energy, oil, and financial companies). He did none of these things—in fact, he widened many of the corporate loopholes—proving beyond a doubt that efficiency has not been his object.

Myth Four. The critics just don't get it. What our tax cuts are really about is improving "supply side" incentives to work, save, and invest.

The marginal tax rate is the tax rate that applies to the last or highest or "marginal" dollar that you earn in a year. Since the late 1970s a core proposition of what has come to be known as the "supply side" argument for tax reform is that reductions in high marginal tax rates can sometimes have a dramatic and positive impact on economic activity and (even) on revenue. In a sensible world, we would all acknowledge that such cuts are an important type of efficiency reform that sometimes works very well—and sometimes does not.

That would be a sensible world. The reality is that supply-side claims have become a theology, ruling out any reasonable discussion of the evidence. Heartened by earlier successes in boosting revenue from high-income Americans with the Kennedy tax cut of 1963 (which lowered the top rate from 91 to 70 percent) and the Reagan tax cut of 1981 (which lowered it to 50 percent), these true believers have moved on to the proposition that they can give us vast efficiency and revenue gains if we only let them keep cutting tax rates—anywhere and at any time.

In fact, there's plenty of empirical evidence that when marginal tax rates are not high, the efficiencies you gain by cutting them may be modest and the impact on economic activity may be ambiguous. By ambiguous I mean that while some people may react to more after-tax income by working or saving more, others may react by working or saving less. The overall impact on production or savings could go either way. In 1993, to choose an apt example, Congress passed and President Clinton signed a deficit reduction package that included a hike in the top marginal federal income tax rate, from 31 to 39.6 percent. Supply-siders predicted doom. What followed was an accelerating seven-year boom in jobs, hours, savings, investment, and productivity—a chapter in economic history that never appears in the supply-siders' texts.

When Bush came to the White House in 2001, the top marginal tax rate was still at 39.6 percent and the average *marginal* rate for both income and payroll taxes (across all U.S. households) was 30 percent. After all of his tax cuts are phased in, Bush expects to reduce these to 35 percent and about 29 percent, respectively. Let's leave aside the fact that these cuts were made "temporary" to save on revenue losses and thus have yet to be permanently paid for. Even if they were writ in stone, they are relatively small cuts in relatively low marginal rates. As such, they are very unlikely to trigger a sizable supply-side response.

Even if the response is both positive and sizable, moreover, the gains will be canceled out—perhaps overwhelmed—by the large economic cost imposed by the deficits needed to pay for it. That's the conclusion reached by the CBO's examination of the new tax plan. The tax-rate-induced gains in labor supply, reports the CBO, would be positive but small, and in any case would be neutralized by the productivity losses due to less business investment, which would in turn result from larger federal deficits. According to some of the dynamic models reviewed by the CBO, the tax plan would actually result in significant GDP losses and further revenue losses relative to the official "static" projection of the plan. Such losses, needless to say, would constitute a humiliating outcome for a tax reform purchased at the cost of trillions of dollars in extra public indebtedness.

Myth Five. Let's be honest. This is all about politics. In the long run, our tax cuts will force Congress to cut back spending and, with that, cut back government.

I know several brilliant and partisan Republicans who admit to me, in private, that much of the supply-side hype about the economics of tax cuts is not really true. But, they say, it's the only way to reduce government spending in a world in which powerful interest groups, allied with the opposition party, stand ready to punish any attempt to cut off the flow of government largesse. A direct approach, they say, is futile. The only practical option is to pursue the indirect but more popular course of revenue reduction, "starving the beast" at its food source. True, deficit financing can keep outlays flowing for a time. But as in the famous story of Solomon, these strategists hope that Democrats will agree to reduce spending rather than slice our children by punishing them with excessive public debt.

This is a clever apologia. But I have three objections to it: it is unfair, it is cynical, and it is hypocritical.

It is unfair because no end, however legitimate, can justify such means. Nothing excuses holding the next generation hostage—any more than your own children—on the dubious bet that another party will have the goodwill to relent. It is cynical because it assumes that our democratic process is broken, that Americans no longer share any common values on which open agreement can be reached, and that subterfuge is the only recourse left. I for one refuse to accept this dismal view. And it is hypocritical. One could take the ostensible goal of the tax cutters—smaller government—more seriously if we saw that the party pushing the tax cut was also at least trying with energy and diligence to reduce government spending, especially in the long term. But we see nothing of the sort. Bush has allowed the "pay-go" rule to expire, vetoed no spending bill, and proposed no significant outlay reduction in a single major entitlement program.

Let me add one more objection: if pressed far enough, this starve-the-beast strategy is almost certain to backfire. What makes the GOP activists so certain that the "enemy" won't employ the same strategy in reverse? What if the Democrats call the GOP's bluff, raise the GOP's ante, and allow a flood tide of debt to sweep forth? What if they come to power and replace the tax cuts with benefit expansions, leaving the growing deficits in place? What next step do these GOP partisans suggest? By the tone of their remarks, one gets the impression that they would truly welcome some political or policy cataclysm, something that would shake America to its roots. But if they read any history, they would be more careful what they wished for. During eras of national crisis, the party of big government *always* crushes the party of small government.

What needs to happen for all the myth-spinning to stop? Nothing can substitute for leadership. The heads of the Democratic and Republican parties need to pause, step back, and assess the potential damage to our nation's future. Voters need to press politicians to adhere more closely to the truth—even if the truth is not always what voters would most like to hear. And if both partisan leaders and partisan voters need a reason to be truthful that appeals to their collective self-interest, here's one: the party that, in its hubris, displays the greatest disregard for truth is almost always the party the loses the next realigning election. "All political parties die at last of swallowing their own lies." So wrote John Arbuthnot, one of the earliest observers of political parties in modern Europe. And, he might have added, the party caught telling the biggest lies is usually the one that dies first.

Chapter 8

•

WHY AMERICA IS CHOOSING THE WRONG FUTURE

During the presidency of Andrew Jackson, Thomas Cole (sometimes called the father of the Hudson River school of painters) unveiled the most memorable work of historical fantasy ever attempted by an American artist. Entitled *The Course of Empire* and now on display at the New-York Historical Society, it consists of five paintings that show the rise and fall of a great civilization against a fixed landscape. The visual epic begins with wilderness and moves to a pastoral republic with austere settlements nestled in nature. It then progresses to a towering cosmopolis, full of bustling markets, glutted spectators, and gigantic public structures. The fourth and climactic picture shows the edifice, now coarse and brittle, at its moment of literal collapse—complete with pillaging barbarians and red sky. The final image is of desolate ruins in the moonlight.

Cole wanted the audience, as it gazed at his paintings, to contemplate the fate of countless empires that have risen to greatness and then disintegrated—from the ancient dynasties of Egypt, Persia, and China to the classical republics of Athens and Rome to the modern monarchies of Spain, France, and (perhaps) Britain. His images bring to mind the social and political forces that gradually transformed each people's greatness into grossness, its virtues into vices.

Many of Cole's visual themes would be easily recognizable today: growing institutional distrust and mounting political dysfunction; a weakening commitment to the future; a strengthening cult of self and a declining sense of social solidarity; grandiose public ambitions alongside widespread cynicism about any public purpose. Only half hidden from view, one also senses the presence of hopelessly polarized political factions and of vast liabilities heaped up on future generations whose fate has essentially been abandoned. This is not surprising, since both themes—factional polarization and endless borrowing from posterity—figure heavily in Edward Gibbon's *Decline and Fall of the Roman Empire*, which Cole took as his inspiration.

Americans have always had mixed reactions to these paintings. Some, resisting Cole's message, believe our nation is exempt from such a fate—either because we are not an "empire" (that touchy word again!) or because we are a chosen or exceptional people whom providence or history has given a free pass. Others agree that the long-term forces pushing us to decline are inexorable; we can delay but cannot avoid the end that Cole depicts.

My own view lies with neither camp. With nations as with people, good outcomes are never guaranteed. They have and always will depend on ceaseless care and effort—and in fact throughout most of our history, starting with our founders, Americans have deliberately safeguarded our republic's ongoing vitality by containing political partisanship and limiting public indebtedness. This chapter is about how we once made the right collective choices—and whether we can start making them again.

Let me preview my conclusion right here. Changing course

won't happen just by trying to enact or repeal a few bills in Congress. Changing course will require educating leaders and then getting them to help educate voters. It will require encouraging young adults to get involved again in public life. It will require mobilizing national opinion. And it will require reversing broad shifts in civic habits and personal attitudes.

Yet such a reversal is possible. Our nation has not so much forgotten about posterity as it has forgotten, practically and collectively, how to serve it. It is within our power to redirect our policies and politics, to revive our nation's commitment to the future, and to avoid Cole's terrible endgame. Most Americans of all ages still sincerely hope our nation chooses a better future—and it is quite possible that the rising generation will soon insist on it.

How the Founders Prevented "the Greatest of Dangers"

America's founding statesmen had one great aspiration and that was to establish a new nation dedicated to "Life, Liberty and the pursuit of Happiness." Shadowing their efforts was one great fear, which was that the new American republic would go the way of so many empires past—the way Thomas Cole would later illustrate in oil colors—to excess, to dissipation, and ultimately to ruin. They were well read in classical history. Most, like John Adams, were prone to pessimistic ruminations over the "inevitable decay" of civic virtue. Of all the great dangers they worried might pull America down before its time, two stand out as remarkably contemporary: burdensome public debt and quarreling political parties.

Many felt so strongly about these dangers that they believed public debts and political parties ought to be banished altogether. Not only that, many believed these two dangers were somehow connected.

Why would a small and largely agricultural society with rudimentary financial institutions worry about government borrowing (or "funding," to use the word most often used in the eighteenth century)? Quite simply because the founders believed that the temptation to enrich a few today at the expense of everyone tomorrow is too potent to be easily resisted. They associated honest and prudent public accounting with principled leadership, a virtuous citizenry, and a prospering economy. Chronic deficits spelled corrupt leadership, political decadence, and economic ruin.

From Benjamin Franklin to Patrick Henry, most of the elder revolutionaries lamented the need to borrow to supply the Continental Army. President George Washington fully supported the advice of his Treasury secretary, Alexander Hamilton, who cautioned that federal debt was a "blessing" only "if it be not excessive." Hamilton later insisted "there ought to be a perpetual, anxious, and unceasing effort to reduce that which at any time exists." Washington's successor, John Adams, similarly warned in his inaugural address that "the consequences arising from a continual accumulation of public debts in other countries ought to admonish us to be careful to prevent their growth in our own."

Thomas Jefferson, our illustrious third president, was a zealous, lifelong enemy of deficit spending in any form. Indeed, he often sounded shrill on the subject. "The public debt is the greatest of dangers to be feared by a republican government," he wrote on one occasion. "To preserve our independence," he wrote on another, "we must not let our rulers load us with perpetual debt. We must make our election between economy and liberty, or profusion and servitude." To Jefferson, a generation that incurred a public debt without paying it off was actually in violation of "natural law" (that unwritten but universal law that tells us what is just and what isn't), for it raised "the question whether one generation of men has a right to bind another." James Madison, with whom Jefferson often corresponded on this topic, agreed. "A public debt is a public curse," Madison later declared.

The very birth of our nation, in short, was attended by leaders whose opposition to chronic deficits was both deep and principled. The founders' aversion to large and organized political parties, meanwhile, was nearly as strong. According to the eminent historian Richard Hofstadter, "the founders saw in parties only a distracting and divisive force representing the claims of unbridled, selfish, special interests." Giving them unflattering names like "factions" or "juntos" for their role in English or colonial politics, the founders often equated parties with conspiracy against the public good. A virtuous republic, they assumed, would attract only public-spirited leaders whose decisions favored the entire commonwealth. Why tolerate a political system based on the war of faction against faction—a distemper known to have destroyed countless ancient republics?

In the Federalist Papers, James Madison concluded that "the common good is disregarded in the conflicts of rival parties." In his farewell address, Washington famously warned "in the most solemn manner against the baleful effects of the spirit of party." During both the Washington and Adams presidencies, it was considered disreputable for any legislator to mention his party connection. The U.S. Constitution, as ratified in 1789, made no allowance for the existence of parties. It stipulated, for example, that in a national election the electors' second choice for president would become vice president, even if the two leaders belonged to opposing factions, like John Adams and Thomas Jefferson. (This flaw was remedied by the Twelfth Amendment in 1804.)

The founders were realists. They understood that a growing nation would inevitably give rise to many self-interested groups and that these would try to influence public policy. But most agreed with Madison that many small factions in a large republic would tend to "counterbalance" each other; none would try to dominate all the rest. Large and organized parties were different—and more dangerous. As each party came to view its own interest as coming at the expense of the other, each would attract exclusive groups of supporters and develop polarized worldviews. And as it vied to attract new supporters, each party would be driven to offer debt-financed public favors that seemed to cost nothing to taxpayers. Jefferson waxed eloquent on this theme, describing how parties in power use debt to reward "retainers and supporters and placeholders" until at last the whole system collapses. "Debt and revolution," wrote Jefferson, "follow each other as cause and effect."

The Founders' Political Legacy

To be sure, the founders' categorical rejection of public debts and political parties did not outlive their own generation—if it even lasted that long. During the War of 1812, President Madison was forced to borrow heavily and reverse Jefferson's policy of steady surpluses. This set a precedent for federal borrowing during military and economic emergencies, and persuaded later administrations to set up efficient financial management systems that could raise funds in a hurry and integrate the government's credit demands with the needs of the economy.

Similarly, when the founders' own children inherited America's top leadership posts during the 1830s, our national two-party system (Democrats and Whigs) was running full bore. By the time Andrew Jackson died in 1845, nearly the whole modern vocabulary of politics had been invented (lobbying, logrolling, gerrymander, bandwagon, caucus, stump, noncommittal, and so on). The founders had been public statesmen who "stood" for election; the founders' children grew up to be party politicians who "ran" for election.

Yet for all of these vast changes, the founders left behind a political legacy—a bedrock of attitudes and habits—that continued to steer the United States for generations to come. Andrew Jackson set the tone for his populist Democrats by agreeing that the national debt was a "national curse." He would let no American rest easy until it was entirely paid off. At the state level, Jacksonians in the 1840s instituted constitutional balanced budget amendments, many of which have remained in force to this day. Their example was thereafter followed by the national leadership of both parties: public debt was only for emergencies, and then was to be paid off as soon as possible. The United States (as James Polk once declared) "owes to mankind the permanent example of a nation free from the blighting influence of public debt."

During the Civil War, the Union had no choice but to finance its nation-saving struggle by borrowing vast sums from the public. But after the fighting stopped, "paying off the debt" became a popular slogan throughout a three-decade tenure of war veteran presidents—all the way from Ulysses S. Grant to William McKinley. In an 1869 article called the "National Debt," the secretary to the British legation in the United States noted that "the majority of Americans would appear disposed to endure any amount of sacrifice rather than bequeath a portion of their debt to future generations." Later, the "Progressives" of Teddy Roosevelt's era took pride in new rational accounting methods that helped keep outlays in line with revenues. Still later, the "Normalcy" Republicans of the 1920s made balanced budgets a bedrock principle of their economic policymaking.

It's often assumed among Americans younger than I am (in other words, among those who lack even a child's memory of the 1930s) that President Franklin Roosevelt and the Great Depression brought a sudden end to our traditional animus against deficit spending. But the truth is that from Black Thursday through D-day, the American public endured deficit spending only for reasons of dire necessity. They hated every minute of it. In fact, Franklin Roosevelt first gained the White House in

1932 by castigating President Hoover for his profligate borrowing. Throughout the rest of the decade FDR was forever defensive about the deficits his administration incurred. ("I have said fifty times that the budget will be balanced for the fiscal year 1938. If you want me to say it again, I will say it either once or fifty times more. That is my intention.") In 1939 an opinion survey confirmed that the majority of Americans—even majorities of the poor and unemployed—preferred spending cuts to more borrowing. As soon as World War II was over and the era of national emergency past, most Americans rejoiced that the country would no longer have to borrow against its future.

Without exception, all of these earlier generations of Americans engaged in furious and partisan battles over those two great questions of political life: Who benefits? And who pays? Farmers battled it out with bankers, southerners with northerners, proslavers with Free-Soilers, westerners with easterners. Unions squared off against corporations, small businesses against trusts, Populists against goldbugs, New Dealers against Liberty Leaguers. Yet throughout those debates, no leader of either major party ever questioned that the issue would have to be settled, one way or the other, among the living. No leader ever stood up and said: "Wait a minute. I'll tell you what. Why don't we both just take what it is we want and stick our kids with the bill?"

Surely the temptation must often have been there. Just imagine the devastation left behind by the Civil War, or the widespread desperation in the wake of the Great Depression. But most Americans just said no, or at least they voted for and approved of leaders and parties who just said no. The leaders and parties, in their turn, usually kept the people's trust by refraining from policies that would undermine their hopes for the future. Very rarely did they take the attitude, so common in public life today, that any recourse is allowable so long as you can't be jailed for it—and that the future can take care of itself.

The founders' legacy was not just talk. It was a legacy of living principles—really, informed habits—that shaped the behavior of our political parties year to year, decade to decade. It kept the fears of the founders at bay. If you look back at the federal budget from George Washington through Dwight Eisenhower and exclude only years of declared war or catastrophic depression, the record is remarkable: 127 years of budget surpluses and 44 years of budget deficits. Even these deficits, on average, were less than 0.5 percent of GDP. Since 1960, the scorecard changes dramatically: just 5 years of surplus and 39 years of deficits, with these post-1960 deficits averaging over 2.5 percent of GDP—a substantial slice of our net national savings. And these figures do not include the much larger liabilities racked up in recent decades, off the books, through unfunded benefit promises.

What Went Wrong? The Great Turning Point

What gave rise to our recent bipartisan flight from fiscal integrity—and when? I believe that most of it happened during the "Me Decades" of the mid-sixties to the mid-eighties, when a socially fragmenting America began to gravitate around a myriad of interest groups, each more fixated on pursuing and financing its own agenda than on safeguarding the common good of the nation. Political parties, rather than helping to transcend these fissures and bind the country together, instead began to cater to them and ultimately sold themselves out. Along the way, they sold posterity out as well.

One could usefully divide this era into two periods. First came the decade of 1964 to 1973, full of optimism and hubris about what the public sector could accomplish, when people talked about how much more everyone ought to get from government. This was the high tide of the benefit expansion, led by an ascendant Democratic Party. Then, following Watergate, came the decade of 1974 to 1983, full of skepticism about the public sector and a growing faith in markets, when people talked about how much less anyone ought to give to government. This was the high tide of the tax revolt, led by an ascendant Republican Party. Both parties today celebrate icons from these periods (Lyndon Johnson and his "Great Society" for the Democrats; Ronald Reagan and his "Opportunity Society" for the Republicans) as a way to distinguish themselves from the other side. In one respect, however, these icons had a common message—Americans could start shedding their civic obligations.

At every level of social life, the theme of these decades was strife and loss of cohesion. Crime rates soared, as did divorce rates. Youths wanted to live apart from their families, as did newly retiring senior citizens heading for Sun City. Some chose to "drop out" by taking drugs, others by dressing down. The Vietnam War and the civil rights movement, the assassinations of Bobby Kennedy and Martin Luther King, Jr., are today all recalled through the fractious passions of that era.

The breakdown of trust in public institutions helped catalyze a new brand of aggressive individualism. The attitude became: "Don't be a sucker. Grab it. There's plenty, and besides you deserve it." America seemed to lose its common bonds of citizenship, its sense of the platoon. Notions of victimization and redress came to replace the idea of the common good as our defining link of citizenship. Arthur Schlesinger, Jr., and Robert Hughes have written two insightful book-length essays whose very titles—*The Disuniting of America* and *The Culture of Complaint*—highlight this era's mood of fragmentation.

This is not to say, of course, that many of the new rights Americans began asserting—above all, civil rights for racial minorities—did not address real and festering injustices. The quest to assert these rights, however, also gave birth to political movements that merely wanted to enlarge their members' share of the consumption pie. And before long those with grievances were not only—or even primarily—the disadvantaged, but a very broad spectrum of Americans at all income levels. We thus ended up with an entirely nonsensical notion: universal entitlements. If we are all victims, the unspoken reasoning went, we all deserved to be on welfare. But if everybody was on the bandwagon, who would be left to pull it?

Out of this evolving political culture came the "entitlement revolution," which has had such a dramatic impact on the federal budget. For each new program, the sequence was the same. First came the law. Then, once the money began flowing out of Washington, came the lawyers, the lobbies, the subcommittees, the constituent phone calls, the expert witnesses, the press conferences, the bound reports, and the campaign slogans for the next election. Very soon you had a program that no politician dared to touch. Later on came a similar rhythm for tax cuts. By the end of this era, growing shares of both federal outlays and the federal tax code no longer justified themselves with a public interest or even pretended to have a public design. Instead, it consisted of rights to debt-financed consumption held by a vast number of entitled groups or "class claimants" who felt they had earned it or needed it or simply wanted it.

Since the mid-1980s we've been living in the backwash of these two decades of social and cultural turbulence. And in many respects America is better off due to the changes they wrought. Our public "safety net" for the poor and disabled has been vastly improved. Deregulation and a reborn ethic of self-sufficiency and entrepreneurship have triggered an acceleration in the productivity of both labor and capital. Above all, Americans take broad satisfaction in their large gains in civil rights, in their freer lifestyles, and in exercising greater tolerance of racial, ethnic, and religious minorities.

Yet Americans would do well to contemplate some of the more worrisome, indeed dangerous changes wrought by those "Me Decades." By pushing us on a relentless path toward public indebtedness and party polarization, they have given rise to the nightmare scenario that haunted the dreams of the founders. The increase in public indebtedness hardly needs elaboration: estimates of our unfunded benefit liabilities go as high as $74 trillion—and the number still grows. The ongoing trend toward party polarization, on the other hand, is driven by two contrary dynamics that merit some mention. One dynamic is the growing extremism of our political leadership. The other is the growing disengagement of our ordinary citizenry.

Most Americans who have followed the news at all over the past twenty years are well aware of the growing extremism of politicians and parties. We see it in their participation in staged "culture war" showdowns—from the Robert Bork and Clarence Thomas hearings to the Clinton impeachment trial, from Earth Day sit-ins to antiabortion human chains—all focused on good-bad "values" questions that don't easily admit compromise. We see it in the growing use of "wedge issues" (designed to divide and weaken the other party), "push polling" (partisans posing as survey interviewers), "negative ads" (which now border on libel), and "scare mailings" (like letters telling seniors that Congressman X is about to terminate their Social Security). Partisan media programming has encouraged what political scientist Norm Ornstein calls the "crossfirization" of policy discourse: don't explain your policy; rip up the other guy's.

We see it also in the growing incivility of leadership tactics, including chronic filibustering and committee room shouting matches, not only to fight the other party but to punish the straying members of one's own party. "I think it's more acrimonious. I think it's more confrontational. I think it's far more bitterly partisan," says Senate majority leader Tom Daschle. "It's like the Middle East," adds Senator Chuck Hagel. "You just keep ratcheting up the intensity of the conflict." Political campaigning has become brutal. During the late 1990s Republican operatives fired up their grass roots by orchestrating rumors that Bill Clinton had been involved in frauds, rapes, murders, drug rings, and official plans to cede U.S. sovereignty to the United Nations. Democratic operatives have recently organized similar ploys against George W. Bush—erstwhile "military deserter," who "stole" the 2000 election and "betrayed" his country over Iraq. One prominent liberal PAC aired a web site ad morphing Bush into Hitler.

Once upon a time, party leaders downplayed the possibility of national crisis or of civic breakdown. Now they play it up, talking often of scorched earth, war rooms, food fights, and train wrecks. In this climate, while candidates may talk publicly about winning over undecided voters, everyone behind the scenes agrees that "mobilizing your base" is the highest priority. A 2004 report by opinion researchers at Wirthlin Worldwide makes this point succinctly: "White House and Democratic party officials say that turning out core Republican and Democratic voters will be more critical to this year's presidential election than winning Independent voters. Pollsters have found that the partisans are much more polarized and that they are turning out in much greater numbers and in greater unity." The niche-targeting media play to this polarization, with nasty talk radio, then "gotcha" books, and then preach-to-the-choir cable TV deliberately homing in on a segment of enraged partisans. Die-hard Republicans have defined the bleeding edge of the trend, but Democrats are catching up fast.

It's not hard to figure out who benefits from this extremism: the party leaders themselves. By projecting a climate of us-versus-them divisiveness, they enhance their leadership power, protect incumbents, and assure friendly donors and interest groups of their vested support. By fostering a mood of emergency, they can shun compromise and punish mavericks, and rest assured that supporters will overlook their unsavory strong-arm tactics and obvious policy contradictions.

Many party leaders, to be sure, insist that they aren't powerful at all. They complain that they are weaker today than their predecessors were back in the "old days" of rigged primaries, compliant media, smoke-filled rooms, and congressional seniority. And in certain respects they have a point. The openness of today's legislatures and primaries along with the independence of today's Internet-age voters have washed away most of the old-boy hierarchies.

But partisan extremism does offer a potent substitute for this sort of traditional control. Most importantly, it has paved the way for the unprecedented emergence of *national* congressional parties. At the grassroots level, Newt Gingrich defined the national party for the GOP with his 1994 "Contract with America." Howard Dean may have started something similar on the Democratic side ten years later with his web-based "Deaniac" movement. At the legislative level, the Republicans are now running Congress with a degree of single-party discipline—complete with closed meetings, party-line votes, and top-down command—never before seen in our history. Many Republicans say the Democrats did plenty of bullying themselves during their long four decades of power and, in any case, fully expect them to play tougher than ever when they retake power. "The Republicans had better hope that the Democrats never regain the majority," warns Senator John McCain.

Leading these trends is the House of Representatives. Thanks to party control over elections and new data technologies that enable ruthlessly partisan methods of redistricting, House members who vote the party line get to design their own districts while members who don't can get gerrymandered out of existence. As a result, most members vote the party line. Since 1991, votes on the House floor have become more partisan, with one party voting one way and the other party voting the other, than at any time since the 1930s. In return, barely 10 percent of House members still come from districts in which they face any realistic threat of competition from a challenger. The other 90 percent are sewn up by safe and very partisan

Democrats or safe and very partisan Republicans—who hardly bother themselves about each other's constituencies. The Democrats need only talk to their own supporters (say, about not touching Social Security) and the Republicans to their own (say, about tax-cutting)—and they will both be happily re-elected.

Meanwhile, as party leaders grow more polarized in their rhetoric and behavior, voters at large have been steadily disengaging from government in general and from party politics in particular. In the mid-1960s, roughly 75 percent of Americans said they "trust the government in Washington to do what is right all or most of the time"; now, only about 35 percent. In 2003 a record share of Americans (64 percent) agreed that "people like me don't have any say in what government does." The Harris Poll's "Alienation Index," which tracks popular frustration with government and leaders, has climbed from an average of 34 percent in the 1960s to 63 percent in the 1990s.

These attitude changes have translated directly into behavior changes. Despite an aging population, the share of Americans who vote has recently fallen to record lows. Of all voters, the share registered as "Democrat" or "Republican" is also hitting record lows (Independents are now the largest single "party"). Parties are so distrusted that, by a two-to-one margin, Americans actually prefer a divided government (where control of Congress and the White House is split between parties) to one-party control. Ever fewer Americans participate in major party events or projects. Indeed, ever fewer want to participate in any civic activity at all. Since the mid-1960s, concludes Harvard sociologist Robert Putnam, Americans are "roughly 40 percent less engaged in party politics and indeed in political or civic organizations of all sorts." He adds, "We remain, in short, reasonably well-informed spectators of public affairs, but many fewer of us actually play the game."

From time to time, grassroots movements arise that try

to circumvent the party establishment. Especially at the state and local level, we've seen a steady growth in referenda, propositions, ballot measures, initiatives, and constitutional amendments aimed at limiting the choices of legislators and executives. At both the federal and state level (from Ross Perot to Jesse Ventura and Arnold Schwarzenegger), we've seen colorful outsiders try to rescue the electorate from partisan gridlock. The results have been disappointing, mainly because rules cannot replace leaders and leaders need an organizational base to build consensus and support over time.

We are left with a scenario that would have distressed the founders: powerful organizations that are not trusted and well-meaning individuals that cannot effect lasting change. Our founders would have predicted what we already know—that this arrangement cannot possibly serve the future of our republic.

Looking for Root Causes—Short-Termitis

For many social critics, America's growing debt-and-deficit challenge needs a bigger explanation than just weakening civic bonds and polarizing political parties. A more powerful force must be behind it all.

Some say it is the result of a decline in the work ethic, or in religion, or in family cohesion, or in geographic "roots." Personally, I enjoy speculating on deeper root causes. But the problem with many of the big causes is that when we try to translate them into trends, we find out that many of them aren't real trends at all. Over the last twenty years, in fact, Americans are working longer hours than ever. They are going to church somewhat more often and think more about religion than they did three or four decades ago. The divorce rate has been declining. And families are moving about less, not more, than they used to. The relative health of the family and of religion in America is especially apparent if you take the rest of the developed world as a baseline.

Others say that our eroding commitment to the future needs no explanation—that it explains itself. They say that impatience, narrowing time horizons, and a decline in what used to be called "deferred gratification" are themselves a long-term trend in our civilization.

Now I confess that I have always had a certain sympathy for this argument. Over my lifetime it's been hard not to notice the briefer-is-better trend in almost every corner of the culture, away from longer art forms (symphonies, novels, journals, debates) to shorter forms designed not to tax anyone's attention span (pop singles, sitcoms, infomercials, sound bites). Each year, newspaper articles cut away more sentences, TV scenes cut away more seconds, ads cut away more words. Even with 24/7 news programming, there is never time to examine any issue with more than a fifteen-second video clip. ("I've heard that. So what's new?") Even pop song fragments can now be purchased in repeatable twenty-second audio chips.

At the same time, at the behest of "postmodern" intellectuals, our sense of national destiny has clouded and grown more contingent. Since history is chaotic, we are now told, talk about "progress" is passé. There is a rising fictional genre called counterfactual history, which assumes that large events could easily have taken a totally different course (the British crushed the American Revolution, Germany won World War II). There is a new academic field called "chaos theory," based on the premise that a fluttering butterfly in China can topple the stock market in New York. The past is beyond explanation. The future is beyond prediction. Perhaps, then, the future is also beyond preparation or bother.

In the late 1980s the phrase "short-termitis" was coined to describe how this trend has shown up in many kinds of economic behavior. More young adults rack up credit card debt with no thought of payback, while more retirees figure out how to plan their estates so they won't leave "too much" behind. I recently cochaired, with now Treasury Secretary John Snow, a Conference Board Commission on Public Trust and Private Enterprise. Among our findings was the growing share of investors who now buy corporate equities to trade rather than to own (causing the average holding period for a share on the New York Stock Exchange to decline from eight years to eleven months over the past quarter century). A growing share of executive compensation, meanwhile, has been dominated by short-term market performance. With everyone adopting a free-agent "Can I cash out yet?" attitude, we hardly recall what it means to provide long-term value to companies, community, and country.

"Short-termitis" has also been used to describe changes in national politics—how rarely, for example, today's politicians refer to "posterity" in their speeches or how often they complain about America's "Pearl Harbor syndrome" (our nation's presumed inability to respond to adversity except when facing an immediate crisis). In the early 1990s OMB chief Richard Darman wrote a colorful memo about voters approaching Congress like "Cookie Monsters." "They want it all, now!" wrote Darman, in a message that struck a chord in the national media.

So is short-termitis a superior explanation? One argument going for it is that its "be here now" message seemed to make a great deal of headway in our pop culture during the 1960s and 1970s, about the same time that we lost fiscal control. If it does provide the right account, the implications for our fiscal future would be dark indeed—since it implies that our national leaders are providing the American people with precisely what they want. Reform would require nothing less than a reconstruction of our core beliefs.

Short-termitis offers an intriguing insight into recent changes in our culture. But it is not persuasive, in my judgment, as a basic driver of behavior. For one thing, many of the trends cited as evidence of short-termitis (like easier consumer credit or faster financial turnover) have other plausible explanations, like new information technology and declining transaction costs. For another, every generation tends to idealize the farsightedness of prior generations and complain about the haste of the present day. Maybe we're being too hard on ourselves. The truth is, people have always required some immediate, self-interested motivation. Abraham Lincoln, commenting on a similar debate in his own day, once remarked: "Few can be induced to labor exclusively for posterity, and none will do it enthusiastically. Posterity has done nothing for us; and, theorize on it as we may, practically we shall do very little for it unless we are made to think we are, at the same time, doing something for ourselves."

The biggest problem with short-termitis is that most of the evidence supporting it is partial. For every example (like the lyric "live for today") you can find a counterexample ("don't stop thinking about tomorrow"). Yes, Americans as citizens are clearly doing a poorer job in getting their public sector to prepare for the future. But in many of their personal attitudes and behaviors, Americans seem at least as future-oriented as ever. Most Americans continue to believe that deficit reduction *ought* to be a high priority, for example, and a record share of Americans today say they favor making real sacrifices to solve such long-term challenges as environmental damage and nuclear proliferation. Over the last twenty years birth rates have risen—and Americans are raising children with markedly lower rates of drug use and violent crime, and markedly higher levels of scholastic achievement and civic confidence. American family trends reflect a growing commitment to the future—not any lack thereof.

The one obvious place where short-termitis poses a clear and present danger is in government policy. And when people see it there, they don't like it, which is one reason why voters are so broadly dissatisfied with government and the leadership of their parties. "Good people, bad system," quipped Ross Perot when asked about the root problem. So we're back to our original explanation—weakening civic bonds that fail to translate sound personal values into sound public policy.

Looking for Root Causes—Generational Change

Let's back up and ask a somewhat different question: Is there any broader explanation for these weakening civic bonds beyond just saying that the whole problem got started in the 1960s and 1970s?

Perhaps there is. In his magisterial study *Bowling Alone*, Robert Putnam includes an exhaustive quantitative examination of the causes of what he calls "the collapse of American community," weighing everything from the impact of TV to the advent of single moms. He concludes that the most important single cause by far—accounting for fully half of the collapse—is generational change. The "civic-minded World War II generation," he observes, was always very community-oriented, even in its youth. By contrast, boomers and Gen Xers born after World War II have always been much less community-oriented. Over time their distinctive brand of individualism and civic detachment has come to prevail throughout society as these younger generations age into the active adult age brackets and as the World War II vets pass on.

In other words, it's not that most Americans ever changed their beliefs. It's that a large group of earlier-born Americans shaped one way by history are slowly being replaced by another group of later-born Americans that was shaped another way. And along with that replacement comes party dysfunction and a sense of civic drift. I think Putnam is onto something. A generational perspective helps us understand just how and when America lost its fiscal bearings.

Consider first the men and women of Putnam's "long civic generation." In 1965, having already used government for so many vast and successful missions—including the New Deal, World War II, the Marshall Plan, and Apollo 11—the men and women of this generation were reaching their high tide of representation in Congress and the White House. They were also just about to retire. At every earlier age, from the Civilian Conservation Corps and the Works Progress Administration in the 1930s to the GI Bill college and mortgage subsidies of the 1940s and 1950s, this generation had always had a special achievement-reward relationship with the public sector. It was only fitting that they would add, as a capstone on their new "Great Society," a generous pay-as-you-go expansion to the rewards due to old age. And it was only natural that grateful younger taxpayers, who were already giving the name "senior citizens" to these organized and politically powerful new elders, would go along without complaint.

Thus did the benefits revolution begin—perhaps enabled by a cultural tide celebrating self over community, but in the first instance triggered by the needs of a generation that everyone believed had served their community well. Largely due to generational replacement, the political attitudes of the elderly totally reversed. In the early 1960s most elders in America were still Republican and disliked big government (in 1964 they split fifty-fifty over Barry Goldwater, even after he promised to slash Social Security benefits). By the mid-1970s they were solidly Democratic and outspoken supporters of big-government programs. By this time, as benefit cost projections began spiraling out of control, the hubris and overconfidence of the benefits revolution became obvious. But these World War II vets, this "can-do" generation whose strong legislative hand might have quickly fixed the problem, were no longer able to set things right. They were disappearing from Congress. Their numbers plunged after the 1974 election, in the wake of Watergate.

Coming up to take their place was a fresh generation of

voters and leaders born in the 1940s and 1950s. Their "mindset," to use a popular buzzword, was very different from that of their civic-minded parents. Another then popular expression was "generation gap," used to describe the vocal passion expressed by many youth leaders against the "establishment" they were inheriting. Under this new boomer influence, the civic mood began to unravel. From the beginning, boomers participated enthusiastically in all the main trends of that era—the desire for confrontation, narrow causes, values showdowns, and symbolic politics, and also the tendency to drop out of the whole voting and party-loyalty "system." Shattering any consensus over national priorities, the new mood threw Congress into fits of gridlock and deterred party cooperation on major new legislation. Even urgent rescue packages for programs facing imminent insolvency (like Social Security) got hopelessly bogged down.

Over the last twenty years a pragmatic new generation born in the 1960s and 1970s has been following boomers into adulthood. This Generation X is frankly pessimistic about reforming our way out of our fiscal problems; more than any other age bracket, they would personally prefer to "opt out" of public benefit programs. Even more than boomers, Xers stay away from most forms of political participation, from voting to running for office. In recent off-year congressional elections (1994, 1998, and 2002), less than 25 percent of adults under age thirty-five have voted—versus 60 percent of adults aged sixty-five and over.

Meanwhile, as boomers themselves have aged into midlife, they have brought much of their famously fractious temperament—a penchant for endless argument and values posturing—to America's top leadership positions. Back when World War II vets ran America, we talked about a "power elite." Today, with boomers, we talk about a "cultural elite."

Both boomers and Generation Xers have no doubt made many positive contributions to our nation's social and economic life. But in the civic arena, today's younger "bowling alone" generations have surely pushed our system of political parties in a negative direction—making them (or allowing them to become) so dysfunctionally partisan that they betray the aspirations of working-age Americans, most of whom really do try to prepare for the future with honesty and patience. Many of today's retirees, meanwhile, make matters worse by exploiting this partisan gridlock. Often expressing distrust of younger boomer leadership, they use their reputation for civic accomplishment and their greater political clout to block any benefit reform and to protect patently unsustainable cost growth. Thus far, unfortunately, the we-first generation of senior citizens has largely declined to set an example of civic self-restraint for the younger generations who will ultimately bear the cost.

If generational change helped maneuver America into this impasse, one might ask: Could such change help get us out again? Several writers have raised this possibility. Putnam himself emphasizes that "American history carefully examined is the story of ups and downs in civic engagement, *not just downs*" (emphasis in the original). He later says it is very possible that "by 2010 the level of civic engagement among Americans then coming of age in all parts of our society will match that of their grandparents when they were that same age." Neil Howe and William Strauss (who coined the now popular name "millennial generation") have likewise predicted the likely appearance of more team-oriented and civic-minded young Americans over the next twenty years.

Indeed, I am struck by the number of public intellectuals who suggest that America is due for a cyclical revival in civic cohesion—from Francis Fukuyama and Robert Fogel to Amitai Etzioni, David Hackett Fischer, and Arthur Schlesinger, Jr. As Fukuyama puts it in *The Great Disruption*, his analysis of the social and cultural consequences of the 1960s, "Any number of signs suggest that, culturally, the period of ever-expanding individualism is coming to an end, and that at least some of the norms swept away by the Great Disruption are being restored . . . Along with this restoration of norms, we have reason to hope for a revival of political consensus, responsible party leadership, and renewed focus on our national future." Very few Americans look with indifference on the final image in Thomas Cole's evocative work, the image he called "Desolation." Americans prefer to hope that their republic is still capable of renewal.

To be sure, a good outcome is never guaranteed. Even if a more community-oriented rising generation is on the way, there is much to be done to prepare their path and make sure we are not planting on barren soil. In the next chapter I will outline some of the changes we need to make in the direction of both our fiscal policy and our party politics. But if self-confidence is a danger, so too is despair. Even at moments of seeming adversity, the founders never gave up on what George Washington called "the experiment entrusted to the hands of the America people." They never lost hope. Neither should we.

Chapter 9

•

HOW WE CAN REBUILD OUR FUTURE— AND OUR POLITICS

What must Americans do to set our republic back on course? We need first to educate each other about what's at stake. We need to raise public awareness about the economic, political, even geopolitical perils of living beyond our means—and from there look unflinchingly at the decisions we must make to keep our fiscal ship afloat and headed in the right direction.

Yet raising public awareness, while vital, is not enough. We also need to reform the way Congress goes about making budgets and setting priorities so that both members of Congress and the rest of us are fully informed about our long-term fiscal choices, and have some way to bind ourselves to those choices once they are made. We also desperately need to fix the dysfunctional polarization of our major political parties—and to enlarge the breadth and depth of the public's participation in politics. All of these goals reinforce one another. When voters are concerned, leaders can start talking responsibly again about our future. When concerned voters are informed, leaders can start taking action. And when concerned and informed voters mobilize and create a nonpartisan consensus—that's when the whole direction of national policy begins to turn around.

In order to achieve this better future, America must act soon on a long-term reform agenda. Some of these reforms do require some sacrifices: yes, more taxes than we like to pay, and yes, fewer benefits than we expect. But these sacrifices are truly minor compared to what we have endured before in our history and to what we and our children are likely to endure tomorrow if we fail to live within our means.

In this chapter I offer concrete recommendations in four policy areas. The first two—reforming Social Security and reforming Medicare—represent the largest challenges in any effort to make the federal budget sustainable over the long haul. Both programs, as we've seen, are on an unsustainable course, and the need to recapture control is beyond debate. Our purpose, of course, is not only to cut spending growth to sustainable levels but to do so in a way that is gradual, humane, and fair. Another purpose is to change people's behavior in positive directions—for example, to get them to plan ahead, to save more, and to live healthier lives.

By focusing on the biggest choices, I necessarily leave many other important budget issues unmentioned. I don't mean to minimize them. Military and civil services pensions, for example, contain huge unfunded liabilities. We must also scrutinize the expensive wish list of procurements guiding our current defense buildup and make sure there is a good reason for every item. And we must roll back the spread of wasteful pork throughout the domestic discretionary budget, including pork that carries the "homeland security" label.

Many Democrats may be disappointed that I don't rank tax hikes along with entitlements reform as a major agenda. Let me be clear: of course taxes will have to go up. The Bush administration was reckless to give away revenues that will eventually have to be recaptured. But Democrats have to keep the relevant magnitudes in perspective. The Bush tax cuts, even if they are all made permanent, will ultimately push federal revenues below their average for the last forty years by just under *1 percent* of GDP. Old-age entitlements, under current law, are projected by 2040 to push outlays above their average for the last forty years by nearly *10 percent* of GDP. Raising taxes is necessary. As a long-term fiscal challenge, however, it simply doesn't rank with controlling entitlement spending.

My third set of recommendations targets our ramshackle federal budget process. We need budget reform to urge leaders to make strategic and long-term choices about total spending and total taxing. Nothing has so tarnished the GOP reputation for fiscal rectitude as the party's sudden contempt for budget procedures that protect posterity—for example, the unaccountable decision to let the Budget Enforcement Act lapse in 2002. Another important purpose of budget reform is to inform the public about how we are or are not safeguarding the future for our kids and our grandkids.

My final area of concern is politics. I have a few suggestions about how we can foster a more constructive political climate. If there is a *root* cause of America's loss of long-term fiscal direction, it is not demographics, nor the budget process, nor the loss of values among the American people. It is something else: the disease of extreme partisanship in our two major parties. We must take direct steps to depolarize our parties. We must do a better job teaching citizens, especially the young, about their rights and duties, both as beneficiaries and as taxpayers. And we must, of course, encourage them to get involved in politics. Nothing better deflates partisan myth-mongering than an educated and involved citizenry.

Reforming Social Security

Social Security, pundits say, is the third rail of American politics: touch it and you die. Yet the day is soon coming when the president and Congress will no longer be able to keep their hands off Social Security reform. Fourteen years from now, the system is projected to start paying out more in benefits than it takes in from taxes. Between 2020 and 2040, Social Security's annual cash deficit will get deeper by roughly an extra $45 billion *each year*. Social Security will thus be adding hugely to the federal deficit problem rather than helping to mask it. No longer will Congress be able to divert the Social Security surplus to pay for Medicare or any other government operation. Instead, other government resources will have to be diverted to keep Social Security checks flowing.

It's not feasible to fill this growing gap just by adding to revenue. To enact further hikes in the payroll tax rate would be to push more resources into a pay-as-you-go system that already offers a poor return on contributions. Young workers would ask why they must pay more than today's midlife boomers for the same (or worse) benefits. And middle- and low-income workers, who pay most of the payroll taxes, would ask why they must pay more to subsidize the high-income old. Some advocate getting the wealthy to contribute more by applying the payroll tax rate to all earnings, without any income limit. But under this proposal you'd still be targeting many young people with large tax hikes to maintain benefits to today's affluent seniors. You'd destroy the whole presumption of a "contributory" system—that what people get back be at least somewhat proportional to what they pay in. And you still wouldn't raise nearly enough new revenue to balance the system.

Until recently I believed that the best way to unwind Social Security's future deficits was to gradually increase the retirement age and then index it to increases in life expectancy, while also changing today's cost-of-living adjustment formula into a "diet COLA" that would more accurately reflect elderly living costs.

In my 1996 book *Will America Grow Up Before It Grows Old?*

I also argued that we should apply an "affluence test" to all federal entitlements. Specifically, I proposed that if your income exceeds $40,000, you would lose 10 percent of your federal benefits for every additional $10,000 of income. If enacted then, the proposal would have eliminated most of Social Security's long-term deficits. I still favor the principle of progressive burden sharing, but I do acknowledge that there are problems with this reform. As one critic noted, "The affluence test is morally objectionable because it penalizes people who make the same income as others their whole life, but who save more and earn a return on these savings." That's true. When combined with the progressive income tax, the affluence test really does punish the thrifty. Enforcing it through the tax code would be difficult. Like a targeted tax hike on the affluent, moreover, it would make contributory programs like Social Security and Medicare seem more like "welfare."

Fortunately, there is a much better way. According to one poll, more young Americans believe in UFOs than think they will ever receive a Social Security check. Imagine how surprised and grateful they would be to learn of the following reform "deal": you are guaranteed future benefit payments that will be every bit as generous as those of today's retirees, after adjusting for inflation. And you will be guaranteed that the system will remain solvent and self-sufficient forever without any need for any tax hikes.

Sounds too good to be true? Well, it's not. One feature of Social Security that few people understand, including some officials high up in government, is that it promises ever higher benefits to each new generation of retirees. The reason is simple. Under Social Security's benefit formula, your pension is calculated as a percentage of your lifetime earnings; but these earnings are "indexed" to the average earnings or "wages" of all workers in the year you reach age sixty-two. Since wages over time tend to grow faster than inflation, each generation receives pensions that have more and more purchasing power.

Here's an example of how this works. A full-time average-wage worker retiring in 2001 received an initial monthly benefit of $1,051. But by 2031 a full-time average-wage worker will be entitled, under current law and projections, to a benefit of nearly $1,460 in today's dollars—in other words, a benefit worth 39 percent more in purchasing power. This happens because, even if average real wages (wages after inflation) grow by little more than 1 percent per year over the thirty years, they will grow by 39 percent overall—pushing "wage-indexed" benefits up by the same amount. Wage-indexing explains why it's impossible to "grow our way out" of Social Security's long-term deficit—even if we faced no demographic pressure. Since benefit levels rise in tandem with wages and productivity, faster GDP growth simply translates into faster total benefit growth.

Wage-indexing was not always part of Social Security. For many years after the program began operation, the benefit formula was not indexed to anything. Congress adjusted it every few years as it liked. As we have seen, these ad hoc benefit hikes got out of hand in the late 1960s and then went haywire after the Social Security expansion of 1972. In 1977 Congress instituted wage-indexing to set *new* benefits. And it's been wage-indexing ever since. This, in combination with yearly 100 percent COLA adjustments for benefits *already awarded*, means that Social Security benefits become continually more generous even as the relative number of workers available to pay for these benefits declines.

Did we have to take this course? Not at all. In fact, just a couple of years after Congress opted for wage-indexing, Prime Minister Margaret Thatcher came face to face with a similar crisis in the British national pension system. As part of her solution, which was later endorsed by Laborites as well as Conservatives, she chose price-indexing instead of wage-indexing to set new benfits. The outcome of this tale of two countries is quickly told. In the United States, projections of insolvency continue to plague Social Security's future. In Britain, sustainability has been totally achieved. Britain's pay-as-you-go pension costs show *zero* projected growth as a share of worker payroll or GDP—a positive fiscal prospect no other nation in western Europe can even dream about.

These realities suggest a three-part plan for reforming Social Security.

Index New Benefits to Prices, Instead of Wages. Under this reform, the average new benefit calculated each year for people reaching age sixty-two would be adjusted upward by the increase in the consumer price index rather than by an index of average wages. As a result, all future retirees—by birth year or by generation—would receive the same average benefit, adjusted for inflation, that new retirees receive today. Under current law, higher real-benefit levels will account for about 30 percent of total Social Security benefit outlays by the year 2050. By saving that extra 30 percent, we would just about bring the system back into balance by then. Social Security's cash deficits, while still rising in the 2020s, would start declining again in the 2030s and would eventually disappear. President Bush's own Commission to Strengthen Social Security projected that indexing new benefits to prices would more than eliminate Social Security's long-term deficit. And this would be true even if we "grandfathered" under the old rule everyone currently over age fifty-five.

Unless there are great leaps in life expectancy, the cost of Social Security under price-indexing would ultimately shrink forever as a share of GDP or worker payroll. There is no reason to let this happen. As soon as the Social Security actuaries foresee, after taking longevity into account, that the program's currently legislated revenue stream comfortably exceeds projected benefit outlays, it could again begin to grant larger real-benefit awards. One shortcoming of the Thatcher reform in Britain is that it did not prevent, in the very long run, this kind of unnecessary shrinkage.

One key reason I prefer this "price-indexing" approach is its *simplicity*. Other multifaceted reform proposals all tend to draw objections from one quarter or another. Critics of means-testing (I prefer the phrase "affluence-testing") complain that it might threaten to someday transform Social Security into "a program for the poor." Unions complain that raising the retirement age would unfairly burden manual laborers whose jobs require strong bodies. Technicians get into endless arguments about how to measure inflation accurately and create a proper COLA formula. More time slips by, and the cost of reforming Social Security mounts.

In political terms, the very simplicity of price-indexing conveys a sense of basic fairness; namely, parents and their kids get the same real benefits. Under this plan, most boomers and all younger Americans would not get the additional real benefits that are currently promised. But they probably are not going to get them anyway, and they know it. Instead, they will have the peace of mind of knowing that they can count on today's real-benefit level. They would also avoid the very likely prospect of huge hikes in payroll tax rates and thereby avoid the potential double whammy of both paying more into the system and getting less out.

Mandate Savings in Personal Retirement Accounts. Since wages usually rise faster than prices, price-indexing will eventually lead to a sizable decline in the *share* of preretirement wages that Social Security replaces. Most workers will want to avoid a large drop, but to do so they will have to save more. To help them, some policymakers suggest allowing people to redirect a portion of their payroll taxes from Social Security to personal accounts. But this is a no-win shell game. What households gain in saving, the federal budget (and future taxpayers) lose in higher deficits. Other policymakers suggest creating more tax incentives for savers. But the track record here is poor, mainly because the tax incentives add to the deficit by cutting federal revenue and succeed mainly in boosting the savings (or just cutting the taxes) of households that already do considerable saving.

My views were importantly influenced by my experience as chairman of the Capital Formation Committee of the Competitiveness Commission, a bipartisan group established by Congress and the President. My committee included a number of America's best tax economists with a wide range of views. Surprisingly, they all agreed that most tax incentives designed to increase savings had a limited, even ambiguous impact on net savings—that is, after considering the cost of these incentives. These experts reminded me that America's propensity to consume and its disinclination to save are deeply ingrained in the public's psyche. At the end of the day, they all agreed that if we needed a significant increase in net savings by households—and no one could disagree with that objective—we would have to make it *mandatory*.

So what does make sense is simply to mandate that all working adults put aside a minimum share of their wages (say, 2 to 3 percent) toward retirement savings, using retirement accounts that are personally owned but highly regulated. Individuals will gain enough in returns to fully make up for the decline in Social Security benefits as a share of preretirement wages, the economy will gain a powerful boost to its household savings rate, and nonsavers will at last start protecting themselves and their families. Most importantly, Congress wouldn't have any chance to spend this money. It would belong to individuals and be beyond government reach. For years Singapore and Chile have used this approach with great success. Australia also requires all workers to pay into fully funded retirement accounts, and not surprisingly Australia is the only developed country that has no worries about either the long-term affordability or adequacy of its pension system.

How would this approach work in an American context? I propose that an independent public/private board oversee the administration of these personal accounts and that the funds themselves be passively invested in global financial markets through *a mix of global equity and fixed-income index funds*. Such an approach has, in my view, several advantages.

First, it would greatly reduce administrative costs, which would be much higher if these funds were managed by individual managers trying to pick and choose the best investments and advertise their results. Most studies show that administrative costs for ordinary mutual funds significantly reduce *net* returns, particularly for the millions of participants with small accounts.

Second, the use of index funds addresses one of the key arguments against government management of investment portfolios, which is the danger of political interference. For example, one can easily imagine a future Congress passing a law that forbade fund managers from investing in companies which do this to the environment or do that for abortion. Or one can imagine a future President pressuring fund managers to invest in companies that have given large campaign contributions. Using an index fund helps to avoid these problems. National security considerations might still lead to a ban against investing in rogue nations. And there might be some political intrigue over which stocks and bonds deserve to be listed on the global index. But by and large, index investing will leave comparatively little room for political manipulation, while also protecting workers from investments that underperform in global markets over time.

Third, a global index offers maximum diversification, which is very desirable in an era of extreme market volatility. As any finance professor will tell you, few if any actively managed portfolios can consistently beat the markets over time. A mix of global equity and fixed-income index funds provides an extra measure of protection. Fourth, as with any individually managed account, workers would receive regular statements showing the size of their accounts. Finally and most importantly, not only would workers be assured that government would not meddle with their funds, they would also be assured that the funds are invested productively in the private sector. This is no small advantage. Americans have already seen what Congress would do if trusted to put aside funds to provide for future benefits: as it did with all the Social Security surpluses to which boomers and other workers contributed over the last two decades, Congress would use the money to boost spending or cut taxes.

Fortify Social Security's Safety Net. If Social Security benefits become a smaller share of total senior income—and if personal savings becomes a larger share—our overall retirement system would grow less progressive. The rich would get a bit richer, the poor a bit poorer. To counteract this, I propose having the federal government contribute into personal accounts on behalf of low-income workers. These workers would have a choice: either the government could pay the worker's mandated contribution, or it could add its contribution on top of what the worker pays. Nothing encourages the savings habit more than having a small nest egg to start with, and nothing helps build a sense of citizenship like having an ownership stake in society. Moreover, it's only fair that the government should help the poor to build assets, since it's doing so much in that department (with large tax breaks for home mortgages and such) for the rest of us. I would also require our means-tested benefit program for seniors, Supplemental Security Income, to boost its payments to the poverty level in all states. With the vast budget savings gained by price-indexing, we could easily afford these safety-net improvements.

Reforming Medicare

Imagine that President Ronald Reagan and House Speaker Tip O'Neill had struck a profile in courage a generation ago and truly made Social Security sustainable forever. Wouldn't that leave today's taxpayers and future generations much less encumbered? Yes, it would. Today, the cost of closing Social Security's deficit over the next seventy-five years is $5 trillion. But to put that number in perspective, Medicare's seventy-five-year deficit is $16 trillion, a bit more than three times as much—because it is growing a lot faster. Congressional Budget Office projections, based on optimistic assumptions about future medical inflation, show that Medicare and Medicaid together will account for more federal spending than Social Security as soon as 2010. Although this section focuses on controlling Medicare spending, the challenge for Medicaid is much the same—to the frustration of Congress and of state legislatures across America.

Controlling these costs will not be easy—or simple. Quite the contrary: I consider the reform of Medicare a far greater challenge than that of reforming Social Security. Medicare is a far more complex system than Social Security. Unlike Social Security, we cannot focus our reform just on a single benefit formula. Medicare pays out benefits according to literally thousands of complex benefit formulas, for different hospitals and physicians and for different treatments and regions. Because Medicare is such a massive purchaser of health care services ($275 billion in 2003), its biases, preferences, rewards, and penalties have themselves reshaped the whole medical-industrial complex over time. To talk about reforming Medicare, then, is also at some level to talk about reforming the way we practice medicine and think about health in America. In the final analysis, this is what makes Medicare reform so daunting: not only does it constitute a much bigger fiscal challenge, but it also raises far more profound, vexing, and even toxic issues—ethical, philosophical, moral, and, indeed, life-and-death issues.

At the first and most obvious level, we need to cut back on the abundance of fraud and waste. In its basic structure,

Medicare is a Soviet-style price-setting bureaucracy. To reimburse health care providers for delivering services, it issues (through regional insurers) thirty checks per second, every hour of every day of the year, according to 45,000 pages of regulations. But it has no way of knowing whether those services actually do anyone any good. It gives doctors and hospitals abundant incentives to overtreat or game the system, while leaving patients indifferent about the cost-effectiveness of their care. Doctors and hospitals decide for themselves what tests and procedures to order up, and how often. Patients get bounced from one specialist to another, with Medicare footing the bill. Even honest providers feel pressure to choose or "recode" their treatments according to the fee schedules that offer the most remuneration. Given this cost-plus "fee-for-service" system, it is little wonder that the share of GDP claimed by health care spending is about twice as large in the United States as in the rest of the developed world, without any significant difference in health outcomes.

It's as though Medicare allowed your auto mechanic to invoice it for any work he did—or claim he did—on your car's engine. Imagine him inviting in several other mechanics to check if you need a new radiator and brakes as well, and then buying the most expensive transmission from another buddy because he thinks it's the best. If he's unscrupulous, he then charges for two transmissions because the first "didn't work." Medicare might release a blizzard of paperwork to try to prevent such waste. But in the end Medicare has no way of knowing and simply pays. The inspector general for the Department of Health and Human Services says that demonstrably "improper" Medicare claims consumed $13.3 billion in 2002, or about 6.3 percent of the system's fee-for-service payments. All the waste that seems "proper" on paper is no doubt much larger.

At the next level, sometimes merging with waste, is the challenge of efficiency and effectiveness. The fact is, modern medicine is far less driven by hard science than you might imagine. Doctors opt for a wide variety of treatments not because there are clinical trials showing that one form of treatment is better than another, but because of professional preference, which may itself be shaped by the local "style" of medicine or the availability of specialists. This truth emerges from studies of regional patterns of care. Again and again, researchers find enormous variation in treatments provided (in expensive treatments especially, from angioplasty to bone marrow transplants) without any variation in health outcomes. One study found that in 2000 per capita Medicare spending was $10,550 in Manhattan, versus only $4,823 in Portland, Oregon—with no measurable difference in quality of care. During the last six months of life, Medicare patients in Miami are treated by twenty-five specialists on average; in Minneapolis, by fewer than four specialists. Yet the result is the same: all of these patients die in six months. Using such data, some experts estimate that nearly one-fifth of total Medicare expenditures provide very little or no benefit in terms of survival or quality of life.

Finally, we have to face the reality that even if we could eliminate all the waste and inefficiency—and that's all we did—health care spending would still keep rising faster than the size of our economy for as long we can forecast. There's the aging of America. There's the bow wave of new technological innovation. And there's the ever-rising expectations about what acute-care medicine can deliver. New drugs will promise to "cure" aging. New treatments will promise better sex, no aching joints, and improved mental and athletic ability. Immortality equals infinity, and infinity is the amount we would pay to live forever, especially if we got to use other people's money. Yet health care costs compete with other worthy and necessary expenditures—for education, national defense, and investment in the private economy—without which there would be no means to pay for health care itself.

I suggest the following strategies.

Move Toward Managed Competition. The federal government knows how to operate an efficient health care system, and it knows how to do so without forcing everyone into HMOs. The Federal Employees Health Benefit Plan (FEHBP) provides federal employees and retirees, including members of Congress, with a benefit package that preserves consumer choice, holds down costs, and promotes quality care. Beneficiaries get to choose from among a wide range of competing plans offered by private insurers. These range from traditional, high-cost "fee-for-service" plans, in which patients get to see any doctor or specialist they like, to low-cost HMOs. All these plans must compete for customers on both price and quality, which is their biggest advantage over Medicare's monopoly position.

Because the system offers consumers so much choice, you might think that the sickest patients would gravitate to the most generous plans. Many do, but this "adverse selection," as it is called, turns out not to be a serious problem. The reason is that consumers pay for what they get. The government bears 75 percent of the premium cost for low-cost plans, and a somewhat lower share for high-cost plans, meaning that if you want expensive fee-for-service medicine, you have to pay more out of your own pocket. This feature, plus the competition for consumers' dollars fostered under the FEHBP, has allowed it to outperform Medicare by a mile in containing costs. Some defenders of the entitlement status quo claim that managed competition (also known as the "premium support" model) would destroy Medicare. Not so. By introducing a few basic marketplace incentives, it will help to control fraud, waste, and inefficiency and thus help to save Medicare.

Promote Cost-Sharing and Gatekeeping. Many people are irritated when they go to the doctor and find that their insurance company or HMO requires them to pay $10 or $20 for the visit. Yet study after study shows that requiring deductibles and copayments on the first dollars that patients pay saves everyone money in the long run, because it cuts back on so much unnecessary care. In one classic study, the RAND Corporation compared two groups of families over fifteen years, one with full medical coverage and the other with a large deductible. The families with full coverage consumed 40 percent more health care dollars than did families with the large deductible, with no measurable differences in health. In its benefit formulas and Medigap rules, and with managed competition, Medicare must require more up-front cost-sharing. To avoid excessive duplication and waste in prescriptions and specialist services, it must also make sure that every patient, even if he or she opts for pure fee-for-service medicine, has a primary "gatekeeper" physician who is required to oversee all acute care and to assign "disease managers" for chronic conditions.

Establish Best Medical Practices. In fiscal year 2003 the National Institutes of Health spent $27 billion on health care research, a budget that has doubled over just the last five years. I'm all for research, but I find it disturbing that only one penny in every dollar goes into research on "health outcomes"—that is, into a systematic effort to overcome our widespread ignorance about which treatments work and which don't. Until we do, each new super-high-tech drug and device we invent will simply be added to the expensive and growing mountain of available services. One reason NIH doesn't fund much outcomes research is that many medical specialists and drug and device manufacturers know that if their products and procedures were put to the test, they'd prove to be either ineffective, too risky, or unreasonably costly. They have little interest in outcomes research, and lobby to quash it at every turn.

The American public, on the other hand, does have a vital interest, and the federal government should greatly expand its efforts in this area. Few biotech breakthroughs will ever generate such vast returns on the research dollar as the discovery, for example, that much back surgery is pointless or that a diuretic costing a few pennies a pill can, in many cases, control blood pressure as well as a beta-blocker costing a dollar a pill. To prevent interference, Congress should create a new institute of clinical studies and give its leadership and staff maximum independence. Not only would such an institute help to put more science and rationality into the health care system, but it could also greatly help to reduce defensive medicine and malpractice suits. It would be hard to win a judgment against a doctor who was following a certified and clinically proven procedure. Similarly, insurers and HMOs would not have to risk being sued for refusing to cover a procedure that is not on the list.

Reduce Litigation Costs by Instituting Malpractice Reform. These litigation costs far exceed those in any other country. No doubt there are many incompetent doctors and poorly run hospitals. According to the Institute of Medicine, "more people die in a given year as a result of medical errors than from motor vehicle accidents (43,458), breast cancer (42,297) or AIDS (16,516)." But current tort law is a highly inefficient and inequitable way to combat the problem. It gives huge rewards to a few who find clever lawyers or sympathetic juries, while leaving thousands without any compensation at all. It encourages too many wasteful treatments and tests—what doctors call "defensive medicine." And it drives up the cost of health insurance for all Americans, especially for families not on Medicare who are paying taxes to support the system.

There are a number of avenues for reform. We should place a ceiling on huge and arbitrary awards for pain and suffering, limit punitive damages, and restrict contingency fees for lawyers. We should modify the doctrine of joint and several liability, which allows plaintiffs to sue "everyone in sight" when they bring a malpractice suit. We should encourage alternatives to formal litigation by the use of dispute resolution agreements, and we should consider adopting the English rule for lawsuits, whereby the loser pays the winner's legal expenses.

Promote Public Health. The U.S. working-age population is growing fatter, more sedentary, and more socially isolated—

trends that have profound implications for the future cost of health care, to say nothing of quality of life. Rates of disability are rising for every age bracket under age sixty. Some researchers estimate that these disabilities will someday cause a 10 to 20 percent increase in the demand for nursing homes over what would otherwise occur from population aging and to a 10 to 15 percent increase in Medicare spending over its already exploding projection. We need to provide incentives for Americans to take better care of themselves. People should get to pay lower premiums for avoiding large and known lifestyle risks (such as smoking and obesity). Regional planners should avoid sprawling development that makes walking impossible. Government at all levels should put more effort into discovering and providing more effective treatments for addiction. Unless we encourage more productive aging, the next generation of elders will present disabilities and chronic conditions that will prevent America from ever aging gracefully.

Initiate a National Reform Agenda. Medicare cannot be entirely "fixed" in a vacuum. We must also begin fixing a few of the broader problems in our national health care system. First, Congress must work with states to develop a low-cost or no-cost health maintenance plan for millions of working Americans who are now uninsured and who often defer treatment until an acute or debilitating illness qualifies them for public assistance. Lack of access generates needless human suffering and economic waste, and triggers haphazard "cost-shifting" to privately insured workers or to programs like Medicare. Second, Congress must stop subsidizing health-care consumption across the board to insured Americans by putting (at least) a tight cap on the tax deductibility of employer-paid coverage. This is an outdated artifact of our tax code. As economist Walter Cadette puts it, "It provides, paradoxically, too much and too little health care—too much for those with comprehensive, employment-based health benefits paid for with pretax dollars and too little for the uninsured, most of whom work, but at jobs too little valued in the U.S. economy to include health benefits in the pay packet."

Then there's the difficult challenge of long-term "nursing home" care, which, when the age wave hits, promises to add hugely to government budgets (mainly through Medicaid, which pays for two-thirds of all nursing residents and about half of all nursing home income). Indeed, it will keep adding for decades thereafter. The fastest growth in pension costs will hit around 2020, when most boomers reach their early sixties. But the fastest growth in nursing home costs won't hit until around 2040, when most boomers reach their early eighties—the age at which the incidence of disability and dementia (such as Alzheimer's) ramps up sharply. To control the growth, we should start by insisting that Medicaid remain a means-tested program. This means tightening eligibility rules. Currently, too many families turn to Medicaid to protect mom and dad's estate—not because they are really in need. We must confront the awkward reality that we lack any broad-based vehicles (save Medicaid) for the financing of long-term care. Private long-term care insurance should be strongly encouraged, though they may never become widely used because the "need" for such care is hard to define and insure against. We should boost ongoing research on cost-saving forms of self-care, home care, and assisted living for the disabled or frail elderly. We need to educate Americans better about the likelihood they will need such care, about what government can and cannot do to help, and about planning ahead for maximum family support.

Introduce Global Caps and Face Hard Choices. All of the above reforms constitute some of the essential tools for controlling the cost of Medicare (and of most other public health care benefit programs). But they will be ineffective without global budgetary caps that many other developed countries use successfully to compel government, providers, and patients to make the difficult trade-offs. I propose that Congress debate and establish a long-term set of cost targets for Medicare and

Medicaid spending. If actual spending exceeds the target in any given year, there should be automatic adjustments to get spending back on track in the following year. The adjustments would include reducing the premium support under managed competition. Yes, these will probably require some painful trade-offs—not just the elimination of faceless "waste." Everything must be on the table, including two specific areas in which America vastly outspends all other countries: "neonatal care" during the first six months of life and, especially, "heroic intervention" during the last six months of life. As Brookings economist Henry Aaron explains, "sustained reductions in the growth of health-care spending can be achieved only if some beneficial care is denied to some people."

Many politicians will say this is rationing. I say it's living within our means. Many politicians will say it's unconscionable. I say, what's unconscionable is for us to take whatever we want and leave the bills to our kids.

Reforming the Budget Process

The federal budget process is a topic of such unfathomable complexity that even veteran Washington hands grow pale and glaze over whenever it is raised. I am reminded of Otto von Bismarck's remark when asked about the origins of an old and tangled dispute between Prussia and Schleswig-Holstein. "Only three people have ever understood it," he replied. "One forgot, the second committed suicide, and the third went stark raving mad."

Perhaps no one understands the federal budget in its entirety. For starters there is no single "process" at all, but rather a haphazard layering of many processes dating back to the 1920s—including such heroic efforts to bring it all to order as the Congressional Budget Act of 1974 and the Budget Enforcement Act of 1990. The result is a thicket of rules, procedures, and definitions that set spending targets for dozens of committees and literally thousands of separate budget accounts. There is a separate track for approving "outlays" (money to be spent this year) and "authority" (money to be spent in any year). There are programs that require annual appropriations ("discretionary") and those that really don't ("mandatory," mostly entitlement benefits). Internal borrowing through trust funds gives rise to several different definitions of the deficit and of total federal debt.

Presiding over this jumble are budget committees that are supposed to ride herd on Congress and get it to create a budget according to an annual timetable. In theory, Congress votes on spending and revenue targets in the early spring and votes again on final budget bills in the fall, in time for the new fiscal year. In practice, nothing quite works. Timetables are seldom met. Vast spending bills are often rushed to a vote in the dead of night as ramshackle "omnibus" measures. Missed deadlines may give rise to ad hoc "continuing resolutions" to keep government from shutting down while politicians argue. And violated budget targets rarely if ever trigger the dreaded "rescissions" and "sequesters" that are supposed to compel enforcement.

In a democratic republic, this unfathomable complexity is itself a serious shortcoming. According to Thomas Jefferson, self-government is only possible when the people are "well informed." But how can citizens be well informed by a process that blurs numbers, evades accountability, and obfuscates basic choices? To his Treasury secretary, Albert Gallatin, Jefferson also wrote: "We might hope to see the finances of the Union as clear and intelligible as a merchant's books, so that every member of Congress, and every man of any mind in the Union, should be able to comprehend them, to investigate abuses, and consequently to control them." Suffice it to say that we have made precious little progress toward Jefferson's goal. Indeed, we seem to be running the other way.

Beneath this complexity lie deeper problems. Despite repeated efforts at reform, the budget process still does not force Congress to make *long-term* choices about the *total* budget in a single debate and binding vote. There are far too many loopholes (like "emergency spending") and elastic deadlines. The antiquated cash-in, cash-out accounting method used by Congress, which the private sector replaced with accrual accounting five hundred years ago, provides too many opportunities to hide spending and double-count revenue. Most seriously, none of the current processes do anything to control the growing cost of existing entitlement programs.

So there is much to be done on budget reform. Yet it's also important to be realistic: in the absence of some sort of national consensus, *process alone cannot possibly bring the budget under control.* Congress is first and foremost a political institution, and it will never ratify a difficult course of action unless it believes the voting public is fully behind it.

Recent history affords several examples of budget-control devices that failed when the political consensus to support them broke down. There was the famous Gramm-Rudman-Hollings budget control act of 1985, in which Congress supposedly bound itself to slash federal spending across the board if it did not meet a specific timetable of future deficit reductions. What happened? Congress came nowhere near meeting the reductions, and as soon as members contemplated the massive automatic program cuts, they deemed discretion to be the better part of valor and quickly voted to scuttle the whole mechanism. Then there was the first major tax cut of George W. Bush's presidency, which would have violated the Budget Enforcement Act (BEA) had not Congress in 2001 simply suspended the BEA in view of the growing (and illusory) surplus projections. The reality is unavoidable: whatever Congress decides to do, it can just as easily undo.

Still, even if the best budget process cannot work without popular support and political consensus, it can render invaluable service by creating a standard of responsibility that rewards legislators who do the right thing and exposes legislators who don't. As I explain below, it can also inform the public about why fiscal control matters to their future, which in turn pushes the public to demand more of Congress. Here are the main measures I would recommend.

Reinstate the Budget Enforcement Act (BEA). In the long and checkered history of budget-control devices, the BEA stands out as a rare success story. Enacted in 1990, it required Congress to follow two simple rules in planning its budget over the next five or ten years: first, don't exceed a fixed-dollar cap on all discretionary spending; and second, don't enact any new entitlements (or tax cuts) without equal and offsetting entitlement cuts (or tax hikes) elsewhere in the budget. This was given the name "paygo," for "pay as you go." Both parties largely complied with the BEA until 1998, when budget surpluses began to erode the political consensus in favor of fiscal restraint. But by that time the caps and paygo rules of the BEA had done their job—by keeping Congress in line while the deficit declined. When it counted most, the BEA worked.

Some budget experts argue that the BEA's success during the 1990s was largely due to temporary good luck. While a strong economy pushed up revenues, outlays were restrained by the post-Cold War decline in military spending and favorable demographic trends. These are all fair points, but I am convinced that there would have been much less improvement in the deficit without the BEA. I have talked to too many members of Congress who tell me it gave them the perfect excuse to turn down constituents. ("Gee, Mrs. Smith, I'd love to help your project, but you know I have to deal with this nasty BEA. By the way, do you know any programs you'd like to cut to make room for yours?")

Issue a Comprehensive Long-Term Budget. The good news is that getting the BEA back in action will help a lot. The bad news is that, on entitlements, the BEA only applies to *new* programs or benefits. Consider, for example, the prescription drug expansion of Medicare, which was enacted in 2003 at an initial ten-year cost projection of about $400 billion. The BEA, had it been in place, would have blocked that expansion unless there were offsetting budget savings. Once enacted, however, the meteoric expansion of this benefit in the first or subsequent decades would lie entirely outside the BEA. Unfortunately, that's where most of our past and virtually all of our future fiscal challenges lie—in already existing programs.

I favor issuing a comprehensive long-term budget. It would offer Congress's best estimate of outlays and revenues in all major programs for at least the next fifty years. If projected earmarked revenues for a program like Social Security or Medicare do not cover benefits, Congress would have to specify how the shortfall would be covered. If Congress fails to cover the shortfall, future beneficiaries would have to be notified about when and how their benefits will be curtailed. (With its annual statement to workers, the Social Security Administration already includes a vague warning; my warning would be official and specific.) The basic idea is to force Congress to clarify its priorities: for example, if future retirees are being promised all their Medicare benefits, where are the resources coming from—tax hikes? debt? cuts in highways or education? At first this budget would serve mainly to inform the public. In time it would help push Congress to enact long-term cost-control reforms in the major programs.

Develop Accrual and Generational Accounting. In the private sector, when investors want to know the value of an enterprise, they can look to the bottom line of a single balance sheet. Here they will find a number that summarizes the "present value" of income and expenses, past and future. It's called accrual accounting. In the private sector, any firm that fails to use it stands in contempt of the law and is shunned by Wall Street, because accrual accounting is the only way to keep track of long-term liabilities. But Congress pretends never to have heard of it. As we have already seen, this oversight allows Congress to ignore its unfunded retirement obligations and leave over a trillion dollars off its annual deficit. Congress should publish an annual accrual-cost balance sheet for the federal government—and specify exactly what its income statement would look like if it were required to follow private-sector accounting standards.

While it is unlikely that Congress would ever pass a law that required the government to meet Sarbanes-Oxley accounting requirements, just imagine the stir some enterprising legislator could create by asking the simple question: If ERISA and Sarbanes-Oxley accounting requirements are good for the private sector, why shouldn't these accounting requirements apply to the federal government? In any event, the proposed legislation could require that the report specify which penalties would apply to Congress under the ERISA and Sarbanes-Oxley laws.

When considering any new spending or tax bill, Congress could similarly be required to calculate its future impact on the budget balance. Call this, if you will, a "generational impact statement." With only a bit more work, such statements could divide up the future costs into those that will be borne by today's adults and those that will be borne by future generations. Would such reporting make a difference? Would Congress care if it knew that a tax cut or a Medicare expansion was about to transfer trillions of dollars from our kids' pockets to our own? I suspect it would. Certainly the public would. If we're going to tax our kids, let's give them representation—in our accounting books, at the very least.

Reforming Politics and Parties

Ordinary Americans have less and less trust in government, and for good reason. We live in an age of extreme and vitriolic partisanship, which has spread virus-like through our political parties. The "base" of each party is so hostile to the other that efforts at cooperation are crippled at every turn. This leads to the failure of common projects, which further inflames the extremists and discredits the moderates.

Meanwhile, what citizen participation in government remains tends to center on defending or expanding existing programs, which these days overwhelmingly means programs for older people. Younger voters get turned off and tune out. No one is appealing to their natural idealism; no one is offering a plan to make their world better. To them, listening to the tone and substance of today's highly charged partisan politics is about as inspiring as listening to your parents having a screaming quarrel down in the living room about whether dad gets a new car or mom gets a new kitchen. Best to just pull your pillow around your head and hope you're all still a family in the morning. Today's kids may have the most to lose from today's politics, but that hardly stirs them to participate in the shouting match.

As the political mood deteriorates, so too does the relationship between citizen and leader—which now too often resembles a codependency in which each thrives off the weaknesses of the other. Former senator Bob Kerrey, a champion of fiscal realism and courageous veteran of both war and politics, once ruefully noted that it is all too easy for a politician these days to elicit a rousing round of applause from any audience. He only needs to do three things: first, identify a terrible "problem" in America; second, declare that this problem is "wrong"; and third, announce that, with his "leadership," America will right this wrong—all at no cost to anyone present, of course. The politician hands a painless promise to the crowd, and they hand him a painless vote.

It wasn't always so. In another era, President Harry Truman once defined leadership as "getting people to do what they don't want to do and getting them to like it." Truman himself knew how to lead. When Truman launched the Marshall Plan, only 14 percent of Americans supported him. Yet with hard work he won the bipartisan support of Congress and an energized American business and intellectual elite. He ultimately persuaded the public to pay for the plan—to devote nearly a sixth of an enlarged but balanced federal budget to aiding countries emerging from the wreckage of war. These public investments helped open the door to a half century of relative peace and global prosperity.

A new and rousing battle to win the affections of ordinary, pragmatic, "middle-of-the-road" Americans—the "moderate majority," if you will—would be good for both parties. In the search for a durable, informed majority, Republicans will sooner or later realize that it won't happen without coming to terms with deficits and debts, and informed Democrats will likewise realize it won't happen for them without coming to terms with entitlements. I am pleased to have been involved in catalyzing one such effort, The Concord Coalition, a national bipartisan organization dedicated to fiscal sanity. To me, it shows what can happen when talented and accomplished citizens choose to withdraw from government service and seek other constructive venues for public discussion. They ask the right questions, they kindle honest debate, and they start attracting sympathetic listeners.

I have no comprehensive "program" for a better politics. Here I simply offer three proposals that might help start us down a better path.

Fix the Gerrymandering of House Districts. When the founders first conceived of the House of Representatives, they envisioned a high-turnover legislative body in which the members would be pragmatic, nonpartisan, and close to all the people. Today, the House is none of the above. The turnover is very low, and many of the leading members are both highly partisan and feel little obligation to work seriously with constituents of the opposite party. Driving this shift is the growing use of extreme methods of computerized gerrymandering by state legislatures. The purpose is either to gain an unfair electoral advantage for one party or to sew up "safe seats" for the incumbents of both parties. Such gerrymandering must be fixed. It threatens to transform our traditional system of decentralized (and mildly partisan) representation by congressional district into a new system of centralized (and highly partisan) control by state and national parties. The recent hijinks in Texas and Pennsylvania, as reported by the media, are nothing less than a scandal.

Many solutions have been proposed. The simplest (adopted by Hawaii, Idaho, New Jersey, and Washington) is for states to appoint bipartisan citizen boards to draw the new districts every ten years. Because appointing a board is itself a political event, this solution is less than perfect. A more radical idea (thus far adopted only by Iowa) is for states to specify neutral mapmaking rules that would generate new districts automatically. This could be easily done with computers. A few experts have even suggested creating large multimember regions in populous states and then allocating winners by proportional vote—a proposal that would require amending the Constitution. One wonders how this might shake up party establishments in heavily gerrymandered states like California—where in 2002, despite palpable voter discontent, not a single challenger to any of fifty-three House seats could even win 40 percent of the vote.

I don't know which reform would work best. But reform there must be, even if it requires a constitutional amendment. We use our amendment process for every other purpose. We might as well use it to make sure our democracy still works as intended.

Neutralize the Campaign Funding Problem. Overall, it's clear that partisanship is worsened by the large amounts of special interest money politicians must raise. Yet it's also clear that most of the laws we've passed to regulate the influence of money in politics have generated more controversy than results. Such laws begin with the dubious premise that there is too much political speech, move on to rules that threaten First Amendment liberties, and frequently trigger entirely unintended consequences—such as protection for incumbents or for super-rich candidates. Most recently Congress enacted the McCain-Feingold bill to limit how parties use soft money. One result has been to drive this money away from political parties and into faceless nonprofits engaging in political organization and advertising, which leaves the press and the public even less able to tell whose money is behind which candidates.

Rather than critique the pros and cons of current legislation, let me propose one simple idea. When you ask candidates running for office why they spend so much time and energy looking for money, they all say the same thing—in order to place TV and radio ads in today's high-priced media markets. Without such ads, they all agree, no candidate can begin to get a fair hearing. As Senator Bill Bradley once put it, "Today's political campaigns function as collection agencies for broadcasters . . . You simply transfer money from contributors to television stations." Well, it just so happens that the public is in a good position to stop this. TV and radio broadcasters control billions of dollars worth of airwave rights, which the public has provided to them for free.

Here's the least we could ask in return. During campaign season, broadcasters would donate a fixed number of free-airtime vouchers to any candidate for federal office who raises some minimum amount in small donations. The well-funded incumbent would still have an advantage, but the new challenger would at least have a fair chance to be seen and heard. Political scientist Norman Ornstein and Paul Taylor, head of the Alliance for Better Campaigns, have been advocating this reform for years. "Rather than restrict speech, we should expand speech," they argue. "Rather than build ceilings, we should build a floor." I agree.

Educate Young People about Fiscal Realities and about Civic Rights and Duties. We are very mindful these days to raise our kids so that they will take care of themselves personally. Seldom do we even think about preparing them to take care of their country publicly. We warn them of the dangers of drugs, but say nothing about the dangers of deficits. We instruct them to beware of advertisers who shade the truth about products they sell, but not about politicians who shade the truth about programs they enact. Even when we teach civics, we often miss the point. We teach kids the names of the capitals of all fifty states, but we don't teach them *what really goes on* in those capitals. We tell youthful citizens why episodic sacrifice in wartime is sometimes the price of freedom. But we tell them little about the routine sacrifices in peacetime that are always the price of national prosperity and social harmony.

I propose that a simple curriculum be developed and taught in the schools that would instruct young people on the full range of rights and duties that belong to all Americans as citizens. It would focus especially on those fiscal dimensions of citizenship that "civics" usually passes over: How does government raise revenue? What is the budget process? Where does the money go? How do our largest programs work? What do these programs really promise you and what are they likely to cost you in terms of added taxes? And how are you expected to take care of yourself? Today's young people can graduate from college and know nothing about how the federal government intends to spend most of their future taxes. Today, most Americans think that roughly half of all federal spending goes into foreign aid and cash "welfare" benefits. (The actual number is well under 5 percent.) That's a failure of education.

It goes against the American grain to have government directly involved in creating curricula—especially about government itself. Moreover, where we've come closest, in the control often exercised by state school boards over textbook publishing, the result has been pabulum or politically correct drivel. But the president would be well served to announce a "White House Conference on Civics Education" that could provide a catalyst to reform efforts, including a nonpartisan process for developing the appropriate educational materials. Meanwhile, foundations looking for a critical, cutting-edge agenda should consider supporting scholarship in civics education.

A Positive Vision of Our Future

If America chooses the right future, it will be because we learn again how to cooperate politically and embrace a positive vision of what our nation can become. Yes, we have to make some tough choices. But instead of obsessing over the tax hike that outrages us, or the benefit cut that shocks us, we need to focus on everything our nation can achieve if we all made an effort to come to terms with our future.

What often makes married couples stop fighting is a good look at their kids. Americans need to ask the leaders and cadre of their two national parties to do the same—to look at our kids. Over the last forty years, we've had many presidents talk about what our country can do for us or what people can do for themselves—but not since Kennedy have presidents asked what people can do for their country. It would be helpful to demonstrate to the next generation that this is a virtue that Americans have not entirely forgotten.

The forces of inertia are great. Even in the face of likely danger, nothing is more human than resistance to change. No matter how firm the numbers or how alarming the opinion of experts, there will always be the temptation of denial (it simply can't be true!), or of delay (we're not quite ready!), or of diversion (let's talk about what our leaders did during the Vietnam War!). Every time the economic outlook brightens slightly, many will hopefully whisper that maybe we don't have to change after all. Every time the outlook worsens slightly, many will despairingly conclude that times are too rough for change.

Year after year passes, and though we fear both acting and not acting, somehow it's never the right time. Livy, the eminent historian in the age of Augustus, noticed a similar mood among his Roman contemporaries. "The people can bear neither their ills nor their cures," he wrote. Like Rome, America too will eventually run out of years.

Chapter 10

•

A LETTER TO THE RISING GENERATION

You may be surprised to know that when I was a boy, parents were generally very different from what they are today. They did not paste "Baby on Board" stickers on their car windows or spring for childproof door locks. Toddlers roamed the backseat without belts. There were no "Amber alerts" or "Megan's laws." Kids in my time ran free and mostly unattended.

Mothers did not spend their afternoons chauffeuring their kids from one organized event to the next; they rang a bell in the backyard when the casserole was ready. Fathers were preoccupied with their work and often emotionally remote. They did not worry about "quality time" with their kids, or about whether their kids enjoyed sufficient "self-esteem." Few families saved to send their sons to college—much less their daughters.

And yet, in a different way, my parents' generation was far more "child-centric" than my own or succeeding generations. They did not vote to provide themselves with massive, unfunded retirement benefits, as my generation did. They did not swoon for political leaders who winked at deficits, or allowed the nation's infrastructure to crumble. Instead, as a generation, they enacted and paid for programs and policies that overwhelmingly benefited people younger than themselves—the GI Bill, the Interstate Highway System, the Apollo program. Nor, rightly or wrongly, did they shrink from challenges that might be put off for another day, such as World War II and the twilight struggle against Communism, even if, for many, it meant sending their own children and grandchildren to fight in Europe or the Pacific, in Korea or Vietnam.

Every generation overshoots. Fifty years ago, most parents probably put too little emotional investment in their kids, even as they overwhelmingly supported government policies designed to benefit the future over the present. By the 1960s this imbalance triggered generational warfare, as America's young rebelled against a nation that seemed oversupplied with military might and material abundance, but spiritually and emotionally impoverished. Then came a new generation of parents, whose emotional investment in their children became more and more lavish, even as government policies increasingly tilted toward borrowing from those same children. Some predict that this new imbalance will also lead to generational warfare—this time, of a very different sort. Let us hope not.

To today's young Americans, I say, You have a right to be angry about the financial encumbrance your elders have collectively placed upon you. But you also have reason to be understanding. Your individual parents and grandparents did not intend to saddle you with this debt. They didn't vote to pick your pocket. Instead, they were misled by various experts and politicians—some of them high-minded, some of them craven—into supporting policies that turned out to be based on false premises.

When your grandparents were in their prime, experts predicted that America was on the threshold of becoming such an "Affluent Society" that future generations would hardly notice the cost of vastly expanding old-age entitlements. Recall again that one famous economist of the day, Paul Samuelson, even went so far as to call Social Security "the greatest Ponzi scheme ever invented." A rapidly growing population and economy, he said, would allow everyone to get back from government far more than they put in. Most old people in those days were poor people, and it seemed only fair that old people be allowed to share more of the bounty that they had helped to create, especially when that bounty seemed to be limitless.

Later, your parents and grandparents were exposed to a new theory called "supply-side economics." It promised that lower tax rates would produce greater economic growth and that growth would itself yield higher tax revenues for the government and higher incomes for us all. But in actual practice, this tax-cutting fever did not produce the promised revenues. Instead, spending increased and your generation was left with the bill.

Maybe in retrospect it seems incomprehensible that anyone ever believed supply-side theory would work. But at the time, figures presumed to have great authority on economic matters, from the editorial board of *The Wall Street Journal* to the President of the United States himself, argued forcefully that it was true. Ordinary Americans in those days were scared about an economy that was no longer producing the bounty their previous leaders had told them would go on forever. The oil shocks of the 1970s, a deep recession, hyperinflation, skyrocketing interest rates, and a general sense of "malaise" had left Americans eager to believe in something new. It was understandable that they might believe in something wrong.

You should know, too, that your elders had little information about how entitlement programs were quietly placing huge liens on your future. The government's budget did not acknowledge these liens. Newspapers would report that the national debt was something we "owed to ourselves" and that gigantic "trust funds" would keep retirement programs in fine shape for decades to come. A more serious and sophisticated media might have explained to the American people how their government, by not funding the cost of future benefits, was borrowing more and more from their children. But the trend in journalism at the time was toward fusing news with entertainment, and there was nothing very entertaining about deconstructing the government's backdoor borrowing.

In such a media climate, your parents and grandparents were highly susceptible to demagoguery from both the Democrats and Republicans. Whether "deficits matter" or not, whether entitlements had to be reformed, became questions decided by sound bites, rather than empirical investigation and serious debate. TV does this. It shows everything about the moment and nothing about the future. Politicians could scare elders into believing that any plan to save Social Security was really a plan to leave them destitute. The White House would become so adept at spinning the press and defining agendas that the country barely noticed as it slid from being the world's greatest creditor to being the world's greatest debtor.

Moreover, even as both political parties were colluding to place new fiscal burdens on the future, they found it easy to distract the public with emotional "wedge issues." Political energy and attention that might have been focused on reforming Social Security and Medicare went instead to debating whether Americans have a right to burn the flag, whether gays have the right to get married, and whether states have the right to mention God in the pledge of allegiance.

Understand, too, that many of your elders did realize how their politicians were conspiring to rob your future, but they lacked the political wherewithal to put a stop to it. Today's older Americans are often referred to as the "Greatest Generation," and indeed they achieved much for our nation. But by the time the era of big borrowing began, the oldest members of this generation were already in retirement and disengaging from public life. Even among those who came to recognize that these programs were effectively borrowing from your future, a majority had lived their lives on the assumption that they would be paid what they were promised. "You've paid your dues. Now collect your benefits," went the classic AARP solicitation letter. Many of this generation compared their own lives with their kids' and said to themselves, "Yes, we *have* paid our dues, haven't we?"

You might be inclined to be harder on your parents—baby boomers and Gen Xers—who had plenty of time to adjust to any entitlement reforms, and who yet went along with a political system that failed to show any fiscal stewardship for your generation. But consider: one reason for this is that so many of your parents' generation took their role as parents so seriously that they neglected their role as citizens.

For many legitimate reasons, baby boomers and Gen Xers lost their faith in government and civic action. They turned inward, celebrating not only the private sector but private life over participation in public affairs. At their worst, they regarded the decay of political institutions with ironic detachment, and put "honesty to themselves" above duty to others. But against this, look at how much emotional and financial investment most members of your generation have received, and are receiving, from your parents.

Again, in my day, far more parents worried about "spoiling" their children than about trampling on their self-esteem or cutting off "communication." My own immigrant parents worked hard to send me to college, but they were unusual, and even they would never have supposed that their parental obligations included providing me with the sorts of advantages many young people enjoy today—from a private room at home, to soccer and ballet lessons, to professional counseling for dealing with life's difficulties.

Maybe now you wish your parents hadn't been so indulgent. Maybe you feel that when it comes your time to have children, you will spend far more effort on working to build a society that doesn't rob their future, and less effort on scripting your children's playtime for "maximum enrichment." And in this, your priorities may well be right. But acknowledge that most members of your parents' generation, in their own flawed way, did try to look out for you, according to the priorities they thought most important.

What can you learn from their mistakes? Some lessons will be obvious. Your parents grew up at a time of relatively easy money. Many racked up huge credit card bills, took out second mortgages, and saved little or nothing for retirement. Chances are that at least some of this free spending went to benefit you—to buy you PlayStations and Game Boys, to get you into a good school district, and to help out with college. But now, after a lifetime of borrowing, your parents' generation is approaching old age with far too little savings. A good number will experience financial disappointment or even real hardship. Others will work far longer than they would like. Don't let this happen to you. Thrift is not some obsolete Victorian notion. In your generation, especially, it will be the difference between those who prosper and achieve respect and those who become a burden to their children and society.

Be careful, too, to avoid the fashionable cynicism about politics that spread when you were growing up. There used to be a joke about Gen Xers when they were coming of age. "Which is worse, apathy or ignorance?" a philosophy professor asked his class. "I don't know and I don't care," came the bored answer from the back of the room. Today, this attitude is far less prevalent among the young. Indeed, your generation's eagerness to volunteer, to take a "hands-on" approach to bettering society by working in soup kitchens or teaching illiterate grown-ups to read, is the single brightest sign of civic renewal in American society. Yet by itself, this "hands-on" approach is not enough to overcome problems that are essentially political, and that only have political solutions. The fact is, old people are three times more likely to vote than young people in a congressional election. Ask yourself: if you were a politician, would you look after the 20 percent you don't even hear from, or the 60 percent who not only vote but who visit you, write to you, send you telegrams and flowers, and organize in lobbies to influence you? In this contest between the silent young and vocal old, guess who is winning? Silent minorities rarely win.

You must find your voice. You must become a vital part of the political action. That means becoming active in your political party. That means joining organizations like The Concord Coalition and the Third Millennium that are devoted to generational equity. That means contacting your political representatives. In short, you must build a lobby for the future.

Citizenship means looking out for one's neighbors and giving a hand to those less fortunate. But it also means understanding the big issues of one's time, seeing past the hype and spin, and working together to hold political leaders accountable. Your time is coming, and when it does, your generation, like every generation, will get the government it deserves. If it is distracted by pseudo-issues and gridlocked by special interests, it will be because too few of you paid attention and made your voices heard.

Finally, realize that we are all in this together. Yes, your generation is fiscally encumbered as no generation before in American history. Yes, you have not only a right but a duty to stand up to those who would borrow still more from you and your children. But remember that as your parents age, they too will bear a burden for the mistakes of the past, and for many it will be a very personal burden. Yes, you can blame them for letting their politicians do this to them and to you, but you can also forgive them. If your parents sacrificed to provide you with a room of your own, with a good education, with free rent after college or help with a down payment on a first house, what do you owe them in return? You may well find that they will eventually need you to return the favor—not only to help them keep their house or their health but to offer them the emotional support they most likely once extended to you.

You can look at that as a burden or as an opportunity. I say, let them help you to raise your children as you labor to pay off their generations' debts. And meanwhile work together to learn from the mistakes of the past. Educate yourself, and educate your parents about the world you have inherited, and work together to rebuild a society based on thrift, stewardship, and justice between generations.

A NOTE ON SOURCES

A book of this scope naturally relies on a vast number of secondary sources, from newspaper op-eds to scholarly monographs, too numerous to mention. Most of the basic fiscal, economic, social, and demographic numbers referenced in this book, however, come from easily accessible primary sources. Many readers will be interested in tracking down these numbers and finding out more about them. To help these readers, and in the interest of full disclosure, let me point the way to a few of the most important sources.

Federal Budget, Historical. Most historical figures on the federal budget (outlays, receipts, debt, investment, R&D, and totals by program, by function, by enforcement category, etc.) come from the President's Office of Management and Budget (OMB), "Historical Tables" volume of the *Budget of the U.S. Government* (latest edition, Fiscal Year 2005; see http://www.whitehouse.gov/omb/index.html) and the Congressional Budget Office (CBO), *The Budget and Economic Outlook* (latest edition, January 2004; see http://www.cbo.gov/). For special topics (e.g., credit, debt, liabilities, federal employment), see the "Analytical Perspectives" volume of the Budget (OMB, op. cit.). Unless otherwise indicated, historical years for the *Budget* refer to fiscal years.

Federal Budget, Projections. Projections of the federal budget over the next ten years typically come from the latest (January 2004) CBO *Outlook* (op. cit.).

The CBO generates many projections, some describing the official "baseline" scenario (in which sunsetted tax provisions expire and discretionary outlay growth is constrained to inflation), others describing what I sometimes call the more realistic "do nothing" scenario (in which all tax provisions are made permanent and discretionary outlays grow with GDP). Beyond ten years, my "do nothing" scenario for the federal budget is the "March 2004 Analysis" from the U.S. General Accounting Office (GAO; see http://www.gao.gov/). This projection is shown in several GAO publications (e.g., GAO, "The Nation's Growing Fiscal Imbalance," 2004); detailed annual numbers are available from the GAO on request. The CBO numbers for the next ten years refer to fiscal years; the longer-term GAO numbers refer to calendar years. The actual projection figures for the long-term "do nothing" GAO projection (2004) described above are as follows:

PERCENT OF GDP

	2004	2010	2020	2030	2040
SOCIAL SECURITY	4.4	4.4	5.6	7.1	8.5
MEDICARE & MEDICAID	3.8	4.5	5.7	7.3	8.9
ALL OTHER SPENDING	10.6	10.1	9.8	9.8	9.8
NET INTEREST	1.4	2.5	4.1	7.8	15.7
TOTAL OUTLAYS	20.1	21.5	25.2	32.1	42.8
TOTAL REVENUE	15.9	17.3	17.7	17.7	17.7
DEFICIT	–4.2	–4.2	–7.5	–14.4	–25.1

Social Security and Medicare. Social Security formally consists of two trust funds (Old-Age and Survivors Insurance, or "OASI," and Disability Insurance, or "DI"); Medicare also consists of two trust funds (Hospital Insurance, or "HI," and Supplementary Medical Insurance, or "SMI"). The benefit programs within SMI (Part B for physicians and Part D for prescription drugs) receive no payroll tax revenue and are funded mostly by general federal revenues. When I discuss the history or projected future of Social Security or Medicare separately from the rest of the federal budget, I rely on the annual reports of the boards of trustees of the Social Security and Medicare trust funds—most recently, *The 2004 Annual Report of the Board of Trustees of the Federal Old-Age and Survivors Insurance and Disability Insurance Trust Funds* and *The 2004 Annual Re-*

port of the Boards of Trustees of the Federal Hospital Insurance and Federal Supplementary Insurance Trust Funds. See http://www.ssa.gov/OACT/pubs.html. The actuaries for the OASDI and HI trust funds calculate detailed seventy-five-year projections according to three scenarios (low cost, intermediate or "official," and high cost, each one corresponding to a set of economic and demographic assumptions spelled out in the report). When I cite one projection, unless otherwise indicated, it is always the official projection. Occasionally, when I cite a range, it is between the official and high-cost projection. The actuaries for SMI only calculate one (official) projection; my "high-cost" projection for SMI assumes the same percentage difference, each year, between the official and high-cost numbers as is the case for HI. The official long-term projections of the Social Security and Medicare trustees are quite close to those of the "do nothing" GAO projection. All years for Social Security and Medicare alone refer to calendar years.

Federal Budget, Unfunded Liabilities. Present-value estimates of Social Security and Medicare benefit liabilities over the next seventy-five years have been tabulated in some fashion in the annual trustees reports (op. cit.) for many years and in the federal budget since the FY 2000 budget (see the "Stewardship" chapter of the "Analytical Perspectives" volume, op. cit.). In 2004, for the first time, the Social Security and Medicare trustees published liability figures for all of their programs (including SMI), for "unlimited" as well for as seventy-five-year time horizons, and for current and future generations. In the 2005 federal budget, the tabulation similarly includes a division into current and future generations. My figures are taken from these sources. The same figures are now very usefully summarized in the *2003 Financial Report of the United States Government* (Financial Management Service, U.S. Department of Treasury, 2003). See http://www.fms.treas.gov/fr/. In Chapter Two, I cite independent estimates of unfunded benefit and overall fiscal liabilities from the following sources: Jagadeesh Gokhale and Kent Smetters, *Fiscal and Generational Imbalances: New Budget Measures for New Budget Priorities* (American Enterprise Institute, 2003); Roberto Cardarelli and Christopher Towe, "Long-Run U.S. Fiscal Imbalance: An Intergenerational Analysis," in *U.S. Fiscal Policies and Priorities for Long-Run Sustainability* (International Monetary Fund, 2004); Liqun Liu, Andrew J. Rettenmaier, and Thomas Saving, "How Large Is the Federal Government's Debt?" (National Center for Policy Analysis, 2003); and Alan J. Auerbach, William G. Gale, and Peter R. Orszag, "Reassessing the Fiscal Gap" (Brookings Institution, 2003). The following unfunded benefit liabilities appear in the "Analytical Perspectives" volume of the 2005 federal budget (op. cit.), all expressed as 2003 present values of benefits minus taxes over the next seventy-five years:

TRILLIONS OF DOLLARS, 2003 PRESENT VALUE	SOCIAL SECURITY	MEDICARE	SOCIAL SECURITY & MEDICARE
FUTURE BENEFITS LESS FUTURE TAXES			
... FOR THOSE AGED 15 AND OVER	+$11.7	+$15.0	+$26.7
... FOR THOSE AGED 14 AND UNDER	–$ 6.8	+$ 0.8	–$ 6.0
TOTAL FOR ALL AGES	+$ 4.9	+$15.8	+$20.7

As discussed in Chapter Two, the 2004 reports of the Social Security and Medicare trustees have recently published much larger present-value figures for the next seventy-five years. These are (total for all ages only) $5.2 trillion for Social Security; $27.7 trillion for Medicare; and $33.0 trillion for both. Of the new Medicare figure, $8.1 trillion is due to the new prescription drug benefit alone.

Economy, Domestic. Historical U.S. figures on GDP, savings, investment, and state and local outlays and receipts come from the Bureau of Economic Analysis (BEA; see http://www.bea.gov/), U.S. Department of Commerce. Figures on national, sectoral, and household wealth are taken from the Board of Governors of the Federal Reserve System (Fed; see http://www.federalreserve.gov/publications.htm), *Flow of Funds Accounts of the United States* (quarterly). Unless otherwise indicated, historical years for state, local, or total U.S. public-sector budgets refer to calendar years.

Economy, International. Historical U.S. figures on international transactions (trade balance, current account, transfers, etc.) come from the BEA. For detailed figures on the "international investment position" of the United States since 1976, see also the BEA. Figures on foreign ownership of U.S. debt are tabulated in the federal budget (see "Stewardship" chapter of the "Analytical Perspectives" volume, op. cit.). For more detail on U.S. debt and official reserves, see the U.S. Department of Treasury and the Fed. For economic indicators on the other developed countries, see the Organization of Economic Cooperation and Development; on all countries, see the World Bank.

Demography. Unless otherwise indicated, all historical data for the U.S. population and households are taken from the U.S. Bureau of the Census (Census;

see http://www.census.gov/). U.S. demographic projections are generally taken from the Social Security Office of the Actuary (as published in the annual trustees' reports, op. cit.). I occasionally use the Census projections, especially for detailed age-bracket data. I compare the Census and Social Security projections in Chapter Three. Demographic projections by age for other countries are taken directly from the "constant fertility" variant of the most recent United Nations projections (*World Population Prospects: The 2002 Revision*; Population Division, United Nations, 2003). See http://esa.un.org/unpp/index.asp?panel=2. Fiscal projections for other developed countries are taken from Richard Jackson and Neil Howe, *The 2003 Aging Vulnerability Index* (Center for Strategic and International Studies, 2003).

Income and Society. My discussions of income, wealth, and poverty (over time, by age bracket and birth cohort, per person, household, and family) rely heavily on secondary sources. Most of the underlying data come from Census and from the Fed. On household wealth, see especially "Recent Changes in U.S. Family Finances: Evidence from the 1998 and 2001 Survey of Consumer Finances" (*Federal Reserve Bulletin*, January 2003). On home ownership, see *The State of the Nation's Housing: 2003* (Joint Center for Housing Studies at Harvard University, 2003). On the distribution of federal benefits by the age of beneficiary (children versus elderly), see *Federal Spending on the Elderly and Children* (CBO, 2000). On "poverty gaps" and many other perspectives on the impact of government benefit programs, see *Greenbook: 2004* (U.S. House Committee on Ways and Means, 2004). On the receipt of federal benefits by income bracket, see *Reducing Entitlement Spending* (CBO, September 1994); estimates updated by the author. On the receipt of tax expenditures by income bracket, see *Estimates of Federal Tax Expenditures for Fiscal Years 2002–2006* (U.S. House Committee on Ways and Means and Committee on Finance, prepared by staff of the Joint Committee on Taxation, 2002). On voter participation by age bracket, see the "Voting and Registration" releases of the Current Population Survey (Census).

ACKNOWLEDGMENTS

I am blessed to be able to work and consult with a great group of professionals.

First on that list must be Neil Howe, with whom I've worked for nearly a quarter of a century. By any standard, he is a first-rate historian and a genuine expert on generational trends, as his several excellent books would readily attest. Neil is joined by Phil Longman, who also has long experience both as a policy analyst and as an author. Richard Jackson is a genuine expert on global aging with whom I have worked for a number of years.

I am also blessed with the access I have to the best group of economists I know anywhere. I refer to the Institute for International Economics and to Fred Bergsten, executive director, Martin Baily, Morris Goldstein, Michael Mussa, and Ted Truman. I am afraid I took advantage of my role as founding chairman to solicit their important views. I could also not forget to mention Bob Bixby, executive director of The Concord Coalition, with whom we reviewed all of our budget projections.

During the course of writing this book I've talked to friends who are far more experienced than I in the ways of today's global capital markets. Stanley Fisher, Steve Roach, Bob Rubin, Anthony Solomon, Dennis Weatherstone, and Paul Volcker were immensely helpful.

None of these fine people bears any responsibility for any errors I have made.

Two people in particular have paid the heaviest personal price, my two assistants Laurie Carlson Oberbeck and Christine Hadlow. I am especially grateful to them for the many frustrating hours working at the computer through endless rounds of revisions. And I must not forget to thank Masood Javed for assisting me at all hours of the day and night. I know they can only be very pleased that this arduous project is over.